"She is more precious than Rubies: and all the things thou canst desire are not to be compared unto her".
Proverbs 3:15

To my loving wife, Natasha.

Special thanks to Thanachoti Sonsa (Graphic Designer), Hathaichanok Malee (Photographer) and Steve Taylor (friend, critic and endless source of good advice); this book is as much yours as mine.

CONTENTS

Please note that related gemstone varieties have been included with the gemstones listed in Chapter 2. Some gemstones also have multiple names. For assistance, please use the index on page 269.

FOREWORD

Why do people buy gemstones? As an early student of gemmology, I was always taught the most important attributes of a gemstone were 'beauty, rarity and durability'. However, over decades of involvement in the coloured gemstone industry, I have learnt that there are much more important aspects to our appreciation of gemstones. When you carefully analyse why one wants to own a gemstone, the main reason invariably is that a particular gem means something special to us: they represent a story, a thought, a desire, or an event. Even if we don't realise it, our choice is a symbol of our thoughts and a reflection of our perceptions.

In *The Clever Gem Buyer* Gavin brings the reader not only the 'gemmological' facts, but also wonderfully prepared information on the less obvious, but much more important, aspects that make us all desire coloured gemstones.

Here is a book that successfully balances science with the romance, myths and history of gems, all presented in an absorbing and entertaining way, and supported by superb photography. Gavin has drawn on his considerable experience in marketing gemstones to produce the perfect companion for those interested in either the single acquisition of a gemstone or the building of a life-long collection.

Terry Coldham BA (Geology)
Fellow of the Gemmological Association of Australia
Chair of the Australian Jewellery and Gemstone Industry Council
Australian Ambassador for the International Coloured Gemstone Association

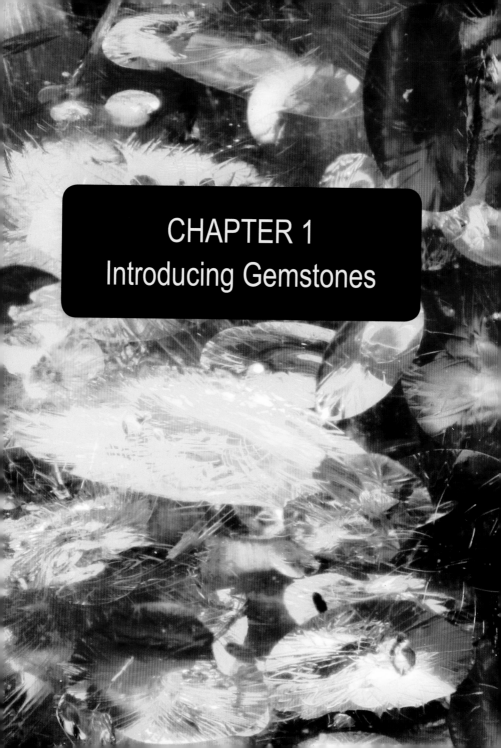

CHAPTER 1
Introducing Gemstones

GETTING STARTED

"Beauty, durability and rarity; such are the three cardinal virtues of a perfect gemstone. Stones lacking any of them cannot aspire to high place in the ranks of the precious stones".

Dr. G.F. Herbert Smith (1872-1953), Gemstones and their Distinctive Characters

Nicely put Dr. Smith, and when it came to gems he certainly knew what he was talking about! As a British mineralogist who worked for the British Museum of Natural History, Dr. Smith was responsible for developing the first efficient jeweller's refractometer (an instrument used to measure the refractive index of gems, see page 246 for more).

My 'first contact' with gemstones happened when I was about 10 years old. I still remember being mesmerised by a small water-filled container full of Opal tailings, given to me by an aunt. My professional love affair with gems started eight years ago under the shadow of Khao Ploi Waen, 'the mountain of gemstone rings' in Thailand's Chanthaburi Province, an international centre for coloured gemstones. My first experience handling gems was certainly anything but illustrious - I shot a gem from my tweezers, almost taking out a colleague's eye! This book is written for people looking for some beginners' tips to clever gemstone buying and appreciation. Hopefully, after reading this book you'll love gemstones as much as I do. Apart from personal experience and published sources, a lot of the information in this book comes from just talking to people. Like any industry dominated by passionate individuals, opinionated discussions are commonplace and always very enlightening. I would also like to point out that the gem industry is not full of villainous scoundrels ready to deceive at the drop of a hat. By and large, gemstone traders, wholesalers and retailers are qualified people looking to turn an honest dollar. Just make sure you are buying from a reputable seller. Look for membership to trade organisations, such as the ICA (International Coloured Gemstone Association) and seek assurance by getting your purchase independently appraised (see page 242 for more).

Mineral or organic materials (see page 50 for more) worn for personal adornment, a gem is only a gem when it is beautiful, durable and rare. Occurring entirely by chance, gemstones truly are amazing miracles of nature. While anyone can appreciate the aesthetic beauty of gemstones, even a basic understanding will make owning gemstones much more rewarding.

In my experience, most people are far more comfortable buying Diamonds than coloured gems, and I guess this isn't surprising considering the amount of money the Diamond industry has spent on advertising. But when it comes to coloured gemstones, most people are unsure what's available, let alone how to determine value. Sure, they might be able to rattle off a few birthstones and some of the more well-known varieties, but unless they or someone they know is 'into' coloured gems, their knowledge barely scratches the surface. This is a pity, because it's easy to become a clever gem buyer. My happiest 'eureka' moments are when people discover they don't have to be millionaires to enjoy coloured gemstones. Coloured gemstones often give a 'big bang' of colour for a reasonable price and many are actually rarer than Diamonds.

Thanks to Diamonds, most people have at least a fleeting recognition of the 4Cs (colour, cut, clarity and carat weight). The 4Cs are a good way to describe beauty in gemstones; they give us an easy value guide to what initially seems like very complicated territory. While the 4Cs are a strong foundation, there are other factors that also need to be considered when purchasing gemstones. We'll cover these below, including their relative importance and interrelationship to a gemstone's final value.

World of Colour

It will come as no surprise that colour is the single most important factor when assessing coloured gems. As a percentage, it is estimated that colour contributes to about 50 percent of a gem's final value. Size (carat weight), cut and clarity all directly impact a gemstone's colour. Considering its importance, I've devoted an entire section to colour on page 16.

A Cut Above

One of the biggest misconceptions of 'cut' is its importance to the overall value of a gemstone. One popular book on gemstones states: *"The cut is subjective and may have little or no effect on the buying price"*. I disagree, ranking 'cut' as the second most important C. Why? Even if a raw gemstone crystal has excellent colour, poor cutting can negatively affect how this colour is communicated to the eye in the finished gem. Inversely, a raw crystal with an average colour can be accentuated by good cutting. Skilful cutting can also reduce the impact of inclusions (see below) by placing them in locations not immediately visible. Please do not underestimate the importance of a gemstone's cut. Much like colour, cutting is so important that it has its own section, starting on page 34.

Bringing Clarity to Clarity

Most gemstones are crystalline and possess a 'crystal structure', a regular, repeating, three-dimensional arrangement of bonded atoms. The majority are comprised of a single crystal (macrocrystalline), such as Amethyst, Sapphire and Tourmaline. Other gems have a crystal structure that is so fine that no distinct particles are recognisable, even under the microscope. Termed 'cryptocrystalline', they include gems such as Agate, Chalcedony and Jade.

Regardless of their crystal structure, very few gemstones grow in nature undisturbed. The process of gemstone formation is often cataclysmic, resulting in tiny natural features

Emerald showing its characteristic inclusions known as 'jardin' (garden)

called 'inclusions', which are sometimes called 'flaws'. To me, this is as inappropriate as calling the slight imperfections in a silk jacket or the knots in a wooden table 'flaws'. In my mind, they are 'natural characteristics', mother nature's hallmarks of authenticity that record a gem's natural relationship with the earth. Inclusions are typically microscopic and most easily glimpsed under magnification, either by using a jeweller's loupe or microscope. A gemstone's clarity is determined by the amount and location of its inclusions, for example, eye-clean (no visible inclusions when the gem is examined 6 inches from the naked eye), slightly included, moderately included, heavily included, and severely included. There are two general rules of thumb regarding clarity:

- The higher the clarity grade, the higher the value of the gem.
- Inclusions that don't interfere with the brilliance, scintillation (sparkle) and fire of a gem, do not affect its value.

However, please be aware that attractive, characteristic or interesting inclusions can add value to a gemstone, for example asterism in Star Rubies (see page 30 and 200 for more).

Related to clarity, but influenced by a gemstone's chemical composition, crystal structure and inclusions, different gems inherently display different levels of opacity:

- **Opaque** is the quality of not allowing the transmission of light. Opaque gems include Agate, Jade and Onyx.

Blue Diamond, a 'classic' transparent gemstone

- **Translucent** gems allow transmitted light to pass through, but objects cannot be clearly seen through a translucent gemstone. Good examples are Fire Opal and Rose Quartz.

- **Transparent** gemstones allow transmitted light to clearly pass through. Objects can be seen through a transparent gemstone and examples include Amethyst, Sapphire and Tanzanite. As it directly affects the communication of colour, the degree of transparency and brilliance is crucial in determining the value of transparent gems.

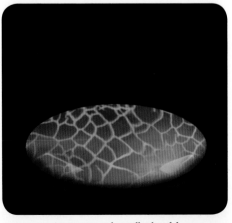

Agate, opaque but still colourful

As you gain experience, you'll begin to expect certain degrees of clarity from certain gems. Some gem varieties always have more inclusions than others. This is neither good nor bad; it's just the way they are found in nature. To make sense of these natural differences, the GIA (Gemmological Institute of America) classifies gems into three types based on the prevalence of inclusions:

- **Type I:** These gems grow extremely clean in nature and usually have no eye-visible inclusions, for example Aquamarine.
- **Type II:** These gems typically grow with some minor inclusions in nature that may be eye-visible, for example Ruby.
- **Type III:** These gems typically grow with many inclusions in nature and they are usually eye-visible, for example Emerald.

Not all gems have been 'type' classified by the GIA, only the more prominent gems at the time of developing the system. Translucent, opaque and cabochon cut gems are not 'type' classified. But whatever you do, please do not incorrectly deduce that a Type III gemstone is inherently inferior to a Type I gemstone.

Weighing In

All things being equal, the bigger the gem, the higher the value. In general, colour and/or optical phenomena, such as colour change or play of colour (see page 32 for more), is more visible in larger gemstones.

Gemstones are traditionally weighed in carats (1 carat = 0.20 grammes/200 milligrammes). For gemstones weighing less than 1 carat, their weight is expressed in units that are 100 times smaller, known as points (e.g. 50 points = 0.5 carats). Originating in the bazaars of the Far East, where carob seeds were once used to weigh gems, carat weight was standardised as one-fifth of a gramme in Europe in 1907. But why did the ancients use

Seeds of the carob plant were used during antiquity to weigh gemstones

carob seeds to weigh gems? They were selected because of their consistent size and weight. Please don't confuse 'carats' with 'karats'. Karat measures gold purity and is only related to 'carat' from the use of carob seeds to weigh the alloys added to pure gold. In the United Kingdom gem 'carat' weight and gold 'carat' purity are both confusingly spelt with a 'c'.

Bigger gems are always rarer than smaller ones. A 4 carat gem is always worth far more than four 1 carat gems of the same quality. However, a group of smaller gems will cost more than a single gem of the same carat weight if the cost to facet the individual gems outweighs the difference in price. Due to their comparative rarity, pairs or rows (suites) of matched gems are more highly valued than single gems of the same size and quality.

Passport Please!

In my mind, the fifth C is 'country' of origin. Much like brand names in sportswear, gemstones with a historical pedigree rich in legend and lore are *sometimes* valued more highly than gemstone's that don't have any historical connotations. But this is not always true, for example, the coveted Paraíba Tourmaline was only discovered in 1989.

Ceylon Sapphire

In a recent article in Coloured Stone magazine, Editor-in-Chief David Federman says: *"Hallowed origins such as Kashmir and Mogok, Burma, are pivotal value factors when pricing Sapphires and Rubies that can make as much as a 40 percent difference in their value"*. While this might make sense if all things are equal and the origin reliably certified, please remember to use your eyes! Paying a premium for an otherwise low quality gem simply because of pedigree has always seemed absurd to me.

The country of origin never denotes quality; good and bad qualities are found in every deposit. Sure, some sources are noted for producing more good quality gems than others, making their origin quality indicative, but this is never an absolute. For example, not all Sapphires from Sri Lanka are of suitable quality to warrant the 'Ceylon' moniker. For me, origin is a collectable curiosity, an interesting attribute that definitely adds to the appeal of gemstones, but not something that is going to make me want to own a gem I don't find attractive.

While including names of geographical locations should only be done when they denote the areas from which gemstones originate, under CIBJO guidelines (see page 255 for more) origin is considered a matter of opinion.

It's a Small World After All

Let's face it, people are becoming increasingly well-informed about global social and environmental issues and in my mind, this is definitely a good thing. At the end of the day, gemstones are pure emotion, and the last thing anyone wants to feel are negative emotions associated with the suffering of others. Accordingly, the sixth C is the 'confidence' that comes from knowing your gems are from legitimate sources not involved in funding conflict or terrorism. With respect to Diamonds, this is largely a given thanks to United Nations resolutions and the Kimberley Process (**www.diamondfacts.org**). With coloured gemstones, always check with the seller.

Are You Tough Enough?

With proper care all gemstone jewellery should be suitable for passing down through many generations (see page 255 for more). Durability is a combination of three properties:

1. **Hardness** is the ability of a gem to resist surface scratching (Mohs' Hardness Scale). See page 246 for more.
2. **Toughness** is the ability of a gem to resist the development of fractures (random non-directional breakage) or cleavage (splitting along well-defined planes). Please note that toughness and hardness in gemstones can be mutually exclusive. Just because a gemstone is hard, it is not necessarily tough and vice versa
3. **Stability** is the ability of a gem to resist physical or chemical damage.

All Gems Are Rare…

By their very definition all gems are rare, but just like in George Orwell's 'Animal Farm', some gems are rarer than others. When buying gems always try to understand why a gem is 'rare', failing to do so makes it lose relevance, becoming a throwaway term. I always cringe when I hear jewellery salespeople endlessly rabbit on about 'rarity' without any contextual qualification. If rarity is worth mentioning, it is certainly worth qualifying. For example, Tanzanite is 1,000 times rarer than Diamonds.

Rarity can be described in three, often unrelated, ways: geological, marketplace and comparative. Just because a gem is geologically rare, this doesn't always mean it has a higher value in the marketplace and vice versa. Beauty, marketing and name recognition also play a big part. Just look at Diamonds. Rarity can also be a double-edged sword, sometimes it jeopardises a gem's commercial viability, for example Tsavorite.

> Just as nobody in their right mind would call their loved one 'semi beautiful', why oh why, do people still call some gemstones 'semi precious'? Derived from the French 'pierres precieuse', the traditional 'precious gems' are Emerald, Diamond, Ruby and Sapphire. When other gemstone varieties gained popularity they also needed a name. For some reason, the industry settled on 'semi precious' and has regretted it ever since. Today, 'semi precious' is regarded as out of date and misleading. This is because it undersells these gems and is no longer a true expression of value. For example, some Rubies can sell for less than $100 per carat, while a fine Paraíba Tourmaline can sell for over $30,000 per carat. That seems pretty precious to me!

Nip and Tuck

To make sure each gemstone reaches its full potential, lapidaries and jewellers employ a variety of techniques. Some of these, like cutting and setting, are immediately visible, while others, such as enhancements or treatments, remain relatively unknown despite being used for thousands of years. Visit page 255 to learn about acceptable enhancements applied to each gem variety, their frequency, and any special care instructions.

Can You See What I See?

When you gaze upon gemstones, what do you see? The following are some important terms used to describe a gem's visual appearance as it interacts with light:

- **Lustre** is the amount of light that is reflected from a gem's surface.

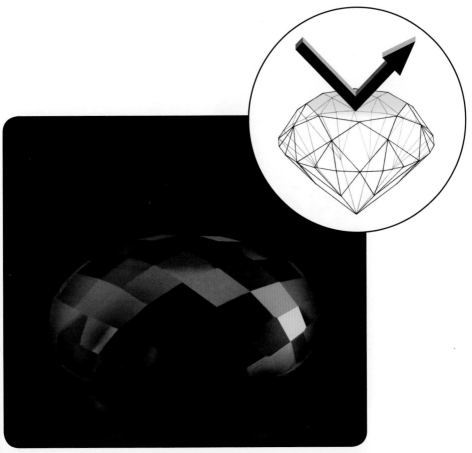

Onyx showing its characteristic lustre

- **Adamantine** is the very bright and reflective lustre displayed by Diamonds. It is derived from the Greek root word for Diamonds 'adamas', meaning 'unconquerable', which is certainly appropriate for the world's hardest natural substance! Sub-adamantine is occasionally used to describe gems with a lustre close to Diamond, such as Alexandrite and Demantoid. While there are other mineralogical terms to describe lustre, these have been omitted because they are of little importance to your everyday appreciation of gemstones.

- **Scintillation** is the play of light (reflections from a polished surface) that causes a gem to sparkle as its relative position to either the viewer or the source of illumination changes.

Incredibly rare and brilliant, this is the only Vanadium Chrysoberyl the author has ever seen

- **Brilliance** is the amount of light (i.e. body colour) that is reflected from a gem's interior. Brilliance is dependant on a gem's optical properties (see page 246 for more), cutting (critical angle), colour, transparency, clarity, polish, lustre and wear.

- **Fire**, also known as dispersion, is the splitting of light into its component colours. This gemmological feature adds both beauty and value. While all gemstones of a large size exhibit fire, the most dispersive gemstones ranked in order are Sphene[1], Demantoid[2], Diamond[3] and Zircon[4].

Diamond showing its characteristic fire

WORLD OF COLOUR

"The best colour in the whole world is the one that looks good on you".
Gabrielle Bonheur 'Coco' Chanel (1883-1971)

Now that's some clever advice. As mentioned previously, colour is the single most important factor when assessing coloured gemstones. But like everything to do with beauty, it is highly subjective and at the end of the day, in the eye of the beholder. This is not to say that there are no colour paradigms in gemstones, there certainly are, but these should never be at the expense of personal preferences. One thing that confuses me is the stance taken by some 'experts' with respect to colour preferences. You should always be aware of how certain colours are valued in the marketplace, but telling someone their prized gemstone is not 'true' because of this or that, not only disregards personal preferences, it can even turn people off coloured gemstones. In my mind, the true gemstone connoisseur is an evangelist never an elitist.

It will come as no surprise that the more attractive a gem's colour, the higher the value. The most valuable colours depend on two factors, fashion and rarity. Fashion is easy to understand, it's all about colour popularity; if no one finds a gem's colour attractive, then its rarity really doesn't matter. Inversely, if a gem's colour is popular and it's rare, such as Paraíba Tourmaline or Padparadscha Sapphire, then you've got a gemstone superstar. In general, intense colours are more favoured than those that are dark or light, but there are exceptions, for example, that Victorian favourite, Rose de France Amethyst.

For most gems, I recommend what I call the 'Goldilocks Maxim', named after the children's story involving a juvenile delinquent and three disgruntled bears. Just like Goldilocks' preferences, the best gems are not too dark or too light, but just right,

Peridot is a 'self coloured' gemstone

Yellow Sapphire is an 'other coloured' gemstone

with the intense 'middle' colours being the happy medium. Most of the time this gauge is reliable, just remember that the 'intense middle colour' can vary for each gemstone variety. As the way a gemstone's colour is described can make people want to own it or avoid it, some gems have specific words or phrases to describe their most desirable colours, for example, 'noble red' in Spinel, 'cornflower blue' in Sapphires or 'AAA' to denote top quality (colour and clarity).

But how does colour actually work? Simplistically, gemstone colour occurs in two ways:

1. **Self Coloured (Idiochromatic):** A colouring element is incorporated into the mineral's crystal structure, always giving it a characteristic colour. For example, Peridot will always be shades of green from its high iron content, which comprises about 10 percent of its total mass.

2. **Other Coloured (Allochromatic):** Colour is caused by small amounts of colouring elements that are not part of the mineral's normal crystal structure and/or crystal imperfections (colour centres). In their pure state, 'other coloured' minerals are colourless, for example Sapphire. Without colouring elements (and/or colour centres), all Sapphires would be colourless.

Most things get their colour due to how they react with light. Some gems, such as Opal, get their colours physically as light is refracted in flashes of colours that change with the angle of observation ('play of colour'). But for most gems, and even most objects, our perception of colour involves an amazing

Several years ago, an elderly American lady took the long bus journey from Bangkok to the gem markets of Chanthaburi to purchase some Rubies to pass on as inheritances for her granddaughters. She was a lovely lady and extremely well-informed. She'd certainly done her homework, reading numerous books and speaking to every 'expert' who'd give her the time of day. In a way, this was her problem. She had become so obsessed with finding 'the perfect colour' that her own preferences had fallen by the wayside. Each time she got an 'expert opinion', she got more confused. I brought her back to earth with a simple question: *"Do you know what Rubies you like?"* She did and within the hour, I thought we'd narrowed the search, but then she asked, *"Is this the best colour?"* In all honesty, she had selected some beauties, intense rich-crimson, not too dark, not too light, so I answered, *"For me, yes".* Anticipating, *"But not for everyone?"* I added, *"These are great collectors' Rubies and assuming that new deposits don't miraculously appear and flood the market, they should hold their value. But don't you think the most important thing for your granddaughters will be that you travelled all by yourself to a small town in Thailand just to buy them some Rubies you love?"* It is true; sometimes you can't see the forest for the trees.

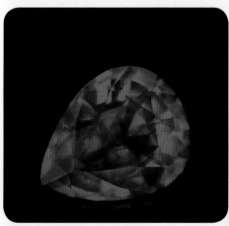

Ruby, the 'king of gems'

transformation. As revealed by rainbows, white light is comprised of the individual colours of the spectrum: red, orange, yellow, green, blue, and violet light. When white light passes through a gem, some of these spectral colours are absorbed. The spectral colours of white light least absorbed combine to produce the colour of the gem. This absorption of certain colours is called the 'selective absorption of light' and is always the same for an individual gemstone. A red gemstone appears red because all the other colours of the spectrum except red are absorbed by the gem. It is changes in a light source's component colours that cause gems to look different in dissimilar lighting conditions. Even a small variation in the light source can produce a big difference in how we see a gem's colour. In extreme examples, this results in the colour change effect (see page 31 for more). While some gemstones look better in natural daylight and others in artificial (incandescent) light, a gemstone's colours should ideally remain beautiful in any light source.

Colour is comprised of three components:

1. **Hue** is the position of a colour on a colour wheel. It is described as the shade, tint or sensation of colour.

2. **Tone** is the degree of lightness or darkness of a colour.

3. **Saturation** is described as the intensity (strength or purity) of a colour.

Even though there are several industry colour grading systems (e.g. GemDialogue, GemEWizard and GIASquare), there is no universal standard for communicating colour in coloured gemstones. This is mainly due to coloured gems being highly subjective, resulting in sellers creating their own grading, such as AAA.

Colour can be a great way to pick the right gem for you, but please note that colour alone is not a reliable way to identify gemstones. Even experts can be fooled. One friend in the industry loves to reinforce this by routinely showing me examples of gems that look like something else. I still remember an exceptionally fine Pezzottaite that at a glance looked like a Pink Sapphire. Once viewed with a loupe, its characteristic inclusions gave the game away. This is an important lesson. Colour helps, but other visual clues such as inclusion patterns, signs of wear (hardness), pleochroism, fire and sparkle are also critical. These features, in combination with gemmological tools such as a microscope, loupe and refractometer, are the only way to be certain.

Below, some popular gems are grouped by their colours - *get back in black* (black gems), *discover heavenly blues* (blue - violet gems), *become a white knight* (colourless/white gems), *make them green with envy* (green gems), *multiply your choices* (multicoloured gems), *warm your heart* (red - pink gems) or *simply brighten your day* (yellow - chocolate gems). One question I have been asked is: *"What colour gem suits every person?"* While blue is one of the most popular choices, its richer tones can be too dark for some people. The colour of the sky and tropical seas, medium or aqua blues suit almost any skin tone. Examples include Aquamarine, Ceylon Sapphire, Paraíba Tourmaline and Turquoise. Don't believe me? Just look at the popularity of blue jeans.

Black Gems

Black Diamond

Black Star Sapphire

Onyx

Other black gems include Black Spinel, Black Tourmaline, Hematite and Obsidian.

Blue - Violet Gems

AAA Aquamarine

AAA Tanzanite

Amblygonite

Amethyst

Apatite

Aquamarine

Blue Diamond

Blue Fire Opal

Blue Green Tourmaline

Blue Sapphire

Blue Spinel

Ceylon Sapphire

Chalcedony

Grape Topaz

Hemimorphite

Indicolite

Iolite

Kanchanaburi Sapphire

Kyanite

Lapis Lazuli

London Blue Topaz

Midnight Blue Sapphire

Ocean Topaz

Paraíba Tourmaline

Purple Sapphire

Purple Spinel

Ratanakiri Zircon

Sky Blue Topaz

Star Sapphire

Swiss Blue Topaz

Tanzanite

Turquoise

Other blue - violet gems include Azurmalachite, Blue Moon Quartz, Blue Opal, Cat's Eye Aquamarine, Sodalite and Sugilite.

Colourless/White Gems

Diamond

Goshenite

Petalite

White Quartz

White Sapphire

White Topaz

White Zircon

Other colourless/white gems include Anglesite, Aragonite, Calcite, Danburite, Howlite, Phantom Quartz and White Kunzite .

Green Gems

AAA Emerald

Amazonite

Amblygonite

Bloodstone

Chrysoprase

Colombian Emerald

Demantoid

Emerald

Green Amethyst

Green Diamond

Green Kunzite

Green Sapphire

Green Tourmaline

Jade

Kiwi Topaz

Malachite

Moldavite

Paraíba Tourmaline

Peridot

Russian Diopside

Tsavorite

Other green gems include Aragonite, Azurmalachite, Chrysocolla, Gahnite, Green Opal, Hiddenite, Idocrase, Mali Garnet, Merelani Mint Garnet, Olive Quartz and Prehnite.

Multicoloured Gems

Alexandrite

Aventurine

Bi Colour Amethyst

Bi Colour Citrine

Bi Colour Quartz

Bi Colour Tourmaline

Black Opal

Cat's Eye Zultanite

Colour Change Garnet

Colour Change Sapphire

Fluorite

Freshwater Pearl

Jasper

Jelly Opal

Labradorite

Matrix Opal

Moonlight Topaz

Moonstone

Mother of Pearl

Mystic Topaz

Neptune Topaz

Rainbow Moonstone

Sardonyx

Semi Black Opal

South Sea Pearl

Tahitian Pearl

Twilight Topaz

White Opal

Zultanite

Other multicoloured gems include Bi Colour Morganite, Boulder Opal, Cat's Eye Alexandrite, Fire Agate, Mabe Pearl, Mookite, Rainbow Quartz, Scapolite, Snowflake Obsidian and Spectrolite.

Red - Pink Gems

Cherry Topaz

Flamingo Topaz

Kunzite

Morganite

Mozambique Garnet

Mulberry Topaz

Noble Red Spinel

Pink Diamond

Pink Sapphire

Pink Spinel

Pink Tourmaline

Pyrope

Red - Pink Gems (Continued)

Red Diamond

Rhodochrosite

Rhodolite

Rhodonite

Rose de France Amethyst

Rose Quartz

Rubellite

Ruby

Star Ruby

Tanzanian Ruby

Other red - pink gems include Andesine, Bixbite, Clinohumite, Pezzottaite, Pink Opal and Umbalite.

Yellow - Chocolate Gems

Agate

Amber

Andalusite

Canary Topaz

Carnelian

Cat's Eye Chrysoberyl

Champagne Diamond

Chrysoberyl

Citrine

Cuprian Tourmaline

Fire Opal

Heliodor

Hessonite

Imperial Topaz

Marcasite

Lemon Citrine

Mandarin Garnet

Orange Sapphire

Padparadscha Colour Sapphire

Padparadscha Sapphire

Smoky Quartz

Spessartite

Sphene

Sunset Sapphire

Sunstone

Tigers Eye

Yellow Diamond

Yellow Sapphire

Other yellow - chocolate gems include Andradite, Bronzite, Cat's Eye Scapolite, Cat's Eye Sillimanite, Cognac Quartz, Epidote, Idocrase, Kornerupine, Malaia Garnet, Orthoclase, Quartzite, Rutile Quartz, Sard, Scheelite, Sillimanite, Star Diopside, Star Sillimanite, Star Sunstone, Unakite, Yellow Beryl, Yellow Kunzite and Yellow Opal.

GEMSTONE SPECIAL EFFECTS (SFX)

"To suppose that the eye... could have been formed by natural selection, seems, I freely confess, absurd in the highest degree".

Charles Darwin (1809-1882), Origin of Species

Gemstones, jewels, bijous, rocks, and 'bling' are much more than just dazzling, multicoloured expensive minerals and organics. Some gemstones also have special optical effects or simply 'SFX'. Called 'phenomena' by gemmologists, these rare and beautiful optical properties are part of a gemstone's structure. Frequently adding value, expert gem cutting can bring out these unique effects to their fullest, or hide them when necessary. So grab the popcorn and turn off your mobile, 'The Clever Gem Buyer' cinema is about to present, 'Gemstone Special Effects'...

Adularescence (Opalescence)

Adularescence mightn't be the easiest word to remember, but it is very easy to spot. Remember 'Moon Shadow' by Cat Stevens? Adularescence is the silver to bluish-white light that shimmers and glides over the surface of that enchantingly romantic gem, Moonstone. Adularescence is due to 'interference phenomena', which simply means the scattering of light by thin crystalline layers. This effect gets its name from a variety of Moonstone found in the European Alps called 'Adularia', and is called 'opalescence' when occurring in Opals.

Rainbow Moonstone showing its characteristic blue adularescence

Opposite: Black Opal & Diamond 9K Yellow Gold Ring

Asterism

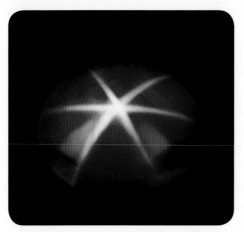

Star Ruby, once aptly known as the 'three swords'

Imagine being the first person to look into a gem and see a luminous star. No wonder star gems were once regarded with so much superstition. Asterism, also known as the star effect or asteria, is a uniquely beautiful, mysterious optical effect especially coveted in Rubies and Sapphires. Asterism is created by the reflection of light from multidirectional, long needle-shaped inclusions that occur in parallel arrangements in at least two different directions. While they come in six rays, four rays, and on the odd occasion 12 rays, all star gems are dependent on a gem being cut 'en cabochon' (cut in convex form and highly polished, but not faceted). Asterism is most visible in a direct, single beam of light. Colour aside, a well cut star gemstone has a distinct star whose rays are straight and equidistant. Stars are typically positioned in the centre of the gem, bearing in mind that they are sometimes deliberately off-centred for aesthetics.

Aventurescence

Another 'scence' word, this one originated in an 18th-century Venetian glassworks, when copper filings accidentally fell into a batch of molten glass. According to legend, the workers exclaimed, *"a ventura"*, which means 'by chance', on noticing their glass with sparkles. In gemstones this phenomenon is caused by glittering metallic inclusions. In Chalcedony Quartz, thousands of tiny metallic flakes create the glimmering rarity called Aventurine and when present in Feldspar, sparkling Sunstone. One 'gem' to be aware of is Goldstone, a manmade glass and copper substitute.

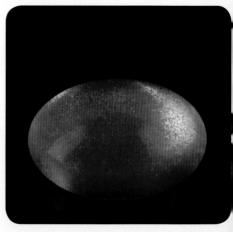

Madagascan Sunstone

Chatoyancy

French for cat, *le chat* is obviously all about our feline friend. Chatoyancy, also known as the cat's eye effect, appears as a single bright reflective line of light, similar to a cat's eye. Chatoyancy is created by the reflection of light from long needle-shaped inclusions occurring in a parallel arrangement. Similar to star gems, the cat's eye effect is dependent on a gem being cut 'en cabochon' and is most visible in a direct, single beam of light. One gem synonymous with this phenomenon is Chrysoberyl, so much so that that if you just say 'cat's eye' to a gem professional, they'll assume you mean Cat's Eye Chrysoberyl.

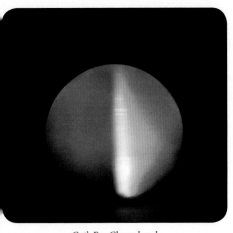

Cat's Eye Chrysoberyl

Colour Change

Manfred Eickhorst M. Sc. Physics, well-known for his innovative lighting and gemmological equipment, states, "*The beauty of gems to the human eye is determined by the gemstone's colour appearance*". Obviously, this beauty is dramatically enhanced if a gem can change its colour. Gemstones that display this phenomenon include the miraculous Alexandrite, which can appear blue-green, forest green, green, khaki, teal or yellowish-green, and combinations thereof in candescent light (sunlight), and brownish-red, orangey-red, red or reddish-purple, and combinations thereof, in incandescent light (candlelight). Also know as the 'Alexandrite Effect', colour change gems show different colours when viewed in two different light sources. As revealed by rainbows, white light is comprised of the individual colours of the spectrum: blue, green, orange, red, violet, and yellow. When white light passes

Brazilian Alexandrite showing its colour change

through a gem, some of these spectral colours are absorbed. The spectral colours of white light least absorbed combine to produce the colour of the gem. It is changes in a light source's component colours that cause gems to look different in various lighting conditions. Although they appear similar to our eyes, sunlight has very strong blue wavelengths, while electric light is richer in red wavelengths. In colour change gems, absorption of different colours of the spectrum from different light sources results in our 'colour change' perception. Other colour change gems include Colour Change Garnet, Colour Change Sapphire and Zultanite. A colour change gem is rated by the strength of its change, and how attractive and distinct its colour is in both candescent and incandescent light. As with all optical effects, the bigger the gem, the more noticeable the colour change.

Iridescence

Derived from the Greek 'iris', meaning 'rainbow', iridescence is a rainbow-like colour effect caused by a gem's structure breaking up light into its spectral colours. With colours that change depending on the angle of observation, some everyday examples of iridescence are soap bubbles and butterfly wings. The 'metallic iridescence' or 'schiller' in Labradorite it aptly called 'labradorescence', while the delicate iridescence seen in Pearl is called the 'orient' or 'overtone'. Examples of other iridescent gems are Ammolite, Fire Agate and Mother of Pearl.

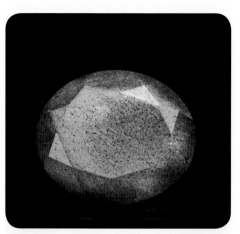

Labradorite displaying its signature metallic iridescence

Play of Colour

Do you remember science class with the prism that displays the spectral colours of the rainbow? If yes, you already understand play of colour. Unique to Opal, 'play of colour' is the flashes of colour that change with the angle of observation. An Opal, whose 'play of colour' flashes are in the rare reds, is generally more valuable than Opals with just blue and green, but as with all gemstones, colour preferences are subjective and should be dictated by individual tastes.

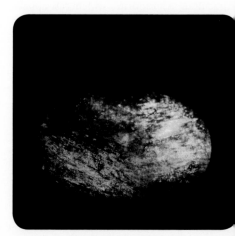

Play of colour in Black Opal

Pleochroism (Double Refraction)

In certain gemstones, atoms are arranged so that light splits into two separate components. If this results in optical doubling, then this is called 'double refractivity' or 'bifringence'. Zircon is a good example of a doubly refractive gemstone. If these rays of light possess different colours visible when the gem is viewed from different angles, then this is called 'pleochroism' or getting more technical, dichroism (two-colours, such as Tourmaline) and trichroism (three-colours, such as Tanzanite).

A common misconception is that double refractivity makes a gem more brilliant. It doesn't. In fact, singly refractive gems can display colours that are purer and more intense than those seen in doubly refractive gems of the same colour (e.g. Noble Red Spinel versus Ruby). Confused? The word that causes the problem is 'double'. While light is being split into two (doubled), the amount of light exiting the gem is not.

Pleochroism affects gem buyers in three ways: the component colours are so similar that pleochroism usually doesn't affect beauty (e.g. Ruby and Sapphire); the component colours are different and not all are attractive, so cutters minimise pleochroism by orientating the crystal to display its single best colour (e.g. Kunzite and Tanzanite); or the component colours are different, yet attractive, so the cutters orient the gem to get a pleasing mix of colours (e.g. Andalusite).

Ratanakiri Zircon is a doubly refractive gemstone

Andalusite displaying its pleochroic colours

A CUT ABOVE

"In the state of nature, the surfaces of gems are generally dull and lustreless; their shape is irregular, and their mass is permeated by flaws and imperfections".
Oliver Cummings Farrington (1864-1934), Gems and Gem Minerals

While it would be wonderful if gemstones came out of the ground ready to wear, this typically just doesn't happen. Raw crystals from the earth are usually called 'rough gemstones' (or just 'rough') and this is actually very apt - rough gems can look pretty rough!

Lapidary (gem cutting) is thousands of years old and is the transformation of raw crystals into dazzling gemstones. It is the art of making the gem assume a certain shape, unlocking its lustre, colour and brilliance. Lapidaries, also known as gem cutters, have two general styles they can choose when cutting gemstones:

1. **Faceted Gems:** Gems with geometrically-shaped, flat polished faces. Today, faceted gemstones are the most popular style, but this was not always the case. Big fans of cabochons, cameos (a gem carved in positive relief) and intaglios (a gem carved in negative relief), did you know that ancient Romans considered wearing faceted gems vulgar?

2. **Non-faceted:** Gems that don't have geometrically-shaped, flat polished faces, such as cabochons. Derived from the old Norman French word 'caboche', meaning head, cabochons are an ancient shaping and polishing technique that remains popular today due to the yesteryear charm and character of what are typically, richly coloured gems.

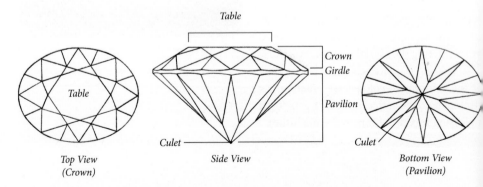

The different parts of a gemstone. Due to the spherical nature of most rough, the oval is the most common shape for coloured gemstones as it typically best balances beauty and weight retention

Because of their different optical properties, coloured gems do not have an ideal 'brilliant cut' like Diamonds (see the diagram in this section for more). Which style, cut and shape lapidaries select depends on the type, shape and quality of the rough gemstone. The cut of a gem directly affects its overall value as the cut determines how well a gem returns its body colour back to the eye.

The lapidary frequently performs a juggling act between beauty and commercial considerations, such as carat weight retention. For every gem, the lapidary is looking for the best compromise between appearance and size, remembering that the value of the finished gem also depends on its carat weight. Maintaining a gem's critical angle (the maximum angle

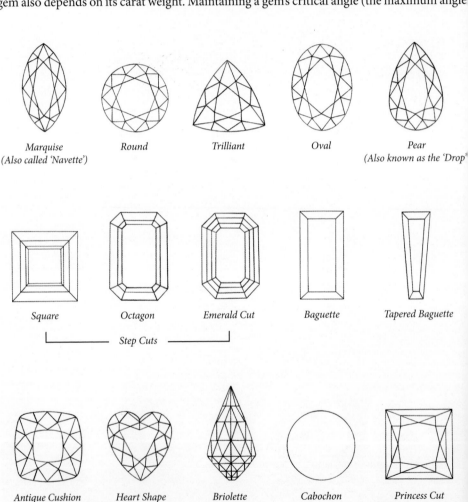

| Marquise | Round | Trilliant | Oval | Pear |
| (Also called 'Navette') | | | | (Also known as the 'Drop' |

| Square | Octagon | Emerald Cut | Baguette | Tapered Baguette |

Step Cuts

Antique Cushion	Heart Shape	Briolette	Cabochon	Princess Cut
				(Also known as the
				'Square Brilliant')

Classic gemstone shapes and cuts

of refraction, see page 246 for more) often unavoidably results in a smaller gem. If you accept a little bulge in the pavilion, the gem mightn't have its very best brilliance, but will weigh more. You also have to consider the impact of windows (areas of washed out colour in a table-up gem, often due to a shallow pavilion) or extinctions (areas of darkness in a table-up gem, all gemstones possess some degree of extinction) on a finished gemstone's beauty. At times, making these decisions is extremely difficult and better suited to a soothsayer than a gemstone professional. For example, several years ago, I encountered a beautiful Canary Yellow Sapphire in my adopted hometown of Chanthaburi, Thailand. At over 35 carats with excellent colour and clarity, it was a very special gem of exceptional rarity. The only minor

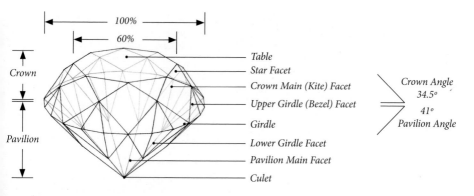

The round brilliant cut possesses the angles and proportions once thought necessary to display a Diamond's best dispersion (fiery flashes of colour), scintillation (play of light) and its characteristic brilliance (white light reflections). While also used for other gemstones, the brilliant cut was developed specifically for Diamonds. The standard number of facets in a round brilliant cut is 57 (or 58 if you include the culet). The brilliant cut was developed by several people, including Vincenzio Perruzzi (an 18th-century Venetian cutter), Henry Morse (he opened America's first diamond cutting workshop in Boston, Massachusetts in 1860) and the Russian mathematical genius Marcel Tolkowsky (a member of a large and powerful Diamond family, he calculated the cuts necessary to create the ideal round brilliant cut in his book, 'Diamond Design' published in 1919).

critique would be that some of its cut proportions were a little loose, ever so slightly reducing its brilliance. Now you could have re-cut the gem, tightening things up to achieve 'optimum brilliance', but this would have reduced its weight by at least 5 carats - not a decision for the fainthearted! Sometimes size does matter and big can be beautiful, but this isn't always the case. Beauty will sometimes be sacrificed to minimise rough weight loss and vice versa.

That's all well and dandy, but how do you tell a good cut from a bad one? No one cut is always more beautiful than another, it's all down to the magic of nature and the artistry of the lapidary. One thing that can confuse is shape versus cut. Sometimes they mean the same thing (a 'princess cut' is always square in shape) and sometimes they don't (a 'step cut' can be square, rectangular or octagon). Like most gemstone authors, I am not too puritanical about this, using both terms interchangeably as appropriate, but the cut is not just a gem's

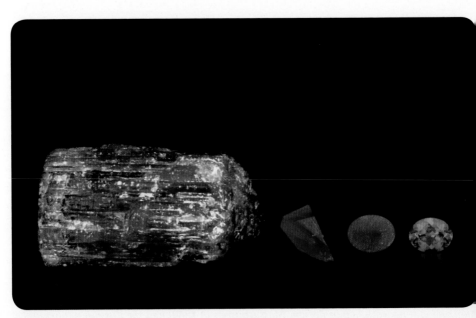

The steps in cutting are slicing (also sometimes confusingly called 'cutting'), pre-forming, shaping and polishing. The first step involves using a Diamond-tipped circular steel saw to slice the rough into pieces. Once the rough has been sliced, it is pre-formed using a vertical steel grinding wheel. The shaper then uses a hand-operated shaping wheel to more accurately present its facets and size. The final step is polishing the gem with Diamond paste on a horizontal wheel to reveal its hidden lustre and brilliance.

shape, it is also the cutting techniques (facet arrangements, finish and proportions) used to finish the gem from the rough. A gem's shape will affect the overall look of the gem, but if it's faceted properly, the shape won't necessarily affect its value. Saying this, certain shapes will sometimes demand a slight premium or be marginally discounted depending on the gem type and the amount of rough lost or retained to arrive at each shape. A diagram of some of the classic shapes and cuts are included in this section. Due to the spherical nature of most rough, the oval is the most common shape for coloured gemstones, as it typically best balances beauty and weight retention. Once you've established your shape preference, simply use the following checklist:

✓ Even, uniform colour with no distinct zoning, unless of cause this is a feature of the gemstone as in bicolour varieties. Remember, gems are designed to be viewed from the table down.

✓ Balance, symmetry and proportion. Some 'fancy cut' gems are deliberately cut asymmetrically, but this is by no means standard. Fancy cut gems are either standard cut variants, create the illusion of a bigger more perfect gemstone, play with the natural shape of the rough or are revolutionary new shapes, made possible by advances in cutting technology.

✓ Acceptable crown height and pavilion depth. The crown is usually one-half to one-third the pavilion depth.

✓ Acceptable brilliance, remembering that brilliance varies amongst different gemstone varieties. Some books suggest always looking for a 'lively gem', but if the species is not noted for its brilliance, this can be misleading.

✓ Acceptable clarity (amount and location of inclusions), again remembering that acceptable inclusions vary among the different gem varieties.

✓ A good polish condition, with no eye-visible scratches or polishing marks.

✓ Acceptable pavilion bulge and girdle thickness.

✓ Acceptable sharpness of the facet junctions.

✓ The majority of the gem's weight is visible from the top.

The diagram below and opposite shows gemstone cuts from antiquity to the present. True 'artists in stone', lapidary has evolved over thousands of years. During antiquity, cabochons were initially the only cutting style available. Guided by the natural facets of the gemstone's crystal structure, the lapidary cut gems in increasingly more complex ways over time. The earliest of these involved removing the tops of crystals. In the last hundred years, technological advances have allowed cutters to develop some breathtaking innovations.

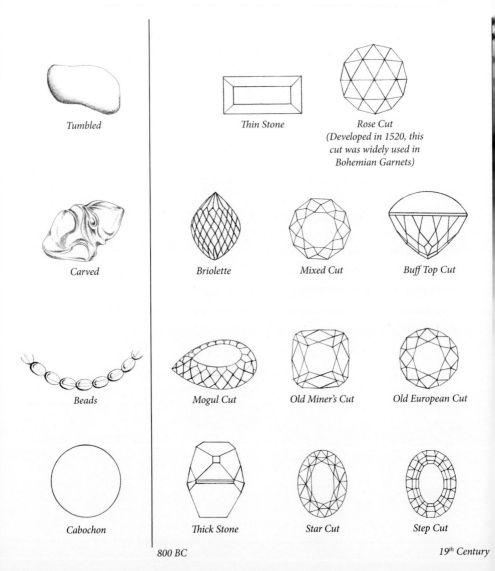

Tumbled

Thin Stone

Rose Cut
(Developed in 1520, this cut was widely used in Bohemian Garnets)

Carved

Briolette

Mixed Cut

Buff Top Cut

Beads

Mogul Cut

Old Miner's Cut

Old European Cut

Cabochon

Thick Stone

Star Cut

Step Cut

800 BC

19ᵗʰ Century

New cuts such as the Wobito snowflake™ would have been difficult, if not impossible, to create just 200 years ago. The general perception is that faceting lower quality rough is not economically viable. When I first started in the gem business, I assumed only lower quality rough was cut 'en cabochon', but this is not the case. Individual preferences vary and today, fine quality gems are cut in both styles. Please don't make quality assumptions based solely on whether a gem has been faceted or not.

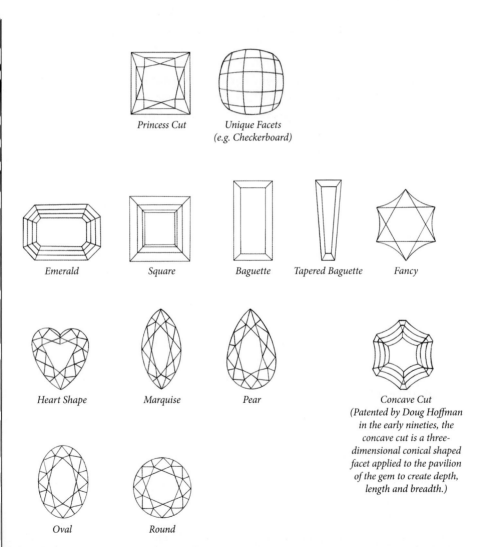

Princess Cut

Unique Facets
(e.g. Checkerboard)

Emerald

Square

Baguette

Tapered Baguette

Fancy

Heart Shape

Marquise

Pear

Concave Cut
(Patented by Doug Hoffman
in the early nineties, the
concave cut is a three-
dimensional conical shaped
facet applied to the pavilion
of the gem to create depth,
length and breadth.)

Oval

Round

A GEMSTONE'S JOURNEY

"The sheen and colouration of precious stones are the same today as they were thousands of years ago and will be for thousands of years to come. In a world of change, this permanence has a charm of its own that was early appreciated".

George Frederick Kunz (1856-1932), The Curious Lore of Precious Stones

This quote by Tiffany's legendary gemmologist and famous gemstone author, George Frederick Kunz, remains a great source of personal insight. I consider myself to be a 'manly man', but like most gem professionals, exceptionally fine gemstones make me act like a giggling school girl! Why? There is something about gemstones that is ingrained in our psyche. To early humans, the mystifying beauty, rarity and durability of gemstones were unexplainable. In a world where people aged, flowers wilted and sunsets disappeared, gemstones alone remain unchanged. For them, the only logical explanation was that they were divine, forever linking gemstones to the spiritual. From Buddhism to Judaism, to Christianity to Islam, this legacy is found within all major religions. To our ancestors, gemstones weren't simply baubles, they meant so much more. They were amulets and talismans that people literally believed could influence their life.

I am not for a second promoting the esoteric attributes of gemstones. My interest in esoteric lore is largely historical, but along with mythology, gemstone history and scientific gemmology, it is critical to understanding the cultural importance of gemstones. Gem lore gives us incredible insight into how our ancestors viewed gemstones and the importance they placed upon them. Today, many people, including my wife, continue to have ideas about the 'healing' power of gems. While some of the 'new age' beliefs and metaphysical properties attributed to gems are certainly intriguing, please remember that little scientific evidence exists to substantiate them.

Created by forces of nature between three billion and several tens of millions of years ago, gemstones have had one heck of a ride. Their journey takes them right back to the genesis of our planet. At 4.4 billion years old, a tiny mineral fragment of Zircon discovered in Western Australia is the oldest known object on earth. This is pretty impressive, considering the earth was formed less than 150 million years before!

Gemstones formed beneath the earth's surface in a variety of different environments, in three different rock types:

1. **Igneous rocks** are formed by the cooling and hardening of magma or molten lava (e.g. basalt and granite).

2. **Metamorphic rocks** are formed when igneous, sedimentary or other metamorphic rocks undergo a physical change due to extreme heat or pressure.

3. **Sedimentary rocks** are formed by the deposition of sediment (e.g. sandstone).

The Earth, Gemstones & You

Earth Formation

Diamond Formation

Gemstone Formation

Users

Heirs

Miners

Purchasers

Middlemen

Cutters

Retailers

Jewellers

Even though some gems form in more than one environment, gemstone formation is broadly classified into four processes: molten rock and associated fluids (e.g. Amethyst, Emerald, Garnet, Ruby, and Sapphire); environmental changes (e.g. Andalusite, Kyanite, Lapis Lazuli, Tanzanite and Tiger's Eye); surface water (e.g. Agate, Malachite, Opal and Turquoise); and formation in the earth's mantle (e.g. Diamond and Peridot).

During antiquity, gemstones were typically accidentally discovered just near the surface of the earth. Even today, prospecting for coloured gemstones still heavily relies on observation and chance. Compared to the intense scientific methods employed in Diamond exploration, prospecting for coloured gemstones is downright primitive. Mechanisation aside, mining coloured gemstones is essentially the same as a thousand years ago, with perseverance, hand tools and elbow grease remaining the key components.

A gemstone deposit is the area where gemstones occur. A deposit is called a 'mine' after it has been worked and one gem deposit can have many mines. Alluvial mining is the most common form of gemstone mining. This method extracts gems from sedimentary deposits, also known as placer or secondary deposits because the gems are not found in the rock in which they formed. These deposits are caused by the erosion of host rocks and include the prospecting of riverbeds, sedimentary deposits beneath the earth's surface and marine mining. The mined earth is either washed with water or sieved, using gravity to extract the rough gemstones.

Rough from alluvial deposits is usually rounded, scratched and cracked due to weathering. This is actually beneficial, as the culling of poorer specimens has already occurred. This typically results in a higher percentage of gem quality crystals in alluvial deposits than primary host rock deposits, where gems are chipped from the rock in which they formed or are hosted.

While they spend a long time waiting in the ground, once discovered, most gems are

Underground fires using thermal shock to split rocks from the 'De Re Metallica' (1556) by Georgius Agricola (1494 - 1555). A mining method common in 16th-century Germany, fire setting is still used in Madagascar

mined and transformed into jewellery within a relatively short time. It typically takes about one to three years from mining for a gem to be set in jewellery and sold, but this can be just a few months or longer than 10 years. The supply chain in the coloured gemstone industry is long and it is not uncommon for a gemstone to pass through seven pairs of hands from the mine to being set in jewellery and then sold to the consumer.

In his book, 'Gemstones: Quality and Value, Volume 1', Yasukazu Suwa states that current annual gem mining production is about one-thirtieth of total past production. Considering that mined gemstones can potentially re-enter the market every 30 years (or so), he estimates that a volume close to that of newly mined gems re-enters the market every year. Saying this, new gemstone deposits are still being discovered (Mozambique Paraíba Tourmaline) and old deposits can start producing again (Russian Alexandrite). Keeping up to date with new discoveries and current availability will help you be a clever gem buyer. Two useful diagrams are included in this section, one that shows the relationship between gems and people, and another that shows the countries in which some popular gemstones are currently mined.

Alluvial gold miners in Russia's Ural Mountains in the early 20th century. It was from deposits like these that Demantoid, a green variety of Garnet, was discovered in 1855

The Origin of Gemstones

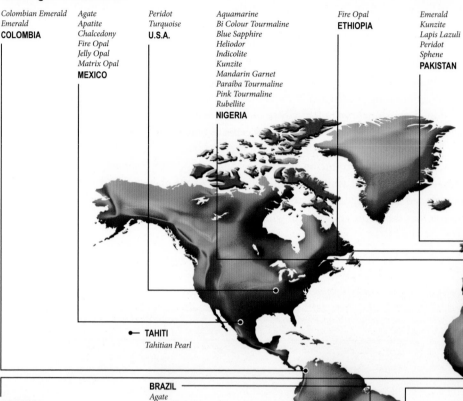

COLOMBIA
Colombian Emerald
Emerald

MEXICO
Agate
Apatite
Chalcedony
Fire Opal
Jelly Opal
Matrix Opal

U.S.A.
Peridot
Turquoise

NIGERIA
Aquamarine
Bi Colour Tourmaline
Blue Sapphire
Heliodor
Indicolite
Kunzite
Mandarin Garnet
Paraíba Tourmaline
Pink Tourmaline
Rubellite

ETHIOPIA
Fire Opal

PAKISTAN
Emerald
Kunzite
Lapis Lazuli
Peridot
Sphene

TANZANIA
AAA Tanzanian Ruby
AAA Tanzanite
Alexandrite
Aquamarine
Blue Sapphire
Blue Spinel
Chalcedony
Chrysoberyl
Citrine
Indicolite
Malachite
Mandarin Garnet
Moonstone
Noble Red Spinel
Peridot
Pink Sapphire
Pink Spinel
Pink Tourmaline
Purple Spinel
Rhodolite
Rose Quartz
Rubellite
Spessartite
Tanzanian Ruby
Tanzanite
Tsavorite
White Sapphire
Zircon

BRAZIL
Agate
Amethyst
Andalusite
Apatite
Aquamarine
Blue Fire Opal
Carnelian
Chalcedony
Chrysoberyl
Citrine
Emerald
Fire Opal
Fluorite
Green Amethyst
Imperial Topaz
Indicolite
Kunzite
London Blue Topaz
Moonstone
Morganite
Mystic Topaz
Paraíba Tourmaline
Petalite
Pink Tourmaline
Rose Quartz
Rubellite
Sky Blue Topaz
Sphene
Swiss Blue Topaz
Tiger's Eye

TAHITI
Tahitian Pearl

Bolivia
Ametine

ZAMBIA
AAA Emerald
AAA Aquamar
Amethyst
Aquamarine
Chrysoberyl
Citrine
Emerald
Malachite

URUGUAY
Amethyst
Carnelian
Citrine

D.R.C.
Blue Green Tourmali
Indicolite

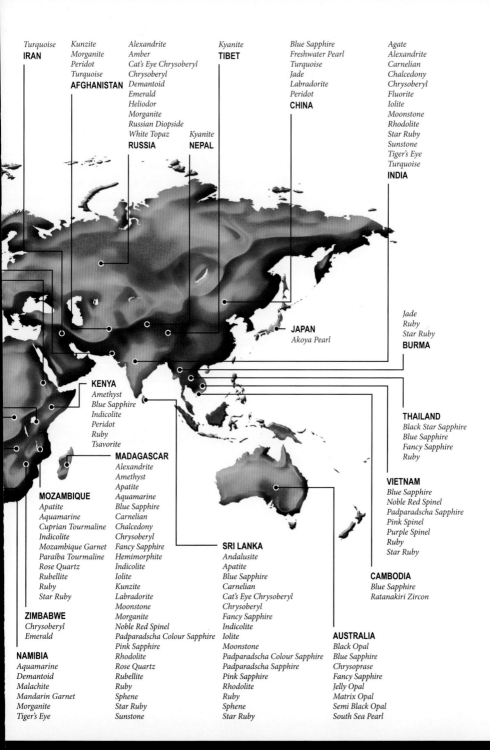

Turquoise
IRAN

Kunzite
Morganite
Peridot
Turquoise
AFGHANISTAN

Alexandrite
Amber
Cat's Eye Chrysoberyl
Chrysoberyl
Demantoid
Emerald
Heliodor
Morganite
Russian Diopside
White Topaz
RUSSIA

Kyanite
TIBET

Kyanite
NEPAL

Blue Sapphire
Freshwater Pearl
Turquoise
Jade
Labradorite
Peridot
CHINA

Agate
Alexandrite
Carnelian
Chalcedony
Chrysoberyl
Fluorite
Iolite
Moonstone
Rhodolite
Star Ruby
Sunstone
Tiger's Eye
Turquoise
INDIA

JAPAN
Akoya Pearl

Jade
Ruby
Star Ruby
BURMA

KENYA
Amethyst
Blue Sapphire
Indicolite
Peridot
Ruby
Tsavorite
MADAGASCAR
Alexandrite
Amethyst
Apatite
Aquamarine
Blue Sapphire
Carnelian
Chalcedony
Chrysoberyl
Fancy Sapphire
Hemimorphite
Indicolite
Iolite
Kunzite
Labradorite
Moonstone
Morganite
Noble Red Spinel
Padparadscha Colour Sapphire
Pink Sapphire
Rhodolite
Rose Quartz
Rubellite
Ruby
Sphene
Star Ruby
Sunstone

THAILAND
Black Star Sapphire
Blue Sapphire
Fancy Sapphire
Ruby

VIETNAM
Blue Sapphire
Noble Red Spinel
Padparadscha Sapphire
Pink Spinel
Purple Spinel
Ruby
Star Ruby

CAMBODIA
Blue Sapphire
Ratanakiri Zircon

MOZAMBIQUE
Apatite
Aquamarine
Cuprian Tourmaline
Indicolite
Mozambique Garnet
Paraíba Tourmaline
Rose Quartz
Rubellite
Ruby
Star Ruby

ZIMBABWE
Chrysoberyl
Emerald

NAMIBIA
Aquamarine
Demantoid
Malachite
Mandarin Garnet
Morganite
Tiger's Eye

SRI LANKA
Andalusite
Apatite
Blue Sapphire
Carnelian
Cat's Eye Chrysoberyl
Chrysoberyl
Fancy Sapphire
Indicolite
Iolite
Moonstone
Padparadscha Colour Sapphire
Padparadscha Sapphire
Pink Sapphire
Rhodolite
Ruby
Sphene
Star Ruby

AUSTRALIA
Black Opal
Blue Sapphire
Chrysoprase
Fancy Sapphire
Jelly Opal
Matrix Opal
Semi Black Opal
South Sea Pearl

ALL IN THE FAMILY

"We are family, get up ev'rybody and sing".
Sister Sledge, We Are Family (1979)

I was nine years old when this song was released. I know it's silly, but a 'pop culture' reference seemed an appropriate lead for a section that some will find immediately useful and others overly technical. If you think you're the latter, your appreciation of gemstones won't be lessened by skipping to the next section, but later you might find it difficult to understand how gemstones' chemical composition (mineralogical class), mineral families/groups and even their colours, all fit together. You'd be surprised how useful considering a gem in relation to its nearest counterparts can be, especially for complicated families like Garnet.

The following charts group gems based on their chemical composition (e.g. silicates, oxides and hydroxides) and mineral families (e.g. Corundum, Beryl and Feldspar).

Borates			
Howlite	-	-	-
Sinhalite	-	-	-

Carbon			
Diamond	Black Damond	-	-
	Blue Diamond	-	-
	Champagne Diamond	-	-
	Green Diamond	-	-
	Pink Diamond	-	-
	Red Diamond	-	-
	Yellow Diamond	-	-

Opposite: The different colours of the Tourmaline family

Carbonates			
Azurmalachite	-	-	-
Aragonite	-	-	-
Azurite	-	-	-
Calcite	-	-	-
Cerussite	-	-	-
Chrysocolla	-	-	-
Dolomite	-	-	-
Malachite	-	-	-
Rhodochrosite	-	-	-
Smithsonite	-	-	-

Halides			
Fluorite	-	-	-

Igneous Rock			
Obsidian	Snowflake Obsidian	-	-

Organics			
Amber	Snowflake Obsidian	-	-
Jet	-	-	-
Pearl	Akoya Pearl	-	-
	Freshwater Pearl	-	-
	Mabe Pearl	-	-
	Mother of Pearl	-	-
	South Sea Pearl	-	-
	Tahitian Pearl	-	-
Shell	-	-	-

Oxides & Hydroxides

Cassiterite	-	-	-
Chysoberyl	Alexandrite	Cat's Eye Alexandrite	-
Cat's Eye Chrysoberyl	-	-	-
Vanadium Chrysoberyl	-	-	-
Corundum	Ruby	Tanzanian Ruby	-
		Star Ruby	-
	Sapphire	Blue Sapphire	Ceylon Sapphire
			Kanchanaburi Sapphire
			Midnight Blue Sapphire
		Fancy Sapphire	Black Star Sapphire
			Colour Change Sapphire
			Green Sapphire
			Orange Sapphire
			Padparadscha Colour Sapphire
			Padparadscha Sapphire
			Pink Sapphire
			Purple Sapphire
			Star Sapphire
			Sunset Sapphire
			White Sapphire
			Yellow Sapphire
Cuprite	-	-	-
Diaspore	Zultanite	Cat's Eye Zultanite	-
Hematite	-	-	-
Rutile	-	-	-
Spinel	Black Spinel	-	-
	Blue Spinel	-	-
	Fancy Spinel	-	-
	Gahnite	-	-
	Noble Red Spinel	-	-
	Pink Spinel	-	-
	Purple Spinel	-	-

Phosphates			
Amblygonite	-	-	-
Apatite	-	-	-
Brazilianite	-	-	-
Lazulit	-	-	-
Turquoise	-	-	-

Silicates			
Amazonite	-	-	-	-
Andalusite	-	-	-	-
Axinite	-	-	-	-
Beryl	Aquamarine	AAA Aquamarine	-	-
		Cat's Eye Aquamarine	-	-
	Bixbite	Pezzottaite (related variety, but not always regarded as a member of the Beryl family)	-	-
	Emerald	-	-	-
	Goshenite	-	-	-
	Heliodor	-	-	-
	Morganite	Bi Colour Morganite	-	-
	Yellow Beryl	-	-	-
Clinohumite	-	-	-	-
Danburite	-	-	-	-
Diopside	Russian Diopside (also known as Chrome Diopside)	-	-	-
	Star Diopside	-	-	-
Dioptase	-	-	-	-
Dumortierite	-	-	-	-
Enstatite	Bronzite	-	-	-
Epidote	-	-	-	-
Euclase	-	-	-	-

Silicates (Continued)				
Feldspar	Andesine	-	-	-
	Labradorite	-	-	-
	Moonstone	Rainbow Moonstone	-	-
	Orthoclase	-	-	-
	Spectrolite	-	-	-
	Sunstone	Star Sunstone	-	-
Garnet	Pyralspites	Almandine	Mozambique Garnet	-
		Pyrope	Mozambique (Pyrope and Almandine	-
			Rhodolite (Pyrope and Almandine)	-
		Spessartite	Mandarin Garnet	-
			Malaia (intermediate composition Spessartite and Pyrope)	Colour Change Garnet
			Umbalite (Pyrope and Almandine with traces of Spessartite)	-
	Ugrandites	Andradite	Demantoid	-
		Grossular	Mali (Andradite and Grossular)	-
			Merelani Mint Garnet	-
			Hessonite	-
			Tsavorite	-
		Uvarovite	-	-
Hauyne	-	-	-	-
Hemimorphite	-	-	-	-
Hypersthene	-	-	-	-
Idocrase	-	-	-	-
Iolite	-	-	-	-
Jade	Jadeite	-	-	-
	Nephrite	-	-	-
Kornerupine	-	-	-	-
Kyanite	-	-	-	-
Lapis Lazuli	-	-	-	-
Lepidolite	-	-	-	-
Mookite	-	-	-	-
Natrolite	-	-	-	-

Group	Variety	Sub-variety		
Opal	Black Opal	-	-	-
	Blue Fire Opal	-	-	-
	Blue Opal	-	-	-
	Boulder Opal	-	-	-
	Fire Opal	-	-	-
	Green Opal	-	-	-
	Jelly Opal	-	-	-
	Matrix Opal	-	-	-
	Pink Opal	-	-	-
	Semi Black Opal	-	-	-
	White Opal	-	-	-
	Yellow Opal	-	-	-
Pectolite	Larimar	-	-	-
Peridot	-	-	-	-
Petalite	-	-	-	-
Phenakite	-	-	-	-
Prehnite	-	-	-	-
Quartz	Amethyst	Bi Colour Amethyst	-	-
		Rose de France Amethyst	-	-
	Ametrine	-	-	-
	Bi Colour Quartz	-	-	-
	Blue Moon Quartz	-	-	-
	Chalcedony	Agate	-	-
		Aventurine	-	-
		Bloodstone	-	-
		Carnelian	-	-
		Chrysoprase	-	-
		Fire Agate	-	-
		Jasper	-	-
		Onyx	-	-
		Sard	-	-
		Sardonyx	-	-
	Citrine	Bi Colour Citrine	-	-
	Cognac Quartz	-	-	-
	Green Amethyst	-	-	-
	Lemon Citrine	-	-	-
	Olive Quartz	-	-	-
	Phantom Quartz	-	-	-

	Rainbow Quartz		-	-	-
	Rose Quartz		-	-	-
	Rutile Quartz		-	-	-
	Smoky Quartz		-	-	-
	Tiger's Eye		-	-	-
	White Quartz		-	-	-
Quartzite		-	-	-	-
Rhodonite		-	-	-	-
Scapolite	Cat's Eye Scapolite		-	-	-
Serpentine		-	-	-	-
Sillimanite	Cat's Eye Sillimanite		-	-	-
	Star Sillimanite		-	-	-
Sodalite		-	-	-	-
Sphene		-	-	-	-
Spodumene	Hiddenite		-	-	-
	Kunzite	Green Kunzite	-	-	
		Yellow Kunzite	-	-	
		White Kunzite	-	-	
Staurolite		-	-	-	-
Sugilite		-	-	-	-
Thomsonite		-	-	-	-
Topaz	Canary Topaz		-	-	-
	Cherry Topaz		-	-	-
	Flamingo Topaz		-	-	-
	Grape Topaz		-	-	-
	Imperial Topaz		-	-	-
	Kiwi Topaz		-	-	-
	London Blue Topaz		-	-	-
	Moonlight Topaz		-	-	-
	Mulberry Topaz		-	-	-
	Mystic Topaz		-	-	-
	Neptune Topaz		-	-	-
	Ocean Topaz		-	-	-
	Sky Blue Topaz		-	-	-
	Swiss Blue Topaz		-	-	-
	Twilight Topaz		-	-	-
	White Topaz		-	-	-

Silicates (Continued)

Tourmaline	Elbaite	Bi Colour Tourmaline	-	-
		Black Tourmaline	-	-
		Blue Green Tourmaline	-	-
		Cuprian Tourmaline	-	-
		Fancy Tourmaline	-	-
		Green Tourmaline	-	-
		Indicolite	-	-
		Paraíba Tourmaline	-	-
		Pink Tourmaline	-	-
		Rubellite	-	-
	Dravite	Chrome Tourmaline	-	-
Unakite	-	-	-	-
Zircon	Ratanakiri Zircon	-	-	-
Zoisite	Tanzanite	AAA Tanzanite	-	-

Sulphates & Chromates

Anglesite	-	-	-
Baryte	-	-	-
Celestine	-	-	-
Gypsum	-	-	-

Sulphides

Marcasite	-	-	-
Pyrite	-	-	-
Sphalerite	-	-	-

Tektites

Moldavite	-	-	-

Tungstates

Scheelite	-	-	-

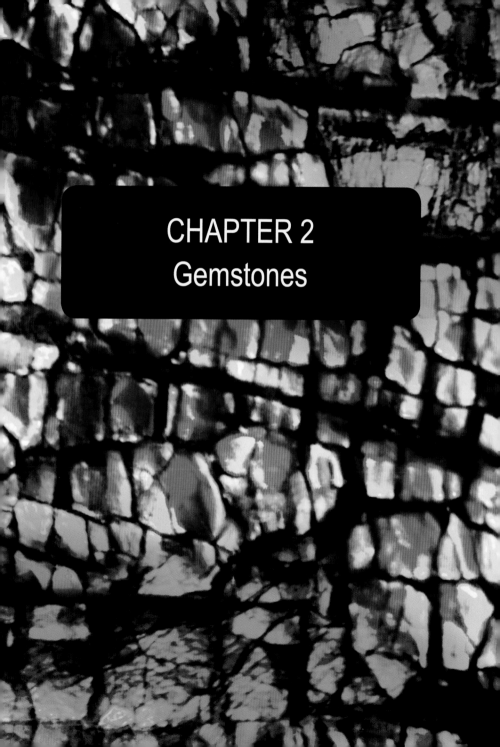

CHAPTER 2
Gemstones

ALEXANDRITE

"Look, here it is, the prophetic Russian stone! O crafty Siberian. It was always green as hope and only toward evening was it suffused with blood".

Nikolai Leskov, The Alexandrite, Mysterious Interpretation of a True Fact (1884)

The 'gem of the tsars', or simply, the 'tsar stone', Alexandrite is a gemstone forever linked to the ruler for whom it was named, Tsar Alexander II of Russia (1818-1881), the country he ruled and the twilight of Russian aristocracy.

Alexandrite is the ultimate gemstone of duality and for me, its twin colours symbolically embody the Russian character, shifting fortunes of hope and hardship. Writing just three years after the death of Tsar Alexander II, Nikolai Leskov cleverly tied together the fates of Russia, the Tsar and the gem that received his name, defining Alexandrite as a prophetic stone. One of the classic Russian writers of the 19th century, Nikolai is regarded by many Russians as, *"the most Russian of all Russian writers"*. Coming to the throne, liberal-educated Alexander knew the path to take to help his people, but at the same time, I guess it's good to be king. Assuming power at the tail end of a humiliating defeat in the Crimean War, Alex thought the time right to modernise. Hailed as 'Tsar Liberator', the hopeful nature of his industrial reforms, new judicial administrations and most importantly, ending serfdom, correspond to Alexandrite's daylight greens or as Nikolai put it, *"green as hope"*.

But by the end of Alexander's rule, these very reforms had created a hotpot of revolutionary zeal, which true to his autocratic legacy, was ruthlessly suppressed. Native languages were banned and over 250,000 people were exiled to Siberia, an irony considering Alexandrite

Tsar Alexander II (1818-1881)

was discovered in the Ural Mountains. These woes came to a head in 1881, when it was third time lucky for the People's Will, a radical revolutionary group that succeeded in assassinating the Tsar. In the end, Alexander's rule, in semblance to Alexandrite's night time reds, was quite literally, *"suffused with blood"*. Even though the writing was on the wall, Alexandrite became a potent symbol of hope and nationalism for Russian tsarists after Alexander's death not only because of its name and alleged discovery on his birthday, but also because this extraordinary gem can echo the Imperial Russian Military colours of red and green. Three tsars later, the Bolsheviks took power and it was finally curtains for the Russian monarchy.

If you haven't already guessed from the above or this section's lead photograph, colour change defines Alexandrite. A member of the Chrysoberyl family, Alexandrite is its most coveted variety. Chrysoberyl was named by German geologist Abraham Gottlob Werner in 1790 using the Greek 'chryso' (golden) and 'beryl' (green gemstone). Chrysoberyl is a particularly brilliant gemstone especially noted for its cat's eye variety (see page 31) and although rare, it

Alexandrite & Diamond 18K Yellow Gold Ring

also changes colour, resulting in Cat's Eye Alexandrite (a favourite with aficionados because it packs a phenomenal double whammy). Most Chrysoberyl is coloured yellow due to iron trace elements, but vanadium very rarely yields vivid green examples (see page 14), while Alexandrite is coloured by chromium. Chromium is the Midas element that gives Emeralds and some Rubies their signature hues.

So it's clear. If Chrysoberyl doesn't change colour, it isn't Alexandrite. Sure, there are other colour change gems, and a few of these are covered in this section, but most of these display a colour shift (a colour change where the two colours are near each other on the colour wheel) rather than the dramatic colour jump of Alexandrite. Alexandrite is pleochroic (see page 33 for more), or getting more technical, trichroic (three-coloured). This means each Alexandrite crystal has three colours, green, red and yellow, whose intensity changes when it is viewed from different angles, but confusingly, this has absolutely nothing to do with its colour change. While you can read more about how colour change works on page

Colour Change Garnet

While colour change gems have been popular since Alexandrite's 19th-century discovery, Colour Change Garnets weren't reported until the seventies and it took the discovery of 'alexandrite-esque' Colour Change Garnets from Tanzania's Umba Valley in 1987 and Bekily in southern Madagascar in the late nineties to really spark interest. Colour Change Garnet is an extremely rare variety of Malaia Garnet (a Pyrope and Spessartite mixture) and its most striking colour change is due to high amounts of vanadium, in contrast to chromium which causes colour change in Alexandrite. Having said this, chromium along with manganese is responsible for the colour change in some varieties. While typically changing from bluish greens to reddish purples or khaki greens to orangey-reds, other varieties of Colour Change Garnet include shades of blue, brown and grey that change to reddish purplish pinks. Usually only available in small sizes like Alexandrite, fine

Colour Change Garnets can be visually mistaken for the 'tsar stone'. While Colour Change Garnet is too obscure for a clarity type classification, moderate inclusions may sometimes be visible.

31, its down to natural (candescent) and artificial (incandescent) light having different amounts of the spectral colours (blue, green, orange, red, violet and yellow light) and the way chromium absorbs and reflects light. Chromium absorbs the yellow spectrum as white light passes through Alexandrite, leaving an even split of blue and green. Sunlight is pretty balanced, proportionally containing more of the green our eyes favour, so it appears green in candescent light, while incandescent light has more red, so its colour changes to red. Simplistically, the better the concentration and configuration of chromium in Alexandrite, the better the colour change.

You may be wondering if the famous Alexandrite description 'Emerald by day' and 'Ruby by night' is really accurate. In his book, Precious Stones and Gems (1898), Edwin Streeter says, *"It has been said that the Alexandrite is an Emerald by day and an Amethyst at night"*.

Colour Change Sapphire

Very attractive, rare and thus highly collectable, Colour Change Sapphires are not regularly available. Typically bluish-purple (candescent light) changing to purplish-red (incandescent light), most Colour Change Sapphires are currently sourced from Tanzania, although they are also found in other countries. While their colours vary depending on origin, Colour Change Sapphires are scarce, especially over 1 carat and are typically cut to maximise rough yield. For example, a very large mixed Sapphire parcel I recently reviewed only yielded 24 Colour Change Sapphires (6x4mm), each weighing around 60 points (0.60 carats). For tips on buying Fancy Sapphires (the collective name for all Sapphires that aren't blue), please see page 140.

and this is telling. In reality, Alexandrite is not dependent on the colours of the change. In candescent light, Alexandrite can appear blue-green, forest green, green, khaki, teal or yellowish-green, and combinations thereof, and brownish-red, orangey-red, red or reddish-purple, and combinations thereof, in incandescent light.

The single biggest value consideration of Alexandrite is its colour change. Any colour change gem is judged by the strength of its change, and how attractive and distinct its colour is in both candescent and incandescent light. Colour preference is subjective, so I am not going to dictate tastes, but the 'ideal' Alexandrite will display distinct medium toned intense colours in both light sources, with the pure daylight greens to night time reds valued highest. Alexandrite that displays a percentage colour change of less than 30 percent or visible greyish, yellowish or brownish tints will be priced accordingly. Nevertheless, Alexandrite with a pure

Zultanite

First collected and faceted by 'rock hounds' (mineral enthusiasts) in the late seventies, Zultanite is now mined commercially. A rare colour change variety of the mineral Diaspore coloured by manganese, Zultanite hails from a sole deposit, a remote mountain area in Anatolia, Turkey. Much like Alexandrite, Zultanite's name also has a royal connection, being named by Murat Akgun in honour of the 36 sultans who ruled the Ottoman Empire in Anatolia in the late 13th century. Noted for its attractive earthy hues, Zultanite's colour change is not limited to two basic colours, exhibiting a range of greens, purplish-reds and yellows in different light sources. Zultanite changes from kiwi greens with canary flashes under sunny skies, to rich champagnes in traditional indoor lighting and raspberry hues in candlelight. With up to 98 percent of the crystal lost during lapidary, Zultanite's very low yield is one of the reasons it is so rare, especially in sizes over 5 carats. The clarity  *standard for Zultanite is eye-clean (no visible inclusions when the gem is examined six inches from the naked eye). Similar to Alexandrite, Cat's Eye Zultanite is also available. Zultanite is a personal favourite and I wrote its page on the ICA (International Coloured Gemstone Association) website: www.gemstone.org.*

You probably read the opening paragraph thinking, *"What does Gavin know about Russia to make such comments?"* Well, my wife is Ukrainian and her mum Russian, so I've been fortunate to add a few old wives' tales to my more conventional understanding of Alexandrite. Getting thoroughly into Russian culture and history, I find the prophetic connection between Alexandrite and the land of its birth intriguing. After the fall of Russian imperialism, I bet many saw a new age on the horizon as green as the hope mirrored in Alexandrite at the start of Alexander's rule. But the horror of WW2, of which Russia bore the brunt, soon saw Alexandrite's reds again linked with the colour of blood, becoming known as the 'widow's stone'. Intriguingly, the name didn't dissuade interest in this gem, so much so that 'fake' Alexandrite was a mainstay of Soviet jewellery. This is doubly ironic considering Alexandrite will forever be the 'imperial' gem, but I guess this embodies the uniquely Russian ability to mix hope with hardship. My favourite Alexandrite folktale is that if you only wear one piece of Alexandrite you will be lonely. Ostensibly due to its two colours requiring a partner, herein lies the problem: Alexandrite is uniquely individual and notoriously difficult to match!

change of 90 percent or more is an impossible rarity for a gem that many regard as the rarest of them all. Good-looking colour, that dramatically change is the pinnacle for Alexandrite, but actually seeing it change colour is dependant on several factors including the intensity and purity of the two light sources, your eyesight, pleochroism, time of day, and even the weather. Standing under kitchen fluorescents with a cigarette lighter is probably not the best viewing environment; please just use your common sense. This alludes to a potentially confusing aspect of assessing colour change, called 'bleed'. This is when a colour change gem's two colours are visible at the same time. As most of us live in places where mixed lighting is the norm, 'bleed' is common, especially for a light sensitive colour change gem like Zultanite. Alexandrites that genuinely show an excessive bleed, diminishing their colour change, will be priced accordingly.

Alexandrite is classed as a Type II gemstone (see page 10 for more), meaning you're probably going to encounter visible inclusions, particularly when over 1 carat. For most gems, I preach the old mantra, *"that as long as inclusions don't effect your perception of beauty, they don't matter"*, but in the case of Alexandrite more inclusions often accentuate the colour change. Whether you select a cleaner Alexandrite with a lesser change or a more included Alexandrite with a better change is up to you, just be aware that colour change is the key value determinant. Because of its intrinsic scarcity, Alexandrite is rare and expensive in any size. Most of what's available is a quarter to a half a carat, with the two, three and five carat markers resulting in exceptional price increases due to their comparative rarity. A fine quality 10 carats plus Alexandrite is either off to a museum or the realm of wealthy private collectors. Again, because of its inherent scarcity, Alexandrite is typically cut to maximise yield, which can result in proportions, windows (see page 37), inclusions and other flaws you'd baulk at if it was in any other gem. As long as the gem changes colour and doesn't look frightfully ugly, this is simply the nature of the beast. In my experience, the most common shapes are cushions, octagons, ovals and rounds.

Often described as the rarest of gemstones, Alexandrite's rarity is inarguably its biggest asset and, along with its colour change, the main reason for its enduring popularity and high price. A lot has been written about the original Russian Alexandrite deposit, with many conflicting tales about when it was unearthed, named and by whom. The Emerald deposit (Izumrudnye Kopi) on the Tokovaya river where Alexandrite would later be found was discovered by chance in 1830 and by 1833 the as yet unnamed Alexandrite was found. Although it was undoubtedly Finnish mineralogist Dr. Nordenskjöld who figured out what is was, suggesting the less politically savvy name of Diaphanite, in 1834, Count Perovskii coined 'Alexandrite', presenting it to the future Tsar Alexander II on his 16th birthday. But if Dr. Nordenskjöld lost out this time, his time would come. Publishing the first scientific paper on Alexandrite in 1842, he later discovered and named one of the green Garnet queens, Demantoid.

Russia and Sri Lanka were the only known sources of Alexandrite for approximately 90 years, despite the fact that no significant Russian Alexandrite was recorded since the 1917 Russian revolution. With the fall of the Soviet Union, rumours of new mining circulated (circa 1995). In 2005, Coloured Stone magazine reported, *"new activity in this area"*, and in October 2006, Tsar Emerald began renewed production of the old Malyshev Mine that originally opened in 1833. While I'm not holding my breath, Russia is a vast land, so who knows what the future will bring. Even though I don't put credence purely in pedigree, some will pay a premium for certified Russian Alexandrite, even if low quality, which makes absolutely no sense to me. While Brazil, Burma, Madagascar, Mozambique, Sri Lanka, Tanzania and Zimbabwe have all produced small quantities of marketable Alexandrite, India is currently the most significant producer. Discovered in Chhattisgarh in 1994 and in neighboring Andhra Pradesh in 1996, Indian Alexandrite production is limited, constituting a tiny amount of the regular Chrysoberyl pulled from the earth.

Without a doubt, Alexandrite is one of the rarest, interesting, phenomenal and collectable of all gemstones. Let's face it, Alexandrite's got it all; beauty, sporadic availability, exclusivity (due to its high price), a cool name, fascinating history, bewitching folklore, is a birthstone for June, and to top it off, it even changes colour!

AMBER

"...it was the 'juice' or essence of the brilliant rays of the setting sun, congealed in the sea and then cast up upon the shore".

George Kunz (1856-1932), The Curious Lore of Precious Stones

Long coveted for its beautiful warm colours, Amber is fossilised tree resin that was create two million to 50 million years ago. Ancient Amber has been with humanity a long tim and I am not just talking about its age; Amber amulets and beads have been found in Ston Age archaeological sites throughout Europe. Being traded far and wide in the ancient worlc along trade routes our ancestors established before the Bronze Age, Amber jewellery datin back to 2600 BC has even been excavated in Egypt.

The word 'Amber' comes from the Arabic 'anbar', meaning 'fragrant substance'. Coming t us via the Spanish, 'anbar' actually referred to ambergris, the aromatic substance create in the intestines of sperm whales that were once used to make perfumes. The confusio possibly originates from the fact that they both wash up on beaches and emit fragrance when warmed, as well as ambergris' historic use in jewellery. Please rest assured, no whale were harmed during the writing of this book.

As suggested by the opening quote, Amber has always been linked to the sun because c its golden colours, light weight (making it easy to wear) and warm to the touch (a poo conductor of heat, Amber feels warm while mineral gems feel cold). Its unearthing in ancien burial sites is no accident. Because of its association with the sun, Amber was regarded as guiding magical light in the afterlife. For Greeks, Amber was 'elektron', meaning 'sun made

In the 'Jurassic Park' movies, dinosaur DNA is extracted from insects trapped in Dominican Amber, which is actually about 25 million years too young to really contain the genetic material of these avian ancestors

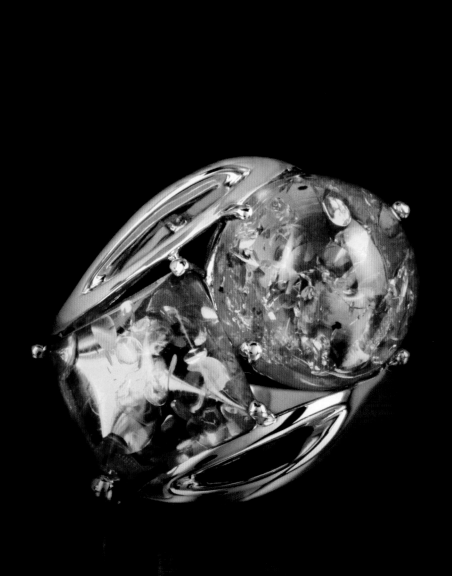

According to their mythology, Phaëton, the offspring of the sun god Helios, begged his father for the right to prove his divine paternity by being allowed to drive the sun chariot across the sky. Giving his son the metaphorical 'keys to the car', things went badly. The earth got cold when he flew too high and then going too low, he accidentally burned most of Africa into desert. His hand forced by Phaëton's poor driving, Zeus the king of the gods, took him out with a lightning bolt. Phaëton's sisters grieved his loss so much that they were turned into poplar trees, forever to weep golden tears of Amber.

Because of Amber's ability to generate a static charge when rubbed, it's from its Greek name, 'elektron', we get the word 'electricity'. In a further nod to its electric personality, the Persians called Amber, 'karabe', which means 'that which attracts straw'. As suggested by its colloquial name 'seastone', Amber floats in saltwater and is collected from beaches on the Baltic coastline, often washing up as far as the British Isles. Romans called Amber 'sucuinum' and it is from this heritage that Baltic Amber is known as Succinite, after its parent *Pinus Succinfera*, a tree common during the Tertiary period 50 million years ago.

A Mexican Amber crystal with two million-year-old leaf inclusions

As it is tree born, Amber is classed as an organic gem and this classification includes any gemstone made or derived from living organisms. While I'll try not to blind you with science, it takes eons for tree resin to transform into Amber and like so much in nature, the process is still not fully understood. The process required for tree resin to become Amber involves molecules combining to form something more complex (molecular polymerisation), oil evaporation, heat and pressure. As soon as it's secreted, tree resin immediately begins to harden and actually has various uses, such as the Frankincense and Myrrh given to Jesus by two of the wise kings at his birth.

Amber's colour is down to its composition (tree species) and what happened after its secretion. Typically transparent to translucent, Amber comes in a huge range of colours including blue, brown, golden, green, orange, red, white, and yellow. While Baltic Amber has apparently been documented in 256 shades, the main colours are broken into three broad groups: old or classic, cognac and lemon. You'll sometimes even see Amber described as 'black', though

Amber & White Topaz 925 Silver Pendant

this isn't really accurate as they are simply the deeper shades of other colours. Since colours don't vary much in price, simply select based on your personal preferences.

Amber often contains glittering natural imperfections and fissures as well as prehistoric inclusions, such as seeds, leaves, feathers, and even insects. Amber with insects entombed millions of years ago is not only highly collectable, but also allows palaeontologists and geneticists a valuable window on the past. The clarity you choose should be down to what you find appealing. For me, a few imperfections that accentuate its natural origin are definitely preferable. As with all gemstones, the way Amber is cut is important as it must be carefully polished to reveal its beauty. Try judging the balance of the tones present, size, finish, shape and proportion in combination with your colour and inclusion preferences. As Amber's popularity can fluctuate with fashion, match,ing pieces to your individual style is also important. For example, the large baroque (irregularly shaped) leather strung Mexican Amber I brought my wife perfectly suits her personality, but I couldn't see it on my mum, who better suits her Amber necklace.

Baltic Amber currently accounts for more than 90 percent of the Amber used in jewellery

With an estimated two-thirds of the world's Amber reserves, Baltic Amber currently accounts for more than 90 percent of the Amber used in jewellery and other decorative arts. Baltic Amber deposits are found in Denmark, Estonia, Finland, Germany, Latvia, Lithuania, Poland, Russia, Sweden and Ukraine, and were formed around 50 million years ago when resin from forests in the Scandinavian Peninsula collected in the area.

The heart of Baltic Amber is the Russian port of Kaliningrad, formally the German city of Koenigsberg. Teutonic Knights were based here during the 15th century, ruthlessly controlling the production of Amber in Europe and punishing illicit collectors with the shape blade of their swords. Today, Kaliningrad is so synonymous with Amber production that it is also known as the Special Economic Zone 'Yantar' (янтарь, the Russian word for Amber). Other Amber sources include Mexico and the Dominican Republic, where tropical Amber is found in the aptly named 'Amber Valley'.

Noble, serene, warm, elegant and ageless are words frequently used to describe Amber's undeniable character. Despite its old age and unquestionable beauty, Amber is also one of those gems that are remarkably affordable. This puts Amber easily within the reach of collectors that will continue to adore a gem that has been coveted since time immemorial.

AMETHYST

"Because of its beauty the very best grade is called the Gem of Venus".
Georgius Agricola (1494-1555), De Natura Fossilium

The 'father of mineralogy', Georgius Agricola, wasn't the first to be enamoured by the beauty of Amethyst. Rich in myth, legend and lore, Amethyst was set into gold rings as early as 2500 BC. Below, I'll decant some of the myths behind Amethyst, pouring some wisdom on what to look for in February's birthstone. But why the wine analogies?

Known as Dionysus to the Greeks and Bacchus to the Romans, this 'bad boy' of Greek mythology was their god of wine. Despite Dionysus's divine mission to end care and worry, he spread his fair share of mayhem, especially after a few quarts of old grape juice. The story goes that a drunken Dionysus, none too happy after being shunned by a passing mortal, swore revenge on the next unfortunate to cross his path. Enter Amethyst, a young, innocent, beautiful maiden (and a big fan of the goddess Diana), followed by two hungry tigers courtesy of Dionysus. As Amethyst screams Dionysus filled his goblet ready for the main event, maiden versus tiger. Divinely unimpressed by Dionysus's shenanigans, all-seeing Diana quickly turned Amethyst into a Quartz statue, as pure as her virtue. While protected from harm, unfortunately the spell couldn't be reversed, causing a guilt-ridden Dionysus to weep tears of sorrow. Collapsing as his tears dripped into his goblet, its contents splashed onto the statue, creating the purple gem we call Amethyst.

Long before Roman emperors donned the bright purple 'toga picta', pharaohs, kings and queens made purple a potent symbol of sovereignty. From the signet of Cleopatra, an Amethyst engraved with a figure of Bacchus, to the Amethyst necklace of Queen Charlotte, wife of George III or

Dionysus, the Greek god of wine and mythical creator of Amethyst

England, Amethyst will forever be linked to power. Because of this heritage, it's not surprising that Amethyst was popular with the Catholic Church in the middle ages. Thought to promote celibacy, it soon became known as the 'papal stone'. Even today, bishops still wear Amethyst rings.

Amethyst has more superstitions than a professional gambler - it's hard to find a malady this gem won't supposedly fix! Leonardo Da Vinci (1452-1519) wrote that Amethyst was able to dissipate evil thoughts and quicken the intelligence, while Pliny the Elder (23-79 AD), Roman historian and author of 'Historia Naturalis' (the world's first encyclopaedia), reported that if the name of the moon or sun was engraved upon an Amethyst hung from the neck by the hair of a baboon it became a charm against witchcraft and beneficial to those petitioning princes.

Ametrine

Ametrine (Amethyst-Citrine Quartz, Trystine or Golden Amethyst) is a bicolour blend of Citrine and Amethyst. Its unusual colour is due to iron in different states of oxidation. While its main deposit in Bolivia (Anahi Mine, named for an Ayoreos princess who married a Spanish Conquistador) has been famous since the 17th century, it's only become commercially available since 1980. Fine specimens display intense colours evenly split.

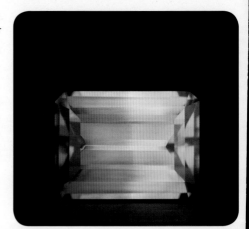

Ametrine

Bi Colour Quartz

While its myths are fascinating, what makes Amethyst tick? A variety of macrocrystalline (large crystal) Quartz that occurs in transparent pastel roses to deep purples, Amethyst owes its colours to iron. Some other popular macrocrystalline Quartzes are included here and you can read about the cryptocrystalline (small crystal) Quartzes on page 106.

Colour is Amethyst's most important consideration, with the deeper shades commanding higher prices. The most valuable Amethysts are medium to dark toned, transparent and pure violet with no shading toward red or blue, although blue or red flashes are desirable and highly coveted. Amethyst crystals occur with reasonably few inclusions, so the standard is eye-clean, with no visible inclusions when the gem is examined six inches from the naked eye. As it's a popular gem for lapidaries and

Bi Colour Amethyst

Caused because of environmental changes during formation, Bi Colour Amethyst is a bicolour blend of Amethyst and White Quartz. Faceted to showcase this feature, fine specimens have a balanced contrast between its colours.

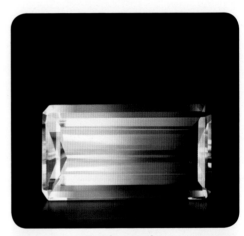

Bi Colour Amethyst

Bi Colour Citrine

jewellers, you'll find more fanciful shapes and cuts of Amethyst than you will for many other gems. Regardless of the cut, look for an even colour and good brilliance.

Found on every continent in varying amounts, Amethyst can vary depending on its origin. First appearing in Europe in 1727, gorgeous Brazilian Amethyst remains prolific, while Uruguayan Amethyst is noted for its spectacular beauty. Deep purple Siberian Amethyst is now historic, although you'll sometimes hear 'Siberian' incorrectly used to describe intensely coloured Amethyst from any locale.

Citrine

Named for 'citron', the French word for lemon, Citrine occurs naturally with Amethyst and is also coloured by iron. It appears in pastel lemon yellow, golden yellow, mandarin orange and 'Madeira' red (for the wine). Caused because of environmental changes during formation, Bi Colour Citrine is a bicolour blend of Citrine and White Quartz.

Amethyst might be a gem of antiquity, but it remains an important fashion gemstone due to its timeless beauty, rich colour and durability. One of the highlights of the 41st Bangkok Gems & Jewellery Fair was 'Purple Evolution'. This outstanding display featured virtually everything purple, eye-catching, rare and unique, including purple gold, Lavender Jade, Purple Sapphire and you guessed it, Amethyst.

Green Amethyst

Ranging from pastel to deep forest green, Green Amethyst is the green variety of quartz. It is also known as Vermarine, Green Quartz, Lime Citrine or by its gemmological name, Prasiolite (from the Greek words 'prason', meaning leek and 'lithos', meaning stone). Olive Quartz is a related colour variety.

Rose de France Amethyst

Hailing from Brazil, 'Rose de France' Amethyst (Lavender Amethyst) is pastel lilac pink. A popular Victorian gem, it often features in antique jewellery.

Rose Quartz

The pink variety of quartz, Rose Quartz is rarely transparent, displaying a beautiful misty appearance.

Smoky Quartz

Coloured by aluminium, Smoky Quartz and its related colour variety Cognac Quartz are earthy transparent quartzes also known as 'champagne on ice'. A variety of Smoky Quartz called Cairngorm (named for its historic source in the Scottish Highlands) is the national gem of Scotland.

White Quartz

Also known as Rock Crystal, the absence of metallic elements makes White Quartz colourless.

Given Amethyst's mythological origin, it should come as no surprise that it was once fashioned into talismans and goblets to prevent drunkenness. But did the ancient Greeks really believe this? After a lot of digging, I think I have the answer. They certainly weren't dummies, yet Amethyst is derived from the Greek word 'amethustos', which means 'not drunk'. Adopting words from other languages, the Greek name is probably a play on the Hebrew for a purple gem, 'achlamath', which itself is possibly derived from the Persian 'shemest'. While legend would have us believe the Greeks really thought Amethyst would prevent intoxication, writing in the 1st century Pliny the Elder was sceptical, remarking, *"the lying Magi promise that these gems are an antidote to drunkenness"*. Yet in his 'Book of Precious Stones', the 13th-century Arabic scholar Mohammed Ben Mansur affirms that, *"wine drunk out of a goblet of Amethyst does not intoxicate"*. At this time, Arabians placed extraordinary value upon Amethyst, so you'd think Ben would've got it right. While it's tempting to dismiss this as fanciful, if you fill an Amethyst goblet with water, it does look a lot like wine, so perhaps this legend has a grain of truth. Doubly so, when you speculate what a good Muslim is doing drinking in the first place. Perhaps this was the ruse. Turn up at a party, Amethyst goblet in hand, look like you can drink Oliver Reed under the table, yet still keep your faith (and your head).

AQUAMARINE

"The Aquamarine was much employed by the ancients for engraving: there is one by Quintillius, of Poseidon mounted on marine horses."

Dr. L. Feuchtwanger, A Popular Treatise on Gems (1867)

In my experience, Aquamarine is one of those gems that most people immediately find attractive. Blue might be one of the world's favourite colours, but it's the crisp cleanness of Aquamarine's blues as well as its resemblance to the sea, that, for many, conveys feelings of tranquillity and calm. Even its name embodies these oceanic connections. Coined by the Romans over 2,000 years ago, Aquamarine literally means 'water of the sea' in Latin, from the words 'aqua' (water) and 'marina' (sea). Given its name, it is no wonder one myth says Aquamarine originated from treasure chests, horded by magnificent mermaids.

During antiquity, Aquamarine was praised for its ability to protect sailors from the wrath of Poseidon (the Greek god of the sea, Neptune in Roman mythology), thereby guaranteeing seafarers a safe voyage. Poseidon certainly was a god you'd want on your side. Keep him happy, and you got new islands and calm oceans, rub him the wrong way and his trident would strike the ground causing earthquakes, storms, drowning and shipwrecks. Sailors back then didn't have GPS, search and rescue, or life jackets, so many would pray to Poseidon for a safe voyage, wearing amulets of Aquamarine to instil bravery in their hearts. At a pinch, these talismans could be thrown overboard as offerings to cool Poseidon's temper, so storms would subside. Several years ago, I learned of a similar local custom from a Thai gem dealer, who maintained that Aquamarine can prevent seasickness and drowning. Given

To calm Poseidon's anger during storms, sailors once tossed amulets of Aquamarine overboard

Aquamarine's mythology, it's not surprising that this gem was also regarded by the ancients as fostering tranquillity, serenity, calmness, purification and wisdom.

Its oceanic mythology aside, what puts the sparkle in March's birthstone? Aquamarine is a member of the Beryl mineral family (from the ancient Greek 'beryllos', meaning blue-green stone), commonly know as the 'mother of gemstones' because of its highly regarded gem varieties. Apart from Aquamarine blues, other Beryl gemstones include Bixbite reds, Emerald greens, Goshenite whites (colourless), Heliodor yellows and Morganite pinks. Aquamarine is coloured by trace amounts of iron, with its relative concentrations causing an extraordinarily beautiful range of pastel to intense deep blues, sometimes with splashes of green.

AAA Aquamarine & Diamond 18K Yellow Gold Ring

Aquamarine is typically eye-clean (no visible inclusions when the gem is examined six inches from the naked eye), occasionally with a very high clarity even under magnification. Because of its high clarity and transparency, colour is Aquamarine's most important consideration. While the deeper, more intense blues command higher prices, they are exceedingly rare; Aquamarine's lighter blues are more readily available.

The deeper Aquamarine blues are often given different trade names that can be potentially confusing for those new to gems. Collectively called 'AAA' or 'double blue' Aquamarine, the names include 'Santa Maria' (rare, intensely deep blue Aquamarine from Brazil's Santa Maria de Itabira deposit), 'Espirito Santo' (medium toned Aquamarine from Brazil's Espirito Santo state) and 'Martha Rocha' (for a 1954 Brazilian beauty queen). 'Santa Maria' colours have also been found in Mozambique (circa 1991) and in other African countries such as Zambia.

Goshenite

Goshenite is the white (colourless) variety of Beryl noted for its exceptional transparency and brilliance. While named for the location of its first discovery, Goshen, Massachusetts, Goshenite has several other names including White Beryl and Lucid Beryl. Its colourless purity gave rise to it being used as lenses in spectacles in ancient Greece and Rome. Today, historians believe that the eye glasses worn by Roman Emperor Nero during gladiatorial bouts probably sported Goshenite lenses, even though the Roman historian Pliny the Elder reported they were Emeralds. Goshenite sources include Brazil, Colombia, Pakistan and Afghanistan.

This has resulted in the trade names 'Santa Maria Africana' and 'Santa Maria Afrique', which conjure a curious mystique over its exact origin. Currently, deep blue 'AAA' Aquamarine is difficult to obtain in calibrated cuts necessary for jewellery above half a carat due to its geological scarcity. Rarely found in larger 'gem quality' sizes in any location, continuous production of the deeper Aquamarine colours just doesn't happen, keeping them in high demand.

For me, the finest Aquamarines are pure blue, with a medium tone and saturation, similar to Goldilocks and her porridge, not too dark and not too light. But as usual, this is simply my opinion and you should develop your own tastes based on your budget and colour preferences. Hints of green often result in extremely beautiful examples that aptly exhibit this gem's oceanic air. Inversely, the more available pastel blues with excellent transparency exude tranquillity, displaying subtle tints reminiscent of surf rising up the golden sands of a tropical beach. Aquamarine that is poorly cut, has too much grey or green, or has

Morganite

Discovered in Madagascar in 1911, this gem was called Pink Beryl until it was renamed by the famous gemmologist, George Frederick Kunz, in honour of his benefactor, the New York banker and philanthropist, John Pierpont Morgan. Sister gem to Aquamarine and Emerald, Morganite is a translucent to transparent Beryl coloured by trace amounts of manganese, which result in its delightful roses, magnolias and peaches. Typically eye-clean, Morganite is currently obtained from Afghanistan, Brazil and Madagascar. Unfortunately, the only limit to Morganite's popularity is its rarity.

prominent inclusions should be priced accordingly. Because colour is such an important value determinant for Aquamarine, lapidaries often employ deeper cuts to accentuate its colour. Aquamarine is typically well cut, with emeralds, ovals and pears the most common. As usual, look for an even colour and good brilliance regardless of the cut or shape.

Prior to the Aquamarine's modern African discoveries, in the early eighteen hundreds (circa 1830), it was the Brazilian gem fields of Minas Gerais, which in Portuguese means 'general mines', and Russia's Urals that ruled the roost, producing the finest quality. Today, Brazil is still a major supplier, but several African nations, including Nigeria (an Aquamarine producer since 1983), Madagascar, Mozambique and Zambia, are the new kids on the block, supplying equally beautiful Aquamarines.

Whether it's Aquamarine's sky or deep ocean blues, this gem is enchantingly beautiful and radiates regardless of eye colour or complexion. In a way, Aquamarine really does seem to have captured the lucid blue essence of the sea.

Morganite & Diamond 9K Yellow Gold Ring

BLACK OPAL

"Of all precious stones, it is Opal that presents the greatest difficulties of description, it displaying at once the piercing fire of Ruby, the purple brilliancy of Amethyst, and the sea-green of Emerald, the whole blended together and refulgent with a brightness that is quite incredible".

Pliny the Elder (23-79 AD), Historia Naturalis

In my mind, Pliny the Elder was the leading authority on gemstones in the classical world, and the reason he's quoted a lot in this book, is that 2,000 years on, many of his observations still ring true. Back in Pliny's day, Opal pretty much came from one place in the world, Czernowitza in modern-day Slovakia (formerly part of Hungary, thus the old term 'Hungarian Opals'). Rome never did manage to make it part of their Empire, so it retained an exotic appeal and genuine rarity, which along with its unique physical beauty, assured its popularity. But before Rome there was Greece, and while Herodotus, Plato and Theophrastus gave Opal a plug, around 500 BC, Onomacritus, compiler and forger of oracles (yep, he got busted) said, *"The delicate colors and tenderness of the Opal remind one of a loving and beautiful child"*. This comparison probably isn't originally his; ancient Greeks and Romans often compared Opal's beauty to that of a favourite child. While both cultures cherished Opals, the Greeks believed it possessed the power of foresight, invisibility and prophecy, while the Romans considered them symbols of hope, love and purity. The Romans even wore them as talismans for protection from danger, which is definitely apt for a gemstone with a rainbow trapped within.

An Opal mine in 1886, located at White Cliffs in the Australian State of New South Wales. Only discovered in Australia in 1849, today around 95 percent of the world's Opal hails from this sunburnt country

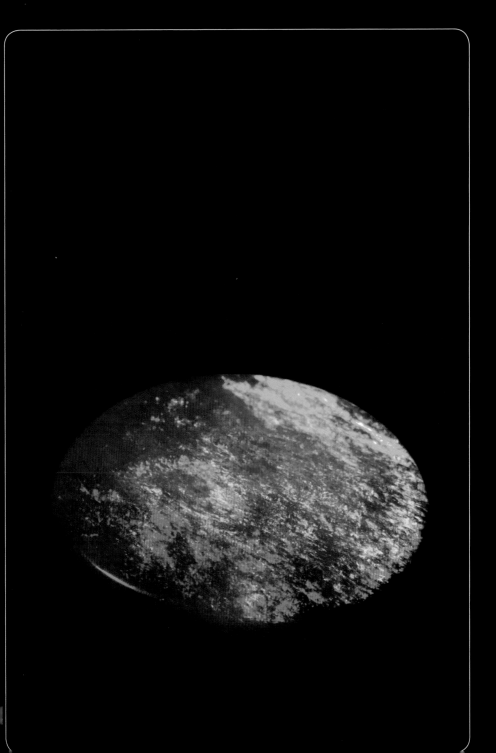

Moving ahead in history, Shakespeare used Opal a lot in his plays to portray lavish magnificence, calling it, *"this miracle queen of gems"* in 'Twelfth Night'. Queen Victoria, much like Cleopatra's second Roman boyfriend Marc Anthony, was a ruler big on Opal. In fact, she actively dispelled myths of Opal being unlucky as a result of people missing Sir Walter Scott's use of metaphor in 'Anne of Geierstein' (1829).

If Pliny liked European Opal, he would have gone wild for the Australian Black, the 'king of opals'. While I try not to play favourites, Black Opal is definitely special to me. After all, since 27th July 1993, Opal has been Australia's national gemstone. This is not surprising, considering 95 percent of Opal hails from my homeland, but I guess we should also remember that Australia's Opal fields are bigger than those found in the rest of the world combined. With only 25 percent of Opal mined gem quality, understanding this October birthstone is easier than you think.

Black Opal & Diamond 9K Yellow Gold Ring

Our modern word for this gem has an interesting entomology. Opal is derived from the Roman 'opalus', which in turn is from the Greek 'opallios', meaning 'to see a change'. While another possible Greek origin is 'opthalmios' (eyestone), the original source of the name is probably the Sanskrit 'upala' (precious stone), lending credence to India once being a source of Opal for ancient Rome.

To understand how Australian Opals were formed, we have to travel back in time 140 million years. Dreamtime legends passed down by storytellers have been part of indigenous Australian culture for over 60,000 years. For tribes from the Andamooka region in South Australia, the Opal was known as the 'fire of the desert' and was linked to creation myths. Their ancestral creator came down to earth on a great rainbow, which turned the rocks it touched into resplendent Opals, coloured with the hues of a rainbow.

Blue Fire Opal

Newness, rarity and beauty are what make Blue Fire Opal special. The debut of Blue Fire Opal has been shifting perceptions in play since the time of the Aztecs; namely, Fire Opal is red, orange or yellow. Blue Fire Opal is transparent to semi-translucent, with a colour similarity to pastel Tanzanite, pretty icy cool violet-blues to steel blues. It also has occasional opalescence, the milky blue appearance of Opal caused by the reflection of light, which combos nicely with its body colour. The first significant production of Blue Fire Opal occurred in December 2007, when it was discovered by sheer chance at the Boca  *Rica Mine in Brazil's Piaui State (pronounced: Pee-Ow-Ee). The Piaui State has garnered praise aplenty for its Opals, being compared to those from Australia. With less than one-tenth of a percent of the rough mined useable, the monthly output of Blue Fire Opal is sporadic.*

In reality, we need to look to a huge inland sea and a resulting geological feature called the 'Great Australian Basin'. The majority of Australia's Opal fields are located in the basin and were formed from the weathering of sandstone deposited over older host rock. The structure of Opals is unique and comprised of tiny spheres of silicon dioxide forming a pyramid-shaped grid, interspersed with water. It's the refraction of light through the spaces between these spheres that produces Opal's characteristic and unique 'play of colour' - the flashes of colour that change with the angle of observation. Interestingly, Opal without 'play of colour' has its silicon dioxide spheres more randomly arranged. Apart from their colourful brilliance, Australian Opals are also valued for their stability, a key consideration for a gem containing around six percent water.

Now famous across the world for its brilliant colours, Australian Opal was discovered in 1849 and by the end of the nineteenth century started to dominate the world's supply. But this wasn't without some initial resistance. Perhaps a little recalcitrant, the Hungarians

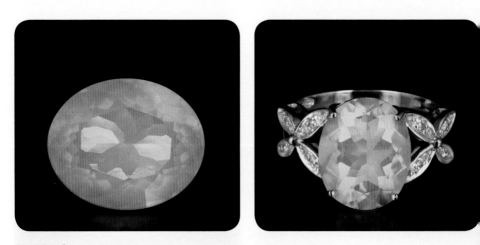

Fire Opal

Fire Opal, also known as Mexican Opal, Mexican Fire Opal, Cherry Fire Opal or Sun Opal, is aptly named for its transparent to semi-translucent fiery reds, oranges and yellows. Treasured in the Americas since the time of the Aztecs, Fire Opals were once called 'quetzalitzlipyollitli' and while I can't pronounce this word, it means 'gemstone of the bird of paradise'. Fire Opal is mainly found in Mexico, but it has also been unearthed in Brazil, Ethiopia, Mali, Tanzania, and occasionally Australia.

laimed Aussie Opal wasn't the 'real deal', despite the fact that by the twentieth century, heir own deposits were pretty much exhausted. Today, most Opal is sourced from a handful of Australian mining areas, including Andamooka (1930), Coober Pedy (1915), Lightning Ridge (1902), Mintabie (1931), White Cliffs (1890) and the Queensland Boulder Opal fields a vast area discovered in 1869 centring around the town of Quilpie).

Before we cover how to judge a Black Opal, it's important to know how different Opals are classified. While there are several classification systems, they all relate to the host rock (also known as 'potch' or 'matrix') on which Opal forms and their resulting transparency and body colour (the base colour on which Opal's 'play of colour' is visible). Black Opal has a black body colour and may be opaque with some translucency, particularly when held to a strong light source. While the main classifications are included under photographs in this section, Grey Opal is a term seldom used, with its specimens typically being grouped in

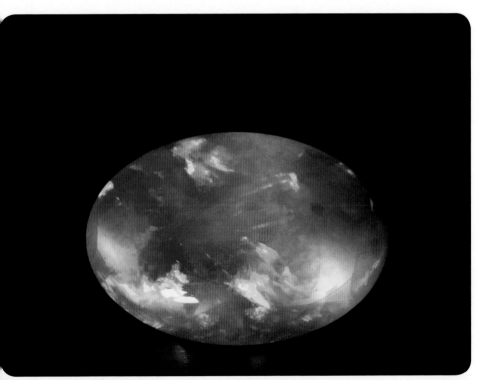

Jelly Opal, also known as Crystal Opal, is transparent to translucent and because of the absence of potch, either doesn't have a body colour or if present is described as White Crystal Opal, Dark Crystal Opal or Black Crystal Opal. While Jelly Opal is found in all Australian gem deposits to some degree, this specimen hails from Andamooka in South Australia

the 'black', 'dark' or 'semi-black' categories, but it is translucent to opaque with a grey body colour. Opaque Opal with ironstone (boulder) potch included in the cut is called Boulder Opal. Take note that not all Opal has 'play of colour'. Fire Opal is transparent to translucent crystal Opal with virtually no 'play of colour', displaying oranges, reds, yellows and, since a recently discovered Brazilian deposit, also blues. Peruvian Opal is a rare variety that exhibits exquisite translucent blues, pinks and greens, also without 'play of colour'. Another variety with no 'play of colour' is the translucent yellow and green Opal from Tanzania.

As each Opal displaying 'play of colour' has its own personality, individual preferences play a big part. Despite this, Black Opal is the most valuable variety, simply because of the contrast and intensity afforded by its black body colour. One way to understand this is to imagine painting a row of windows black (Black Opal), grey (Semi Black Opal), white (White Opal) and colourless (Jelly Opal), then randomly spray painting each window in all the individual colours of the spectrum: blue, green, orange, red, violet, and yellow. Obviously, the window

Matrix Opal, also called 'opal with matrix', is any Opal where the host rock is visible face up. This specimen is from Central Queensland and shows a black host rock (matrix) embedded with brilliantly colourful flashes of Opal

painted black is going to make the colours appear more intense. This is key to appreciating Opal, because when 'play of colour' is present, its value lies in the brilliance, brightness and strength of colours displayed.

Superficially, assessing Opals appears incredibly simple, but when an expert starts dissecting the combinations of colours and patterns possible, much like Jade, you're heading into complex territory. But thankfully, there are some easy to understand paradigms that not only apply to Black Opal, but any Opal displaying 'play of colour'. Just be aware that for darker coloured Opal (black and semi-black) opacity demands a premium and in lighter Opals (white and jelly) transparency demands a premium. In the marketplace, there is a definite hierarchy of colours, with red being the most valuable, followed by orange, yellow, violet, green, and then blue.

Opals whose 'play of colour' flashes in the rare reds are generally more valuable than those with just blue and green, but as with all gemstones, colour preferences are subjective.

Semi Black Opal (also known as Dark Opal) is translucent to semi-translucent and has a body colour in-between grey and black. As Black Opal is generally more opaque, opacity is the criterion that divides black and semi-black Opal. This example is from Mintabie in South Australia

An Opal with a 'play of colour' comprising more than half of one colour is named for it primary hue, while an Opal with three or more hues is called 'multicolour'. Even though the presence of red increases a Black Opal's rarity and value, it's typically valued lowe than a multicolour that shows several colours. The patterns of colour also affect value, with large patches of colour priced higher than those with small patches of colour. Professional often communicate these patterns using colourful self-explanatory names such as Chinese writing, harlequin, peacock and pin-fire. While 'play of colour' and strong opalescence (the silver to bluish-white light that shimmers and glides over an Opal's surface) rarely exist together, Opal with an opalescence that reduces the brilliance and intensity of its colour play will be priced accordingly. The biggest thing to remember is that due to its layered colours Opal is probably the most 'artistic' of all gemstones. So when making your selection, try remembering the old saying, *"I don't know much about art, but I know what I like"*.

White Opal, also known as Light Opal, is the darling of everyday fashion jewellery. It is translucent to opaque with a white body colour. Coober Pedy in South Australia is the main source for this variety. Named for its Opal miners, 'Coober Pedy' means 'white man's hole in the ground' and is a corruption of a local indigenous Australian phrase, 'kupa-piti' (boys' waterhole)

Once you've settled on a colour play you find appealing, you must consider the cut. Thankfully, assessing cabochons is straightforward, just look at their finish, shape and proportion. While symmetrical ovals will demand a premium, Opal that is cut too thin or thick, whose dome is too shallow, or has a finish that is cracked or crazed, will be priced accordingly. Due to their rarity, slithers of Black Opal are sometimes joined with other material to create doublets (Opal plus a backing material) or triplets (Opal with a top as well as a back). These are understandably more affordable, but do be aware that these are manmade composites that should be sold as such. Although Opal is relatively durable, it does have some special care requirements (see page 262 for more). While Black Opal is primarily sourced from deposits at Lightning Ridge in New South Wales, production at Lightning Ridge is half of what it was 10 years ago. Unfortunately, this is somewhat echoed at all of Australia's major Opal deposits, markedly increasing scarcity. Apart from Australia, other Opal sources include Brazil, Ethiopia, Mexico, Peru, Tanzania and the U.S.A.

Thanks to Australian movies, television and tourism advertising, you're probably already aware of some classic Australian slang like 'G'Day Mate', but unless you've visited an Opal field, terms like 'floaters', 'noodling' and 'ratters' will probably fall on deaf ears. Well, I'm here to help! Floaters are Opal that is visible from the surface and typically indicative of an underground deposit, noodling is hunting through old mine tailings to find Opal that others missed and ratters are people who poach Opal from another's claim - a big no, no that was once arbitrarily and severely punished!

As colourful as its country of origin, Black Opal is definitely a gemstone with its own unique personality and character. Like Australia itself, Black Opal is easy to appreciate; it's easy to become enchanted by its unrivalled beauty. In the words of the famous Australian poet Dorothea MacKellar: *"An Opal hearted country a wilful lavish land, all those who have not loved her you will not understand"*.

BLUE SAPPHIRE

"When I thought that my chivvying had reached the limit of their patience, I drew from my pocket a magnificent Sapphire, a rare specimen piece, from which I had long refused to be separated, despite most attractive offers. "Now, friends," said I, "as you have shown me the best you have to offer, I will show you what kind of gem interests me, so that when I come again you will know what to bring me".

Louis Kornitzer, Gem Trader (1939)

Blue Sapphire is a truly mesmerising gemstone with a rich history, potent symbolism and a popularity spanning over 2,500 years. Having honed my passion for gemstones in Chanthaburi, Thailand, an international centre for coloured gemstones, the above story has a special place in my heart. The wheeling and dealing of an open-air gem market is a unique experience. Exciting and challenging, unless you're an experienced professional, you had best remain a silent observer. With approximately 70 percent of the world's Sapphire output passing though Thailand on its way from the mine to the wearer, Sapphires are to Chanthaburi what belts are to trousers. Along with Ruby, these two gems hold everything together.

Ruby and Sapphire are colour varieties of the mineral Corundum (crystalline aluminium oxide), which derives its name from the Sanskrit word for Rubies and Sapphires, 'kuruvinda'. Corundum produces 'other coloured' gemstones (see page 18 for more), meaning that trace amounts of elements such as chromium, iron and titanium are responsible for producing its rainbow of colours. While 'Sapphire' alone refers to its blues, I favour adding 'blue' to the front of Sapphire not only to avoid confusion, but to also indicate that other colour

The age-old technique of river mining for Sapphires in Sri Lanka, exactly as Captain Ribeyro described in his 17th-century 'History of Ceylon'

exist. Collectively described as 'Fancy Sapphires' or assigned a colour prefix, Sapphire's other colours are featured on page 140. Sapphire's name is derived from the Latin, 'sapphirus', which in turn comes from the Greek 'sappheiros', meaning blue. This name is believed by some to originated from either the Hebrew 'sappir' (precious stone) or the Sanskrit 'sanipriya'. Used to describe a dark precious stone, 'sanipriya' means 'sacred to Saturn' and this entomology is lent credence by the fact that Sapphire is regarded as the gem of Saturn in Indian astrological beliefs. Historically, 'sappheiros' usually referred to Lapis Lazuli rather than Blue Corundum, with the modern Sapphire probably called 'hyakinthos' in ancient Greece. Believe it or not, Sri Lankan Sapphires were reportedly used by the Greeks and Romans from around 480 BC, which once again provides evidence of the ancient trade routes used by our ancestors.

Ceylon Sapphire & Diamond 18K Yellow Gold Ring

Like all famous gemstones, Blue Sapphire features in mythological and religious stories. Whether these really referred to what we know as Lapis Lazuli or blue gems collectively during antiquity is uncertain, but one thing's for sure, our modern Blue Sapphire certainly fits the bill! While Persians believed Sapphire's reflections gave the sky its colours, this gem also scores several mentions in the good book. In Exodus (24:10), the throne of God is paved with Blue Sapphire of a heavenly clarity. It is also one of the 12 'stones of fire' (Ezekiel 28:13-16) set in the breastplate of judgement (Exodus 28:15-30). As one of the 12 gemstones set in the foundations of the city walls of Jerusalem (Revelations 21:19), Sapphire is also associated with the Apostle St. Paul. More lore in a minute, let's get our heads around how to judge the quality of one of the most popular of all gemstones, Blue Sapphire.

Blue Spinel

Spinel derives its name from either the Latin 'spina' (thorn), for its characteristic octahedral crystals or the Greek 'spintharis' ('spark), in reference to its bright red hues. Historically confused with both Ruby (see page 202 for more) and Sapphire, Spinel occurs in a plethora of colours, including blue, orange, pink, purple, and red. Confused due to the proximity of their deposits, Spinel and Corundum (Ruby and Sapphire) are actually fairly easy to tell apart. Spinel is singly refractive, while Ruby and Sapphire are doubly refractive. Available in pure blues, along with blues with violet or green tints, a

variety called Cobalt Blue Spinel (coloured by trace amounts of cobalt) is arguably some of its finest hues. I have seen similar coloured Blue Spinel from Tanzania that has this colour without the cobalt. True Cobalt Blue Spinel demands a marketplace premium. While highly saturated pure blues with good transparency is the benchmark, simply select a colour you find beautiful in a gem, with a good shape and overall appearance. Good cutting that accentuates its inherent brilliance is also an important value consideration. While Spinel is a Type II gemstone, meaning it typically occurs with some minor inclusions that may be eye-visible, the standard is eye-clean (no visible inclusions when the gem is examined six inches from the naked eye), except in lighter colours or in larger gems. One of the gem industry's best kept secrets, this beautiful gemstone's public recognition and marketing impact is limited by its low production. Sources include Madagascar, Tanzania and Vietnam.

Blue Sapphires are transparent gemstones, whose colours include blues, violet blues, greenish-blues, and combinations thereof. While you should ultimately be guided by your preferences, for Blue Sapphires the reliable Goldilocks maxim is good advice; not too dark or too light, just right. Intense 'middle' colours are the happy medium, with pure blues being the marketplace ideal. Blue Sapphires that are too dark (inky), too light, or have too much grey or brown are priced accordingly. While some violet tints in Blue Sapphires are attractive and desirable, excessive greenish-blues are usually more affordable. While Blue Sapphires are pleochroic (different colours visible from different viewing angles), this is not usually a concern, but gems with table-up pleochroism that detracts from its beauty, will also be

Blue Star Sapphire

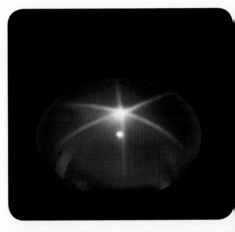

A unique and rare gemmological phenomenon, Star Sapphires are traditionally the most popular of all star gemstones. Due to an optical special effect called 'asterism' or the 'star effect', parallel needle-like inclusions create a reflected luminous star of light that moves across the gemstone. For Corundum, reflections from a whole host of tiny rutile needle inclusions, also known as silk, cause their stars. The ultimate love charm, a Blue Star Sapphire is said to have been responsible for Helen of Troy's conquests. This is intriguing, considering they are also known as the 'stone of destiny' (the three bands symbolising faith, hope and density). Historically a common talismanic gemstone, Star Sapphires are said to be a protective 'guiding star' for travellers. They are even purported to bless past wearers once passed onto other hands. All star gems are dependent on a gem being cut 'en cabochon' (cut in convex form and highly polished, but not faceted). Assessing cabochons is straightforward - just look at their finish, shape and proportion, favouring attractive smooth domes with a desirable symmetry. While asterism is most visible in a direct, single beam of light, a well-cut star gemstone has a distinct star whose rays are straight and equidistant. The norm is a six rayed star, but twelve rayed stars also occasionally occur. Unlike Black Star Sapphires, where the virtually opaque dark body colour markedly enhances the star effect, in Blue Star Sapphires the distinctiveness, intensity and transparency of the blue body colour are also important value considerations. While the gem gravels of Sri Lanka is the world's 'classic' source, once contributing 90 percent of the Star Sapphires on the market, the gem pictured hails from Madagascar. Star Corundum come in shades of red (red to violet) and blue (blue to grey), but orange and yellow Star Sapphires do not exist.

priced accordingly. As usual, the visibility of pleochoism is determined by crystal orientation during lapidary. The aesthetic impact of colour unevenness due to zoning (location of colour in the crystal versus how the gem is faceted) or excessive windowing (areas of washed out colour in a table-up gem, often due to a shallow pavilion) is also an important value consideration for Blue Sapphire. Finally, pay attention to how transparency and inclusions affect Blue Sapphires' colour beauty and subsequently, value. Simply be guided by your colour preference and pocket, bearing in mind that top quality Blue Sapphires are one of the world's most expensive gems. While gemstone lighting is a book in itself, a gemstone's colours should ideally remain beautiful in any light source. Blue Sapphires usually look their

Iolite

Iolite is named after the Greek 'ios' (violet) and 'lithos' (stone). Historically compared and confused with Blue Sapphires, Iolite's blues and transparency explains its common name, 'water sapphire'. Despite the name, Iolite is actually fairly easy to differentiate from Blue Sapphire due to its pleochroism or getting more technical, trichroism (three-coloured). This means each Iolite crystal has three colours, deep blue, colourless to very slightly brown and colourless to very slightly blue, whose intensity changes when it is viewed from different angles. The beautiful violet blue in a finished Iolite gemstone is due 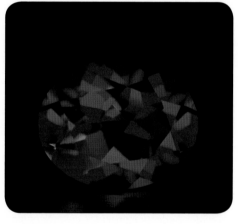 *to its intrinsic trichroic colours, accentuated by appropriate cutting techniques. Simply look for a high transparency with a table-up violet blue colour you find attractive, noting that its other colours may be visible when viewed from different angles. This gemmological curiosity has a cool story you can use when showing this feature to others. In Scandinavian sagas the magical 'sunstone' of Norse seafarers is portrayed as a miraculous means of allowing navigation on overcast days when the sun wasn't visible. Known as the 'Viking's compass' or 'Viking's stone', they actually used thin pieces of Iolite as the world's first polarizing filter. Dark or milky Iolites will loose transparency and despite being a Type II gemstone (minor inclusions in nature that may be eye-visible), the standard for Iolite is eye-clean (no visible inclusions when the gem is examined six inches from the naked eye). A beautiful gemstone in its own right, whose colours and characteristics are immediately obvious to the expert eye, Iolite is predominately sourced from India, Madagascar and Sri Lanka.*

best when viewed outdoors in natural light or under fluorescents. Incandescent lights are the bane of Blue Sapphires. The most prized colours of Blue Sapphire are 'royal blue' (dark blue with 10 to 15 percent violet) and 'cornflower blue' (medium blue with five to 10 percent violet). While the prefix 'Ceylon' is often used to identify fine Sri Lankan Sapphires, just make sure you're buying the gem, not the name.

While both Ruby and Sapphires are classed as Type II gemstones (gems that typically grow with some minor inclusions in nature that may be eye-visible), Sapphires are usually cleaner (and larger) than Ruby, with an eye-clean clarity (no visible inclusions when the gem is examined six inches from the naked eye) being the typical standard. Fine microscopic inclusions (called 'flour', 'milk' or 'silk') in some Blue Sapphires can impart a 'velvety' or 'sleepy' appearance that boosts both beauty and value. Once you've settled on a colour you

Kanchanaburi Sapphire

An important source in the eighties, the Bo Ploi Sapphire mines were discovered in 1918 and are located in Thailand's western province of Kanchanaburi, which is best known for the Bridge over the River Kwai. In comparison to the violet shades that provide Ceylon Sapphires with their signature royal and cornflower blues, Kanchanaburi Sapphire often has greyish tints that sometimes provide a bluish steel colour (see example pictured). Heavily mined in recent decades, the Bo Ploi mines must excavate over 50 tonnes of alluvial soil to get just 1 carat of Kanchanaburi Sapphire crystals.

ike, look for a good shape and overall appearance (finish, outline, profile and proportions). While ovals are the most common, Blue Sapphires are available in a huge array of shapes and cuts, almost as diverse as their colours. Blue Sapphires are also cut 'en cabochon' (see page 34 for more), not only for its star varieties, but also for examples whose clarity makes them unsuitable for faceting.

A review of Blue Sapphire wouldn't be complete without introducing some of its major sources. The 'classic' source for Blue Sapphire, Ceylon (renamed Sri Lanka in 1972) holds the earliest record for the mining of Sapphires. To put its antiquity into context, King Solomon reportedly wooed the Queen of Sheba with Sri Lankan Sapphires, sourced from gem gravels surrounding the town of Ratnapura ('gem city' in Sinhalese). Just outside Ratnapura, I had the opportunity to river mine for Sapphires, finding a spectacular example that cut an impressive

Kyanite

Even though Kyanite was named in 1789 from the Greek 'kyanos', meaning 'blue', it was sold to Europeans as Blue Sapphire until the turn of the 20th century. This is not surprising, considering its finest colours have a visual resemblance to superb Blue Sapphires. An interesting mineralogical attribute of Kyanite is that it is a polymorph, meaning it has two different hardnesses. This makes Kyanite challenging to cut well and thus Kyantie's faceting quality is important. Kyanite's most famed origin is the Kali Gandaki region of west central Nepal and Tibet, whose deposits were only discovered in 1995.

star. While it was exactly as Captain Ribeyro described in his 17th-century 'History of Ceylon', it was extremely physical and very tiring, despite the picturesque surroundings. Although Blue Sapphires traditionally hail from Sri Lanka and Burma (Mogok), other sources include Australia, Cambodia (Pailin), China, Kenya, Laos, Madagascar, Nigeria, Tanzania, Thailand, the U.S.A. (Montana) and Vietnam. Even though Australia produced approximately 70 percent of the world's Sapphires during the eighties, the poor old Aussie Blue Sapphire is much maligned, often unfairly pigeonholed as too inky or overly green. The truth is fine Blue Sapphires do hail from the sunburnt country, but because of negative marketplace perceptions, they sometimes unethically get Sri Lankan citizenship when they leave the lapidary! Historically known as the 'Beryl Island' due to its abundance of gemstones and minerals, Madagascar has been the new kid on the block for Sapphires since the early nineties.

Midnight Blue Sapphire

Mined in a wide variety of countries, including Australia, China, Madagascar, Nigeria, Thailand, and Vietnam, Midnight Blue Sapphires are characterised by rich, deep, over-colour blues that are beyond vivid; to get a mental image, try picturing a clear night's sky. Midnight Blue Sapphires are affordably priced due to their tone and saturation reducing transparency, something that actually accentuates the gem's lustre, complementing its flashes of colourful brilliance. This is visible in this gem from China's Shangdong province.

Blue Sapphires from Madagascar have really impacted the gem world's perception of this country, reportedly accounting for around 20 percent of the world's Sapphires. Arguably the world's finest Blue Sapphires were discovered in Kashmir (India) around 1881, with the deposit ostensibly depleted by the nineteen thirties. Occasionally re-entering the market in antique jewellery or as collectors' investment gemstones, Kashmir Sapphires are especially noted for a fine silk that imparts a soft velvety blue, with only minor areas of darkness in a table-up gem (extinction).

If you believe your Greek mythology, the first person to wear September's birthstone was Prometheus. Apparently, he took a Blue Sapphire at the same time he 'borrowed' the fire that got him into so much trouble. I for one am glad he did and while Blue Sapphires are certainly 'mainstream' because of where I live, I feel a great connection to these gemstones. Once regarded as bringing peace and joy to their owners, there is nothing esoteric about this. Stare into the photographs on these pages and you'll see exactly what I mean.

Blue Sapphires have long symbolised faithfulness, innocence, sincerity and truth, so it's not surprising that for hundreds of years they were popular engagement ring gemstones. This use is also leant credence by a belief held by renaissance lapidaries that Blue Sapphires cure anger and stupidity. As anyone who's been married can attest, the absence of these emotions definitely helps smooth things along! Apart from being one of the world's favourite hues, blues are also psychologically linked to calmness, loyalty and sympathy, again, all positive emotions conducive to good relationships. While Blue Sapphire's popularity as an engagement gemstone was somewhat upstaged by Diamonds since the fifties, they are making a comeback. For example, in 1981 Prince Charles gave Lady Diana an engagement ring set with a stunning 18 carat Ceylon Sapphire. Being avidly passionate about coloured gemstones and their history, I had really only one choice when it came time for me to tie the knot. You guessed it, Blue Sapphire! I spent a lot of time looking for the 'perfect' gemstone and probably the most surprising thing is that I didn't pick one from a 'classic' source. My wife and I fell in love with a gorgeous Madagascan blue. This just goes to show that while origin is an interesting attribute that definitely adds to the appeal of gemstones, at the end of the day, use your eyes and be guided by beauty, the cornerstone of gems.

CHALCEDONY

"The first Roman who wore a Sardonyx (a variety of Chalcedony), according to Demostratus, was the elder Africanus, since whose time this stone has been held in very high esteem at Rome".

Pliny the Elder (23-79 AD), Historia Naturalis

Friends, Romans, countrymen, lend me your ears: I come to tell you of a gemstone of antiquity, one bequeathed to us from our ancestors and worthy of me ripping off Shakespeare. Seriously, Chalcedony was a big part of the ancient's gemstone repertoire, playing an important role in Mesopotamian (modern-day Iraq), Hittite (modern-day Turkey), Egyptian and Greek civilisations. To put its heritage into context, Agate (banded Chalcedony) beads dating back to 7000 BC have been excavated in Turkey. As you've probably already guessed, the Romans particularly prized Chalcedony. They used Chalcedonies as magic amulets, seals, signets, cameos (a gem carved in positive relief) and intaglios (a gem carved in negative relief), setting them in rings, brooches, bracelets, fibula (ornamented clasps) and necklaces. Thankfully, Chalcedony's heritage didn't lapse at the end of the classical period; its esteem remained intact during the middle ages and renaissance. Today, Chalcedonies continue to be popular with lapidaries, jewellers and collectors, both as a gemstone and in the decorative arts.

Chalcedony is potentially confusing because it is not only the family name of cryptocrystalline (small crystal) Quartz, but also a gem within the family. Another trap for the beginner is its pronunciation; Chalcedony is correctly pronounced 'kal-ced-on-ee'. Chalcedony's name

The Romans greatly prized all varieties of Chalcedony

is derived from one of its classic sources, Chalcedon, a port of Bithynia, an ancient region, kingdom and Roman province in modern-day Turkey. Continuously mined since Roman times, fine translucent Blue Chalcedony from Turkey, also known as Blue Turk Chalcedony, remains highly regarded.

Chalcedony is typically translucent to opaque, coming in a huge array of colours including shades of black, blue, brown, green, grey, orange, pink, red, white, yellow, and combinations thereof, including patterns such as banding, mottling and spots. Despite being a gem and

Agate

The banded form of Chalcedony, Agate's name comes from the river Achates (now Dirillo) in Sicily. Agate's banded patterns are caused by the oxidisation of manganese, iron and other minerals. Coming in a huge array of colours and an infinite number of patterns, Agate's numerous varieties have a plethora of descriptive prefixes.

Moss Agate

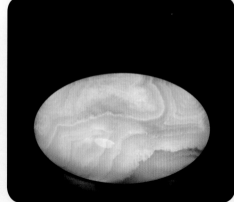

Crazy Lace Agate

a family name, Chalcedony is also a sub-group within the family that covers its uniformly coloured members. Its multicoloured varieties are all come under the Agate umbrella. Popular Chalcedony Quartz gemstones include Agate, Aventurine, Bloodstone, Carnelian, Chrysoprase, Jasper and Onyx. You can read about the macrocrystalline (big crystal) Quartzes on page 72 and the table on page 54 shows how all the Quartzes fit together.

Given the multitude of varieties within this family, where do you start? For Chalcedony, colour is king, but because of the prevalence of banding, mottling and spots in some

Aventurine

While you can read about this gem's name origin on page 30, Aventurine is typically a green Chalcedony whose small inclusions of mica, goethite, hematite and fuschite create a sparking effect aptly called 'aventurescence'.

varieties, personal preference is the ultimate caveat. For the solid colour varieties, specimens with a uniform distribution of an intense colour and greater transparency are valued higher. Banded, mottled or spotted Chalcedony is assessed by judging the beauty and intensity of the colours and patterns present. Usually polished as cabochons, Chalcedony is also frequently used in carvings, cameos and intaglios. Assessing cabochons is straightforward - just look at their finish, shape and proportion. While carvings, cameos and intaglios are probably best left to personal preferences, as a general rule, look for the intricacy of detail and the position of colour within the context of the design.

Carnelian

Carnelian is the orange to red variety of Chalcedony named from the Latin 'carneus' (made of flesh) due to its colouration. In reality, vegetarians needn't worry, there is nothing meaty about Carnelian, as its oranges and reds are caused by iron oxide. Symbolically, the Romans regarded darker Carnelian as masculine and lighter Carnelian as feminine and, according to our Roman friend Pliny, "among the ancients there was no precious stone in more common use". Carnelian is also a gem with deep religious and spiritual connections, featuring in Egyptian, Tibetan Buddhist and Christian traditions. A gemstone

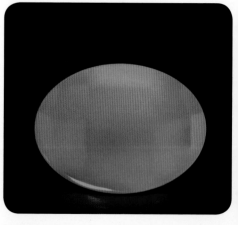

revered by Muslims, Carnelian is also known as the 'Mecca Stone' because Muhammad used an engraved Carnelian silver ring as a seal. Napoleon allegedly found a large octagonal Carnelian engraved with "the slave Abraham relying upon the merciful" from a battlefield during his Egyptian campaign.

Given its cultural prominence throughout history, it is no surprise that Chalcedony features in Jewish, Christian, Islamic and Buddhist religious traditions. During antiquity, gemmology wasn't the science we know today, but rather more a religious or esoteric pursuit, with a bit of basic lapidary and occasionally some alchemy thrown in for good measure. Gems weren't just worn purely for adornment; they possessed potent connections with the netherworld, making them powerful talismans. While this practice has decreased in modern times, Chalcedonies are uniquely beautiful gemstones that connect us with a bygone era. I don't know about you, but every time I slip on a Chalcedony ring I feel like going off to conquer Gaul!

Chrysoprase

One of the most prized Chalcedonies, Chrysoprase is named from the Greek 'chrysos' (gold) and 'prason' (leek), in reference to its green colour. Chrysoprase's green varies due to the hydrated silicates and nickel oxides present. It is sometimes confusingly and incorrectly called 'Australian Jade' due to this prodigious origin, Chinese naming practices and its resemblance to Imperial Jade. In his book, 'Secrets des vertus des Herbes, Pierres et Bestes', renowned medieval philosopher and theologian Albertus Magnus relates a story of how Alexander the Great wore a Chrysoprase in his girdle to assure victory.

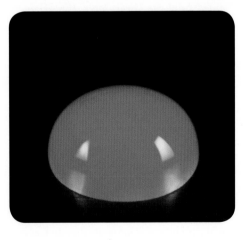

Jasper

Jasper is Chalcedony's spotted, blotched and veined variety, named from the Latin 'iaspis', which means 'spotted stone'. Coming in over 50 different colour and pattern varieties, Jasper is historically associated with a mind-boggling array of esoteric powers.

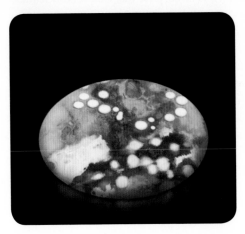

Onyx

Named from the Greek 'onyx' (fingernail or claw), Onyx was mythologically created when Cupid trimmed the fingernails of a sleeping Venus. Colloquially known as 'black magic', Onyx is typically perceived as a black gem, but as a variety of Agate, is actually banded with white. Finely textured, Onyx also comes in banded chocolate, green, reddish-brown and white. Sardonyx is the reddish brown and white variety of Onyx. Sardonyx was highly valued in Rome as a seal stone because it apparently doesn't stick to wax. The importance of this shouldn't be underestimated. During antiquity, your seal was your passport and credit card all rolled into one. Roman General Publius Cornelius Scipio was a big fan of Sardonyx and many legionnaires went into battle wearing Sardonyx's engraved with Mars (the god of war) for courage.

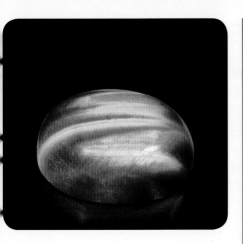

Tiger's Eye

The chorus of the Survivor classic, "It's the eye of the tiger, it's the cream of the fight", is a good match with the gem of the same name, once being favoured by Roman legionnaries for protection in battle. The best known variety of cat's eye or chatoyant Quartz (see page 31 for more), Tiger's Eye has lustrous yellow and golden brown stripes. Named for its resemblance to the eye of a tiger, Tiger's Eye is actually a macrocrystalline Quartz (large crystal), but is included here because of its appearance. Varieties include Bull's Eye (reddish-brown) and Hawk's Eye (bluish-green). The quintessential 'masculine' gem, it is a perennial favourite for signet rings and cufflinks.

If you look carefully at the end of 'Indiana Jones and the Raiders of the Lost Ark', where they crack open the 'Ark of the Covenant', you'll see René Belloq (filling in as high priest) wearing 12 sacred gemstones set in a breastplate. According to legend, the divine power of these gemstones was due to God creating them on Mount Sinai (Mountain of God). Apparently, they also once belonged to Lucifer, but were taken away when God stopped talking his calls. Known as the 'stones of fire' (Ezekiel 28:13-16) or 'the jewels of gold', they each represented a tribe of Israel and are the impetus for birthstones in Western culture (see page 250 for more). Given the gems on the Mountain of God, Moses followed God's instruction (Exodus 28:15-30) and set them in the breastplate of Aaron (high priest and brother of Moses), also known as the 'breastplate of judgment'. Said to have the power to summon angels, they were probably called the 'stones of fire' because they were thought to control the awesome heavenly power of the ark. Of these 12 gems, four are Chalcedonies: Agate, Jasper, Onyx and Sardius (Carnelian). Jumping ahead a testament, in Revelations (21:19-21) we are told of a different group of 12 gemstones set in the foundations of the city walls of Jerusalem. Once again, Chalcedonies take centre stage, with Chalcedony, Chrysoprase, Jasper, Sardius (Carnelian) and Sardonyx making up five of the 12. These gems are directly linked to the apostles in the bible (Revelations 21:14) and Andreas, the Bishop of Caesurae, paired them up as follows in the 10th century; Carnelian (Apostle: Philip), Chalcedony (Apostle: St. Andrew), Chrysoprase (Apostle: St. Thassaeus), Jasper (Apostle: St. Peter), and Sardonyx (Apostle: James).

CULTURED PEARL

"All art is autobiographical; the Pearl is the oyster's autobiography".
Federico Fellini (1920-1993)

Humble in origin yet unquestionably beautiful, Pearls are one of the world's oldest and most enduring gemstones. They mightn't have the 'bedazzle' of some other gems, but I agree with Fellini, there is something inherently artistic about Pearls; they embody a subtle sophistication, which is probably why they have such a lasting appeal. Pearls truly are natural wonders and just like Amber, they're not your average gemstone. The progeny of oysters, mussels and clams (or collectively, molluscs), Pearls are classed as organic gems and this classification includes any gemstone made or derived from living organisms.

Our modern name for this June birthstone is actually pretty new. Pearl is derived from the Latin 'perna' (ham) in reference to the shape of some Pearl mussels, but has only been in play since the 18th century. Prior, the English called them 'unions' (from the Latin 'unio', meaning 'unity' or 'a single large Pearl') or the old Greek and Roman name, 'margarita'. Nothing to do with that famous 1889 pizza, some associate 'margarita' with 'marine' because Pearls are waterborne, but I like to think it comes from the Persian 'murwari'. Meaning 'child of light', this helps explain why Pearls have long been a symbol of purity and innocence. As suggested by their name for this gem, the ancient Persians believed Pearls to be created by moonlight shining magically into open oyster shells. The Persian Gulf is the genesis of humanity's fascination with Pearls and even today, continues as a source for 'natural' Pearls, whose only significant remaining market is the Middle East.

Kokichi Mikimoto (1858-1954) devoted his life to perfecting Pearl farming and is the 'father' of the modern Pearl industry

Delicate, incomparable, luminescent, lustrous, radiant, and unique, Pearls might be quintessentially feminine gemstones and a timeless symbol of refined taste, but what exactly are they? The ancient Chinese told their children they were tears of sharks, but after watching the remorseless 'Jaws' as a boy, I would have found this hard to believe. For the ancient Egyptians, Pearls were for Isis, the goddess of healing and life, while in the Greco-Roman pantheon they were the tears of joy wept by Aphrodite (Venus), the goddess of love and beauty. To the Romans, Pearls were born when oysters swallowed dewdrops filled with moonlight that fell into the ocean. At school, I was taught that Pearls where caused by grains of sand entering the oyster and this isn't incorrect, just a romantic over-simplification. In truth, beautiful Pearls are the way molluscs respond to infection. When an irritant, such as a piece of coral or parasite, enters the mollusc's soft tissue its natural defence mechanism

Akoya Pearls

Akoya Pearls (Pinctada Fucata Martensi) are named after the Japanese word (akoya-gai) for the saltwater Pearl oyster originally used by Mikimoto. Today, pollution in its original habitat has resulted in the Akoya Pearl also being farmed in China, Tahiti and Vietnam. Akoya Pearls typically grow for eight months to two years and can be nucleated with up to five bead implants, but two is most common. Usually two to six millimetres in diameter, Akoya Pearls are rarely over nine millimetres in size. Approximately one out of five nucleated Akoya oysters produce Pearls and only a tiny fraction of these are of gem quality.

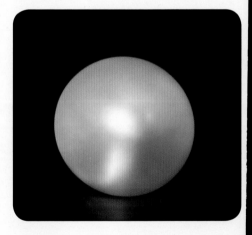

kicks in, coating the intruder with a cocktail of calcium carbonate, better known as 'nacre', from the Arabic for shell, 'naqqarah'. Left to its own devices and a *lot* of luck, this process *might* yield a marketable Pearl over time. The problem is, this rarely happens in the wild and even if it does, you've still got to find it! This is the reason Pearls were for centuries considered among the most valuable gemstones and a potent symbol of power, prestige, social status and wealth. Over 2,000 years ago in ancient Rome, Pearls were the most valuable thing money could buy. Julius Caesar, Roman general, dictator and (believe it or not) Pearl aficionado, once paid 60,000 gold pieces for a single Pearl and in the 1st century BC enacted a law forbidding the lower ranks from wearing them. Even Caesar's failed invasion of Britain was to secure its coveted river Pearls. Back in the glory days of the British Empire, Queen Elizabeth I was so enraptured by Pearls she was called the 'Pearl Queen'. The historic esteem

Chinese Freshwater Pearls

It doesn't matter whether you call it a clam or a mussel, the freshwater Hyriopsis Cuingii produces Pearls in a plethora of affordable colours and shapes. When tissue nucleated, up to 50 Pearls can be produced from a single clam, making them affordable. Typically baroque-shaped because they are solid nacre, they are also very luminous and colourful. Chinese Freshwater Pearls can also be bead nucleated, producing Pearls up to 14 millimetres in diameter.

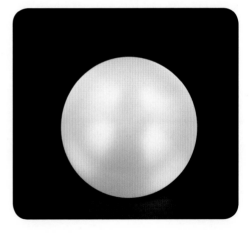

of Pearls is even recorded in religion. In Matthew (13:45-46) Jesus compares the kingdom of heaven to a *"Pearl of great price"*, while in the Koran (35:33) the kingdom of heaven has *"gardens of perpetual bliss will they enter, therein to be adorned with bracelets of gold and Pearls"*.

All this changed for the better in 1908, when a Japanese noodle maker, Kokichi Mikimoto, started the world's first commercial Pearl farm. Rudimentary Pearl farming had been practised in China as early as the 5th century, but it was Mikimoto, aptly called the 'Pearl King', who managed to shuck the proverbial oyster, culturing perfectly round Pearls and marketing them to a willing world. Since the sixties, cultured Pearls have become the market norm and trust me, this is a good thing. What was previously an aristocratic luxury reserved for high society has now become an extravagance everyone can afford. Also, let's not forget that Pearl greed once decimated Central American oyster populations and resulted in the near extinction of Scottish rivers mussels (pearling has been banned in the UK since 1998).

South Sea Pearls

South Sea Pearls (Pinctada Maxima) are farmed in Australia, Indonesia and the Philippines. This oyster is noted for producing white, silver and golden Pearls. South Sea Pearls typically grow for two to six years and while they only accept one nucleus at a time, they can be nucleated several times and even returned to nature to lend their genes to future generations. South Sea Pearls are some of the largest Pearls and while they are typically 10 to 16 millimetres in diameter, they can grow up to 20 millimetres. Due to its compatibility with Caucasian skin tones, whites remain the most popular and expensive.

Defined as a natural process with human intervention, culturing is just giving nature a helping hand. Cultured Pearls are propagated by 'nucleation', which simply involves introducing an implant (nucleus), either a bead (typically made from rounded and polished oyster shell, Mother of Pearl) or a piece of tissue, into the mollusc so it's coated with nacre, thus triggering the formation of a Pearl. After they've been seeded, the molluscs go back into the water to grow. The depth of the nacre has a big impact on a Pearl's value (more below) and depends on the rate of nacre accumulation, which in turn is determined by environmental conditions and its species. This takes time, anywhere from eight months to six years, during which everything can go wrong. Relying on luck as much as skill, Pearl farming is a risky business. Uncontrollable factors, such as disease, storms, temperature fluctuations and water pollution, can wipe you out overnight. For example, two tropical storms killed off millions of Pearl oysters in south eastern China in August 2007. Having visited the freshwater Pearl farms of China's Zhuijiang Province, I found that Pearl farming is big business, but are they still rare

Tahitian Pearls

Named for the tropical isle in French Polynesia, Tahitian Pearls (Pinctada Margaritifera) are arguably the most coveted of all Pearls, despite only being introduced to Europeans in 1845. This is primarily due to the dramatic contrast between their grey, silver or black body colours and their colourful orients. Tahitian Pearl orients are typically blue, green, pink or purple, their rarest and most valuable orients being 'peacock' (green pink combo) and pure purple. Green is the most common orient colour in Tahitian Pearls and dark green is commonly called 'fly wing'. A pink orient produces a colour called 'eggplant' 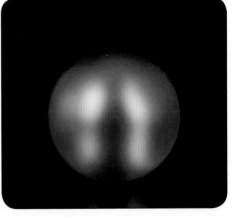 *when combined with a black body colour. Tahitian Pearls typically grow for four to five years and while they only accept one nucleus at a time, they can be nucleated several times and even returned to nature to lend their genes to future generations. Typically eight to 16 millimetres in diameter, Tahitian Pearls are some of the largest Pearls. While Tahitian myths associate this Pearl with a beautiful princess called Bora Bora, it was Empress Eugenie, wife of Napoleon III, who boosted Pearl's Western popularity.*

enough to really be gemstones? In my mind, yes! Only half of the cultured Pearls harvested are marketable and less than five percent are top-quality perfectly round Pearls. Natural and cultured Pearls are instinctually the same, they both come from a mollusc not a science lab, which is why many in the gem industry were horrified by the United States Federal Trade Commission's recent ruling, allowing the term 'cultured' to be used to market synthetic gemstones. Even though they are farmed, Pearls remain a coveted natural product and as with all gemstones, perfection is rare.

Seed Pearls are 'young' Pearls that first gained popularity in the Victorian period as jewellery accent gemstones

Apart from their lustrous beauty, part of Pearls' classical appeal must have been that once out of their shell, they're pretty much ready to wear and don't need the time-consuming lapidary of mineral gems. But how do you judge a Pearl? Firstly, forget the 4Cs (colour, cut, clarity and carat weight) as they don't apply to Pearls. Secondly, provenance is critical as different Pearls from different locations have different qualities and prices. The four main Pearl types are Akoya, Chinese Freshwater, South Sea and Tahitian. Species aside, Pearls are judged by their body colour, translucency, orient (overtone), lustre, surface clarity or texture, size, shape and symmetry. Like all gems, beauty is of paramount importance and for Pearls, lustre and orient are the two most important factors. Regardless of your taste

Appearing in an attractive array of iridescent colours, Mother of Pearl was named by Queen Elizabeth I in the 15th century. Beautiful yet remarkably affordable, as its name suggests, Mother of Pearl is the lustrous inside of mollusc shells

or budget, the good news is that cultured Pearls offer a huge range of shapes and colours that vary depending on their species, nucleus shape, shell position and growing conditions.

Close your eyes and think of a Pearl and I bet you see something white and round. This might be the *classic* perception, but the reality is that the basic body colour of Pearls offers a myriad of choices: apricot (yellowish-orange), black, blue, bronze (reddish-brown), champagne (pinkish-yellow), chocolate, cream, golden, green, grey, orange, peach (pinkish-orange), plum (reddish-violet), purple, red, violet, white, yellow and everything in-between. While some professionals regard green tints in Akoya and South Sea white Pearls as less desirable and greys should be silvery not dull, colour is subjective and ultimately, a matter of personal preference. Regardless, a Pearl's body colour alone isn't that important in assessing its beauty. The real determinant is how a Pearl's body colour, translucency, lustre, and orient all work together. A good guide is to choose a body colour that compliments your skin tone. In his book, 'Secrets of the Gem Trade', Richard Wise describes this *"compatibility with the skin of the wearer"* using the Italian word, 'simpatico', which means 'pleasing' or 'sympathetic'. This excellent terminology actually embodies the almost symbiotic relationship between Pearls and people. It has long been known that Pearls look more beautiful if worn regularly and English ladies of the 18th century were quick to adopt the Indian practice of having their servants wear their Pearls so they were always warm and luminescent.

The orient or overtone is the secondary colour of Pearls, and along with lustre, is what makes the finest examples. This overtone of translucent colours moves over a Pearl's body colour, accentuating or contrasting as well as adding depth and glow. Orient comes from the Latin 'oriens', which means 'the rising of the sun' and this is definitely apt; it often looks like an internal sun breaking through a lucid dawn. It occurs because a Pearl's nacre is deposited in

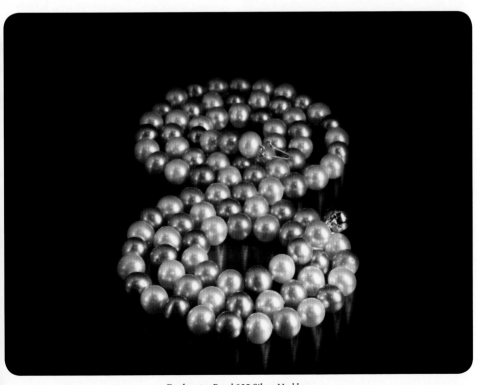

Freshwater Pearl 925 Silver Necklace

While Pearl oysters' scientific name *Pinctada* distinguishes them from edible oysters known as *Ostreidae*, Roman historian Pliny the Elder (23-79 AD) tells the story of how Cleopatra put this to the test. Competing with Marc Anthony to see who could host the most lavish dinner party, she trumped him by dissolving a Pearl from her earrings in vinegar and downing it. Movie myth has it that she crushed it in a glass of wine. However the Pearl was consumed, at the cost of 80,000 gold pieces, she really did drink the 'wealth of nations'. Now you've probably heard this story before, along with the old wives' tale about how you can rub the surface of a Pearl over your teeth to tell if it's fake (smooth) or real (bumpy). Now, before you start sticking your Pearls in your mouth, this is not a reliable test. Sure the premise has some validity, but for cultured Pearls this no longer *always* rings true. A bespoke jeweller once told me about a male customer shopping for his wife, who insisted on performing this test on a selection of expensive Tahitian Pearls. Undoubtedly the real McCoy, our jeweller was a little apprehensive given their value, but the customer is always right. Reluctantly agreeing, he glanced away for a second to answer the phone. Turning back to continue the sale, the red-faced customer admitted he'd accidentally swallowed one! Now jokingly referred to as 'pulling a Cleopatra', it mightn't have cost him the 'wealth of nations', but I would've loved to see how he explained that credit card statement to his wife!

thin layers that bend light into one or many spectral hues. While the orient is typically monotone, how many colours are visible, and their intensity, is down to the Pearl species and nacre thickness. The orient is most visible on the crest of a Pearl's horizon, but not all Pearls display orient. Even if the species produces orients, if a Pearl isn't given enough time to grow, the nacre will not be thick enough to diffract light. Because of the way they are cultivated, Akoya Pearls have thin nacre, so they rarely display orient. As most Chinese Freshwater Pearls are tissue nucleated, they are almost all nacre and sometimes display unique rainbow iridescence, particularly when irregularly (baroque) shaped. In my experience, orient is most visible in Tahitian Pearls, which is not surprising, considering the contrast afforded by their black body colour (just like Black Opals) and that their nacre is comprised of thousands of layers up to 10 millimetres thick.

Generally, Pearls with colourful orients are more valuable than those that have little or no orient, but a high lustre is also significant, especially if orients aren't typical for the species. For me, lustre largely defines the beauty of Pearls and is as important to Pearls as brilliance is to transparent gemstones. A Pearl's lustre should be bright, snappy and reflective, not dreary, blurry or lazy. Much like orient, lustre is also related to nacre thickness, but like inclusions in transparent gemstones, a Pearl's surface clarity or texture is also important. Pearls with smooth silky surfaces will reflect light greater and more evenly than ones with significant imperfections. Of course, if you can't see them, blemishes don't affect a gem's beauty, so clever jewellers often set Pearls in a manner that hides imperfections. As with all gems, size matters and all things being equal, the bigger the Pearl the higher the value. Because of the size of their oysters and their prodigious nacre creation, South Sea and Tahitian are usually the largest cultured Pearls. While it is said that Caesar could judge a Pearl's value simply by weighing it in his hand, today his skills wouldn't be much use; Pearls are typically measured by their millimetre size, not by their weight. In the 'Shu King', a 23 BC Chinese manuscript, a lesser king's tribute of *"strings of Pearls not quite round"* is belittled by the scribe and while perfectly rounds are still valued highest, Pearls actually come in many shapes. One of the biggest misconceptions is that culturing guarantees rounds. It doesn't, and most Pearls aren't round. Pearls are either spherical (perfectly round or nearly round), symmetrical (buttons, drops, ovals and pears that are balanced and regular) or baroque (abstract or irregular). Ultimately, the 'best' shape is best left to personal preferences, but please consider baroques, their artistic irregularity often accentuates this most artistic of gems. Unless deliberately part of the design, suites of Pearls should always match.

In her recent article 'Pearls in Politics', published by Coloured Stone, Deborah Yonick says, *"Pearls stand alone, unique and unfettered by excess, with a simple, no-nonsense approach to dressing for success. Pearl jewellery affirms that women are strong, independent and in control. They project a balance of both power and beauty"*, and I couldn't agree more, but thanks to the 'Pearl King' you now don't have to be a 'Pearl Queen' to afford them.

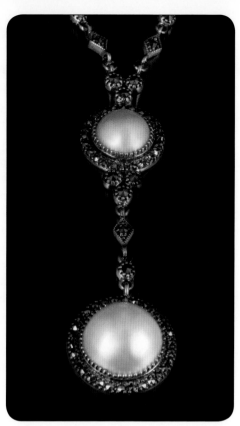

In the 5th century, the Chinese experimented with Pearl culturing by placing little lead Buddha's inside mussels. By the 14th century, they were the first to master the art, particularly with respect to culturing Mabe Pearls (pictured). Mabe Pearls are hemispherical shaped Pearls, grown against the inside of the mollusc's shell

DIAMOND

"I never worry about diets. The only carrots that interest me are the number of carats in a Diamond".

Mae West (1892-1980)

Whenever I give a talk on gemstones, I always begin by asking women what their favourite is. Not surprisingly, given the millions pumped into their marketing, Diamonds invariably emerge as the flat-out winner. Clever global marketing along with famous movies, have made Diamonds iconic cultural symbols deeply ingrained in modern society. Take for example the 1953 classic, 'Gentlemen Prefer Blondes' where Marilyn Monroe sang 'Diamonds Are a Girl's Best Friend' and 'Breakfast at Tiffany's' (1961) with the petite Audrey Hepburn. Other classics include the dashing Sean Connery as 007 in 'Diamonds Are Forever' (1971) with Shirley Bassey singing its unforgettable theme, Quentin Tarantino's ultra-violent, but totally cool 'Reservoir Dogs' (1990), Guy Ritchie's Brit-flick 'Snatch' (2001), and Leonardo DiCaprio's, 'Blood Diamond' (2006). Considering that their mainstream popularity is very much a post-fifties phenomenon, particularly with regard to engagement rings, this is actually pretty astounding. That is not to say I have anything against Diamonds, mind you. How could anybody have anything against them? Indeed, 'the girl's best friend' and April's birthstone has it all. Antiquity (most Diamonds are between one billion to 3.3 billion years old), durability (they're the hardest known natural material ever), blinding brilliance (white light reflections), fantastic fire (the ability to split light into its component colours), sizzling scintillation (play of light) and, last but not least, remarkable rarity, for 80 percent of all

Diamond revenues enable every child in Botswana to receive free education up to the age of 13

Diamonds mined are only good enough for industry. It takes one million Diamonds to get one 1 carat gem quality Diamond! No, I have nothing against Diamonds at all, it's just that, like the myriad of shapes, characters and individual styles personified by the women who usually wear them, the gem kingdom has a lot more going for it than sparkling, yet plain old whites. But here's the thing, Diamonds also come in colours and there are other rare gemstones that possess greater fire. More on these later.

Formed in mantle at the very heart of the earth, Diamond derives its name from the Greek 'adamas', which means 'unconquerable', certainly appropriate for the hardest and one of the most valuable of all gemstones. The only gemstone comprised of a single element, Diamonds are crystalline carbon, making them long lost relatives of coal and lead pencils. Given its unique mineralogical attributes, it's not surprising that Diamonds have an encyclopaedic array of mythological origins, purported attributes and esoteric abilities. Greek philosophers thought Diamonds were 'alive' with celestial spirits, Romans thought them tears of the gods or splinters from falling stars, while Hindus believed they were created by lightning striking rocks. According to Jewish tradition, a Diamond held before a guilty person will darken, while a Diamond held before an innocent will increase in brilliance. From the middle ages to the renaissance, they were purported to possess a variety of esoteric abilities to counter life's

Diamond Platinum Ring

roubles, including instilling bravery, courage, invincibility, strength, and virtue; the power to drive away nightmares, ward off evil spirits, soothe savage beasts, and even protect your house from lightning!

While Louis IX of France once decreed Diamonds exclusively the domain of royalty, since the 15th century these gemstones have slowly made their way from monarchs to the masses. The 4Cs (colour, clarity, cut and carat weight) are the foundations of Diamond valuation. As these are covered in detail in Chapter 1, we'll briefly recap these in the context of accessing Diamonds. Due to their homogeneity, judging a Diamond's colour and clarity is now relatively straightforward, thanks to the 'Diamond Clarity Scale' and 'Diamond Colour Scale' developed by the GIA (Gemmological Institute of America). Both of these scales are included in this section.

For Diamonds beautiful brilliance is king and this is true for both single solitaires destined for engagement rings to melees (> 0.2 carats) used in cluster designs or in a supporting role as accent gems. We are looking for the best balance of dispersion (fiery flashes of colour, see page 15 for more), scintillation (play of light) and its characteristic brilliance (white light reflections), which is a combination of its internal brilliance and its unique adamantine lustre (see page 14 for more). In bright illumination, Diamonds can display the entire colour spectrum of the rainbow (blue, green, orange, red, violet, and yellow) in all their individual glory, and as the gem is moved its facets sparkle in the play of light (scintillation). The problem is the lapidary must use angles to balance these three signature characteristics, and as fire and brilliance are odd bed fellows, maximising both is simply impossible. Much has been written about the 'ideal' cut proportions for Diamonds and the maintenance of these uniform ideals to get the best out of them. However, research by the GIA, using computer

GIA Diamond Clarity Scale

Clarity	Description
Flawless (FL)	Shows no inclusions or blemishes under 10x loupe.
Internally Flawless (IF)	Has no inclusions when examined using 10x loupe and only insignificant minor surface blemishes.
Very Very Slightly Included (VVS1 & VVS2)	Contains minute inclusions that are difficult to see under 10x loupe.
Very Slightly Included (VS1 & VS2)	Contains minute inclusions when observed under 10X loupe.
Slightly Included (SI1, SI2 & SI3)	Contains inclusions that are noticeable under 10x loupe. The Rapaport Diamond Report, the definitive pricing guide for Diamonds, added SI3 to its price list after the EGL (European Gemmological Laboratory) started issuing certificates with the SI3 grade.
Included (I1, I2 and I3)	Contains inclusions that are obvious under 10x loupe.
Pique (PK)	Eye-visible inclusions.

modelling, has established that there are actually several proportions that can maximise either brilliance or fire. Simply put, the idea of an 'ideal' cut for Diamonds is not finite, and judging the quality of cut in terms of visible brilliance rather than against mathematical proportions is the current trend. Personally, any criterion that throws out the cookie cutter and favours visible beauty has my vote. For example, I am still amazed that many smaller accent Diamonds (1mm rounds) actually look better when not cut with the traditional 57 facets of a modern brilliant cut (see page 37 for more). This is intriguing, considering the modern brilliant cut may result in a loss of more than 50 percent of the rough crystal. Apart from its cut, a Diamond's brilliance will also be determined by its colour, inherent transparency (clarity), and fluorescence. As with all gems, the better the brilliance, clarity and cut, the higher the price.

While the Diamonds most people want to own are colourless (or as clear as their bank

Coloured or Fancy Diamonds are extremely popular and are sometimes described as 'two gemstones in one' because they give you colour plus the characteristic sparkle of a Diamond. Referred to as Z+ by the GIA as their colour intensity is outside the normal range, their colours include black, blue, brown, green, grey, olive, orange, purple, red and yellow. Diamonds are comprised of carbon and because of their compact atomic structure, trace elements that colour other gemstones just can't get in. So instead of being coloured by chromium, titanium and vanadium, Fancy Diamonds owe there hues to boron, hydrogen and nitrogen, as well as crystal imperfections (colour centres). Not surprisingly, Coloured Diamonds are exceedingly rare in nature, resulting in the vast majority of what's available in the marketplace being colour enhanced (see page 259 for more)

balance will allow), in reality, they can come in an array of colours. To the untrained eye most Diamonds look colourless, but to the expert, minor differences can equate to big price differences. While true colourless Diamonds are extremely rare and priced accordingly, near colourless Diamonds or those with barely perceptible yellowish tints offer better value for money. Don't be bullied by a salesperson into spending more on something you can't see! One factor that confuses many is the impact of fluorescence on a Diamond's brilliance and colour. Fluorescence is a material's ability to glow in ultraviolet light and about one-third of Diamonds possess this attribute. While invisible to us, a Diamond's bluish fluorescence can actually make a yellowish Diamond appear whiter. This might seem like a good way to get more 'bang for your buck', but the problem is fluorescence can also somewhat reduce a Diamond's daylight brilliance, negatively affecting its beauty. The key is a balance of all its attributes (body colour, brilliance, clarity, cut, dispersion, fluorescence, scintillation, size and transparency), with a beautiful brilliance the ultimate consideration.

With rounds accounting for the bulk of Diamond sales worldwide (approximately 80 percent), ask women, *"What shape is a Diamond?"* and they'll probably say, *"Round"*. They're lovely, they're popular and they sell well, but there are many other beautiful shapes and cuts that warrant serious consideration. You can meet these on page 36. Not wanting to conform to the norm, I selected two 45 point pear-shaped Diamond accent gemstones for my wife's Blue Sapphire engagement ring. Some branded Diamond cuts exist and just like labels on jeans, these sometimes incur a premium.

With the reducing marketplace influence of the DeBeers Diamond syndicate, emerging sources in Russia and Canada, and the 'blood diamond' fiasco, origin has become increasingly discussed for one of the world's most homogeneous gemstones. Until Brazilian Diamonds were discovered in 1725, India had been the world's only source, with records dating back to

GIA Diamond Colour Scale

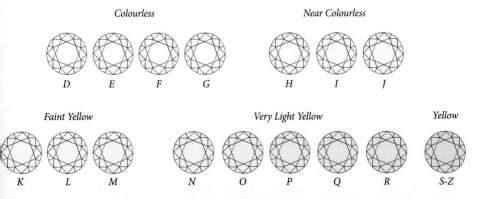

The GIA 'Diamond Colour Scale'. Not wanting to confuse their system with existing grades, the GIA started afresh, beginning with the letter D

at least 800 BC. Ancient Europeans were probably introduced to Diamonds via the Persians, scoring their first mentioned in Roman literature in the 1st century. Today, approximately 65 percent of the world's Diamonds come from African countries.

Brilliant, beautiful, symbolic and iconic, Diamonds are deserving of their marketing hype. Whether they will still be the 'engagement' gemstone of the future or Blue Sapphires' popularity again re-emerges as the 'choice' for those tying the knot, one thing's for sure, Marilyn was right, *"Square-cut or pear-shaped, these rocks don't lose their shape, Diamonds are a girl's best friend"*.

Demantoid

A favourite of the famous Russian jeweller Karl Fabergé, Demantoid was discovered and named by Dr. Nordenskjöl in 1855 (the same guy who identified Alexandrite). The original source was in Russia's central Urals, in alluvial deposits at the Sissersk District and the Bobrovka River (hence one of its colloquial names, 'Bobrovka Garnet'). A colour variety of Andradite, Demantoid and the Grossular Garnet Tsavorite are the two green members of the Garnet family (yes, Garnets come in hues other than reds and oranges). Until Dr. Nordenskjöld took a closer look, Demantoid was assumed to be Emerald; hence it's other

colloquial name 'Uralian Emerald'. Dr. Nordenskjöld took its name for the old German 'demant', which means 'diamond-like'. Demantoid was named in reference to its adamantine lustre (see page 14 for more), extreme scintillation and dispersion (fire) higher than in Diamonds. Like Emeralds, Demantoid is coloured by chromium and ranges in colour from green to yellowish green. As with most coloured gems, the happy medium is the ideal and for Demantoid this is an intense 'emerald-green'. Due to its body colour, Demantoid's fire is often not as discernable as in Diamonds, leading some to prefer lighter greens that accentuate its characteristic fire. As a Type II gemstone, Demantoid typically grows with some minor inclusions that may be eye-visible. In fact, Demantoid over half a carat usually isn't eye-clean (no visible inclusions when the gem is examined six inches from the naked eye), with the majority mined smaller than 1 carat. A fine Demantoid over 2 carats is exceptional and anything over 5 carats is a museum specimen. While Demantoid was hugely popular in Europe in the years after its initial discovery, no significant production was recorded since the 1917 Russian revolution, until the fall of the Soviet Union saw small-scale Demantoid mining recommence around 1991. Beautiful Demantoid is also found in Namibia. Russian and Namibian material is differentiated by Russian Demantoid's 'horsetail' inclusions, radiating strands that appear similar to a horse's tail. With 'classic' greens, impossible rarity, and a fire greater than Diamonds, Demantoid Garnet is a true connoisseurs' gemstone.

Sphene

It's not easy being a Sphene. Sure, you might be new, rare, have dispersion (fire) greater than Demantoid and Diamonds, but so what? You might even have a strong pleochroism (different colours visible from different angles) that makes you appear to change colour, have amazing adamantine (Diamond-like) lustre and double refractivity that lends optical depth. But who cares? The fact is nobody has ever heard of you! Named from the Greek 'sfena' (wedge), because of its wedge shaped crystals, Sphene is also sometimes called Titanite. Most Sphene is green to yellowish-green, but its intense fiery brilliance can display every spectral colour (blue, green, orange, red, violet, and yellow). Possessing an intense natural beauty, Sphene when faceted creates brilliant, fiery gems, but is notoriously difficult to polish. Usually smaller than 1 carat, large eye-clean Sphene is extremely rare. While Sphene hails from Brazil, Pakistan and Sri Lanka, Madagascar is currently its main source.

As I said earlier, gems are pure emotion and the last thing anyone wants to feel are negative emotions associated with the suffering of others. This is especially true if that gemstone has become the 'symbol' for love, romance and marriage. But regrettably, this same thing happened. If you've seen Leonardo DiCaprio's, 'Blood Diamond' movie, you already know the premise. But what you may not know is that the Diamond industry dealt with this issue long before the movie's release. 'Blood Diamonds', also known as 'conflict diamonds' are Diamonds mined in a war zone and sold, usually under the table, to finance fighting. The United Nations mandated 'Kimberley Process' eradicates 'blood diamonds' via a government-regulated system adopted in 2000 by more than 40 countries; only participating countries may legitimately export rough Diamonds and only to co-participating countries. The World Diamond Council (WDC) strengthened the government programme via a voluntary system of warranties that requires seller invoice affirmations that that the Diamonds have been purchased through authorised channels every time they change hands. Today, thanks to the Kimberly Process, over 99 percent of the world's supply of Diamonds is conflict-free. While the movie heightened public awareness, it also made us perhaps a little cynical to Diamond public relations initiatives like **www.diamondfacts.org**. This site is full of great 'feel good' facts, such as an estimated five million people having access to appropriate healthcare globally, thanks to revenues from Diamonds. Revenues from Diamonds are instrumental in the fight against the AIDS pandemic and an estimated 10 million people globally are directly or indirectly supported by the Diamond industry. I'm going to close with a quote from Mr. Festus G. Mogae, former President of the Republic of Botswana, *"For our people in Botswana every Diamond you buy means food on the table, better living conditions, better health care, safe drinking water, more roads and much, much more"*.

EMERALD

"Indeed there is no stone, the colour of which is more delightful to the eye... there being no green in existence of a more intense colour than this".

Pliny the Elder (23-79 AD), Historia Naturalis

When I was a boy, long before I knew or cared who old man Pliny was, I thought Jim Henson's Kermit the Frog was pretty fantastic. Having grown up on 'Sesame Street', the 'Muppet Show' was a programme we enjoyed as a family, with many happy memories. I remember Kermit singing, 'It's Not Easy Being Green', when he starts lamenting about being the colour of ordinary things, ending positively in full realisation that green is good: it is cool, friendly, the colour of Spring, and big important things, such as oceans and mountains. In a way, Kermit's journey of self realisation mirrors my experience with Emeralds. Initially, I couldn't understand them, their intricacies, personality or character. Trying as I might to get into their 'ins and outs', I was just out. After a while, I began to see them for what they are, truly ancient and fantastic gemstones. No wonder Mesopotamians (modern-day Iraq) reportedly traded Emeralds 4,000 years ago. From Cleopatra to conquistadors, the lust for its rare, beautiful greens has made Emeralds one of the world's most valuable gemstones. But the birthstone for May isn't as easy to understand as other gems; so hold my hand as we get clever with Emeralds.

Emerald is a member of the Beryl mineral family (from the ancient Greek 'beryllos', meaning blue-green stone), and commonly known as the 'mother of gemstones' because of its highly regarded gem varieties. Apart from Emerald greens, other Beryl gemstones

Legend has it that Cleopatra's favourite gemstones were Emeralds

Historically, Emerald was the mean green beauty machine of the ancient world; Mesopotamians, Egyptians, Greeks and Romans all coveted the 'greenest of green' gems. For those looking for Emeralds in early civilisations surrounding the Mediterranean, they'd have been best off seeing the Egyptians, because this was the place where Emerald's story begins.

Tsavorite Garnet

Campbell R. Bridges, the legendary Scottish geologist who was the first person to bring Tanzanite to the GIA (Gemmological Institute of America) for identification, discovered Tsavorite in 1967 in Tanzania and in 1971 in Kenya's Tsavo region. A Green Grossular Garnet, Tsavorite is the trade name created in 1974 by Campbell and Tiffany's Henry B. Platt (great grandson of Louis Comfort Tiffany), and is named in honour of Kenya's Tsavo National Park. Having had lunch with Campbell, I found him an interesting man, relaying colourful stories of living in a tree house to protect himself from leopards and  *even placing a python in among Tsavorite rough to prevent theft. He actually challenged yours truly to a race up a shaft at his Scorpion Mine, but I was unable to travel to Kenya, so the jury's still out on that one. While Emerald's greens are frequently touted as being 'unparalleled in the gem kingdom', Tsavorite is the one gem that can give it a run for its money. Tsavorite is coloured by trace amounts of vanadium, and occasionally chromium, the same elements that give Emerald its characteristic hues. In terms of colour, a pure 'emerald-green' is considered by the marketplace to be the finest, but as will all gems, be guided by your preferences. The reliable Goldilocks maxim again rings true (see page 16 for more), with intense midpoints being favoured. Dark 'blackish' Tsavorite that loses transparency and overly yellow specimens will be priced accordingly. Tsavorite is available in a wide variety of cuts, so look for a good shape that accentuates its innate brilliance due to its high index of refraction. In this respect, Tsavorite has a crisp brilliance that 'snaps' when compared to the 'satiny' brilliance of Emeralds. While Tsavorite is classed as a Type II gemstone (see page 10 for more), like most Garnets, it possesses few inclusions. While the market norm is eye-clean (or as close to that ideal as possible), larger gems with a few eye-visible inclusions are forgivable due to their scarcity; most Tsavorite is under 3 carats. Despite being heavily marketed in seventies by Tiffany & Co., 40 years on, Tsavorite never did manage to usurp Emerald as the greenest of greens. It may be cleaner, rarer and more brilliant than Emerald, but Tsavorite is plagued by scant availability. Only a handful of its notoriously difficult to mine deposits in Kenya, Tanzania, Madagascar and Zambia are commercially viable, keeping prices high. Exceptionally beautiful, Tsavorite's unique properties have crowned it the 'king of garnets', but due to little public awareness it remains a choice gem for the connoisseur.*

Perhaps mined as early as 3500 BC, Egypt's Emerald mines were located in Egypt's eastern desert region and were rediscovered in 1816 by Frédéric Cailliaud, a French mineralogist and explorer. Even Greek miners braved heat, scorpions and snakes to unearth Emeralds there for Alexander the Great. This isn't to say there weren't other Emerald sources; the Habachtal region in the Austrian state of Salzburg might have yielded a few Emeralds, and Roman earrings featuring Emeralds from the Mingora Mine in Pakistan's Swat Valley have been discovered. There is also a legend that the Scythian Emeralds mentioned by Pliny in his 'Historia Naturalis' were actually from Russia's Urals, but as far as supply is concerned, Egypt had a near monopoly. Cleopatra, last Pharaoh of Egypt, was big on Emeralds; she wore sumptuous Emerald jewellery, decorated ornamental objects with them, and presented dignitaries with Emeralds carved with her likeness. While it's tempting to think they were her favourite simply because of their beauty, Cleopatra was shrewd, intelligent and politically savvy. She understood the importance of symbolism, glamour and prestige in power and politics. Emeralds were more than just pretty gems to the Egyptians, they were potent

Peridot

Peridot (correctly pronounced 'Pair-ee-doh'), derives its name from the Arabic 'faridat', which means 'gem' and was called the 'gem of the sun' by the ancient Egyptians and the 'evening emerald' by the Romans. The 'classic' source for this gemstone is Zeberget (St. John's Island), which is located approximately 80 kilometres off the Egyptian coast in the Red Sea. Due to this deposit having a high nickel content it was visually similar to Emerald and you guessed it, many of Cleopatra's 'Emeralds' were actually Peridot. Rich in legend and lore, Peridot scores several mentions in the bible (using its old name Chrysolite, 'golden stone')

and was even a favourite of pirates, who were said to have used them for banishing evil spirits and terrors of the night. Coloured by iron, Peridot is the gem variety of the Olivine mineral and ranges in colour from green to yellowish-green, with its 'pure' green hues demanding the highest prices. Peridot has an attractive 'sleepy' appearance with a shining glow, which is why Peridot was mined at night during antiquity, when the gem's natural glow made it easier to spot. While it can be eye-clean when small, as a Type II gemstone, Peridot typically has eye-visible inclusions, especially in larger sizes. Although the world's largest Peridot deposit is located in the San Carlos Apache Reservation, Arizona, China has recently become a key player. But in my humble opinion, the best of the best hails from the Nanga Parbat region of Pakistan.

patriotic symbols of national pride and she knew this. When Cleopatra finally consolidated her power base in 47 BC, with a little help from her Roman boyfriend Caesar, she was quick to claim the countries mineralogical riches as her own. Despite being discovered some 2,000 years before her birth, the Egyptian deposits will be forever known as 'Cleopatra's Emerald Mines'.

Since Egyptian times, Emeralds have been linked to fertility, immortality, rejuvenation, and eternal spring, so it's no surprise they are the birthstone for May. Pliny bestowed the benefits of Emeralds to refresh and sooth strained eyes and even today, we have 'green rooms' to relax presenters in TV studios and 'hospital green' to calm patients. Having looked at a gem parcel or two in my time, there is some truth in this. Emeralds (and other green gems) are definitely easier on the eyes.

When getting ready to choose your Emerald, you'll need to understand four criteria and how they impact value: purity of colour, transparency, clarity and brilliance (brightness). As with so many gems, colour is king for Emerald, and the wise Goldilocks maxim (not

Zambian Emerald & Diamond 18K Yellow Gold Ring

too dark or too light, just right) is heading in the right direction. But all things being equal, a slightly deeper richer bluish green than the middle point is equally desirable. What is critical is your 'purity perception' of its green in different light sources, remembering a gem should ideally look good in all lighting conditions, and for the marketplace, the purist green possible is the most valuable. The tricky thing is that 'pure' greens are the unicorn of Emerald, with different experts differing on their preferences. A little bit of yellow (typically up to 15 percent) can enhance a pure green, balancing its colour in incandescent light, while a little bit of blue brings depth, richness and warmth. Colour preferences are subjective, so if you like them pastel because of your complexion, I'm not going to argue, but if you want to stick to the marketplace norm, the best Emerald for you is *your* best perception of green. Emeralds with too much blue, brown, grey or yellow will be priced accordingly.

Transparency and clarity are best described as two different, albeit related, things in Emerald. In general, a transparent 'lively' Emerald with a few bigger visible inclusions will be valued higher than an Emerald whose inclusions are so fine they create a murkiness that negatively impact transparency. Emeralds' inclusions and tiny fractures are termed 'jardin', from the French for 'garden', and this is definitely apt. As a Type III gemstone (see page 10 for more), Emerald has visible inclusions that we tolerate. In fact, you stand a better chance of seeing

Russian Diopside

Emerald? Not! Russian Diopside is a chromium-rich Diopside known for its green to bluish greens and is predominately mined in Russia (Siberia), although deposits also exist in China. Coloured by one of the trace elements also responsible for the 'classic' greens of Emerald (and sometimes Tsavorite), Russian Diopside is also known as Chrome Diopside or Imperial Diopside. Extremely rare, the supply of Russian Diopside is inconsistent. While it is usually eye-clean, Russian Diopside is mostly small sized, with anything over 5 carats virtually impossible to obtain. Diopside derives its name from the Greek 'di' (two) and 'opsis' (appearance), in reference to its double refractivity (see page 33 for more).

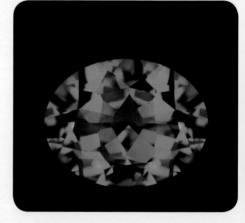

a flock of pigs than an eye-clean (no visible inclusions when the gem is examined six inches from the naked eye) Emerald above 1 carat. If I'm honest, this took some time for me to get used to, but now all is forgiven. In Emeralds, inclusions are the nature of the beast and are a characteristic trait, like a beauty spot, not a blemish. Why? Emeralds grow slowly within metamorphic rocks (rocks that have undergone a physical change due to extreme heat or pressure), which limits their size. This violent environment, combined with chromium and vanadium trace elements, creates a veritable inclusion fiesta. All things being equal, cleaner large Emeralds are worth more simply because of geological scarcity.

Last but not least, you need to appreciate the unique brilliance of Emeralds. Influenced by colour, cut and clarity, the 'brightness' of an Emerald is often described as satiny, silky, warm, soft, glowing, or my favourite, 'green fire'. You won't get the brilliant snap, crackle and pop of Paraíba Tourmaline in Emerald, but nor should you. Emerald has an elegance all of its own. Quality of cut is very important for Emeralds as a skilled lapidary can locate its inherent eye-visible inclusions in a way that minimises their impact on beauty. In terms of cut and shape, the famous equidistant steps of the 'emerald cut' are designed to reduce cutting pressure, accentuate Emerald's satiny brilliance and, in the case of Colombian Emerald, maximise rough yield. While this traditional cut is synonymous with Emerald as red is to Ferraris, because of the shape of the rough, ovals and pears are common for Emeralds from Brazil and Zambia. Material not suitable for faceting is often fashioned into cabochons and beads. As with all gems, look for a good shape and overall appearance. Although Emerald is relatively durable, it does have some special care requirements (see page 259 for more).

While Egypt's Emeralds are long gone, since the 16th century and the exploits of the infamous conquistadors Hernando Cortés (who campaigned against the Aztecs from 1519) and Francisco Pizarro (who campaigned against the Incas from 1526), a Colombian pedigree has become synonymous with Emeralds of exceptional quality. By reputation and experience, Colombian Emerald is the 'in demand' marketplace heavy weight of Emeralds, but supply is scarce. To put this in context, my gem dealing friend Tony Diniz on his last buying trip to Colombia was only able to source less than 30 pieces of Emerald from thousands examined that met his quality standard. As with all sources, there are good and bad from Colombia, so just make sure you're paying for the gem, not the name. Discovered in 1931, Zambia has the world's second largest Emerald deposit and is also known for producing fine quality. Other Emerald sources are Afghanistan, Brazil, Pakistan, Russia (Ural Mountains), and Zimbabwe.

Emerald's unique beauty requires a little understanding to fully appreciate its character, but once initiated into their secrets, you'll agree with Kermit: *"I am green and it'll do fine, it's beautiful! And I think it's what I want to be"*.

FANCY SAPPHIRE

"Hail the jewel in the heart of the lotus."
Buddhist Mantra

The above nicely introduces the most prized of all Fancy Sapphires, the mighty Padparadscha Sapphire, the pinkish-orange to orange-pink princess of gemstones. But back to her shortly, first let's get our heads around how Sapphires aren't always blue.

As mentioned earlier, Ruby and Sapphire are essentially the same deal, being colour varieties of the mineral Corundum (crystalline aluminium oxide). Corundum is derived from the Sanskrit word for Rubies and Sapphires, 'kuruvinda'. Corundum produces 'other coloured' gemstones (see page 18 for more), meaning that trace amounts of elements such as chromium, iron and titanium are responsible for producing its rainbow of blues, greens, oranges, reds, violets, yellows, and combinations thereof. There are even Colour Change Sapphires (see page 31 for more). Corundum's reds are of course called 'Ruby', while 'Sapphire' alone typically refers to its blues. All its other hues are collectively described as 'Fancy Sapphires', with prefixes used to denote specific colours. 'Fancy' is often defined as 'fantastical imagination', and with respect to these Sapphires, it is extremely apt; their colours truly are fantastic and uniquely beautiful, firing the imagination. I favour adding 'blue' to the front of Sapphire not only to avoid confusion, but to also indicate that other colours exist. Now some puritans will say this is akin to saying *"green Granny Smith apple"*, but we'd all do well to remember that not every gem owner has the time or inclination to delve into nomenclature complexities. The key thing is that September's birthstone offers a lot more than just blue. For more on the history and mythology of Sapphires, see page 96.

Nelumbo Nucifera Speciosa, the pinkish-orange lotus flower from which the famed Padparadscha Sapphire is named

These Sapphires certainly tickle my fancy, but how do you choose the right one for you? In his book, 'Gemstones: Quality and Value, Volume 1', Yasukazu Suwa states, *"When choosing fancy-coloured Sapphires, it is important to look at the stone for yourself and select one your find truly beautiful, concentrating on quality without being influenced by name"*. Arguably good advice for any gemstone, for Fancy Sapphires he's definitely right on the money. Called

Black Star Sapphire

Back in black, these beauties are a personal favourite. Why? Apart from the sheer 'rock n' roll' coolness of a black gem with a white or golden star that mysteriously glides across its surface, the world's only Black Star Sapphire deposit is the Ban Kha Ja district of my adopted hometown of Chanthaburi, Thailand. In fact, the mines are about five minutes' drive from my house, on the way to an awesome seafood restaurant. Due to an optical special effect called 'asterism' or the 'star effect', parallel needle-like inclusions within the gemstone creates a reflected luminous star of light that moves and dances across the gemstone.

Black Star Sapphires differ from other Rubies and Sapphires in that its inclusions not only produce the star effect, but also mechanically colour a blue, green or yellow Sapphire, deep black chocolate. When present in an otherwise blue or green Sapphire, the Star's rays are white, while in yellow Sapphires it makes the star golden. All star gems are dependent on the gem being cut 'en cabochon' (cut in convex form and highly polished, but not faceted). Assessing cabochons is straightforward, just look at their finish, shape and proportion. While Asterism is most visible in a direct, single beam of light, a well-cut star gemstone has a distinct star whose rays are straight and equidistant. Stars are typically positioned in the centre of the gem and one of the best things about Black Star Sapphire is the marked contrast of a sharp white or golden star against the intensity of a black body colour. Currently, there is little mining occurring in Chanthaburi, with most Black Star Sapphires traded locally probably from earlier production. Because its sole deposit is depleting, this gem is a real geological rarity that will most likely become unavailable in the future.

the 'gem of the heavens' or the 'celestial gem' because their colours can mirror the sky's many moods, Sapphire's kaleidoscopic spectrum of colours is truly mind-blowing. While colour preferences are subjective, especially for diversely colourful gemstones like Fancy Sapphires, the reliable Goldilocks maxim is good advice; not too dark or too light, just right, with the intense 'middle' colours being the happy medium. Nevertheless, it's more affordable pastel

Green Sapphire

Once called 'Oriental Emerald', Green Sapphire colours include bluish-green, green, green-blue, and yellowish-green.

Orange Sapphire

Rich juicy fruits abound with Orange Sapphire whose hues run the gambit from orange to reddish-orange and yellowish-orange.

Padparadscha Sapphire

Along with fine blues, Padparadscha are Sapphire's rarest and most coveted colours. "That which spreads its rays like the sun, is glossy, soft to the touch, resembling the fire, like molten gold and not worn off is padma raga" is how a medieval Indian text on gemmology (*Thakkura Pheru's Rayanaparikkha*) describes Padparadscha Sapphire. Yet, despite its fame, seductive beauty and extreme scarcity, this colour prefix has been both confused and misused. When I first started in the gem business, I was perplexed as to what was and wasn't 'Padparadscha' as its exact definition seemed to vary from book to book and person to person. Writing in 2001, gemstone author Yasukazu Suwa echoes this confusion with, "there is no universally accepted definition of Padparadscha Sapphire" and this isn't surprising considering its history. While its name is derived from the gem's semblance to a pinkish-orange lotus flower (*Nelumbo Nucifera Speciosa*), our modern word 'Padparadscha' is in fact an English corruption of a German corruption of the Sinhalese 'padma' (lotus) and 'raga' (colour). Thankfully, since 2006 the name's exact meaning has been clarified. Members of the Laboratory Manual Harmonisation Committee (LMHC) have standardised the nomenclature they use to describe a Padparadscha Sapphire, defining the gem as "a variety of Corundum from any

Padparadscha Colour Sapphire

Padparadscha Sapphire

geographical origin whose colour is a subtle mixture of pinkish-orange to orangey pink with pastel tones and low to medium saturations". Even though this description provides clear boundaries, it has enough room for individuals to explore the sublime intricacies of this impossibly rare connoisseurs' gem. While yellow flashes from its facets are acceptable, Padparadscha Sapphire should not have any secondary browns. Just as attractive yet more affordable, Padparadscha Colour Sapphire's colour is identical (and sometimes even superior) to Padparadscha Sapphires, owing their hues to recent gemstone enhancement innovations (see page 264 for more). Sources for these gems include Madagascar, Sri Lanka, Tanzania and Vietnam.

and over-coloured examples, can be as equally enticing. Looking at the colour, an attractive brilliance should sparkle (scintillate) throughout the gem, but this will be affected by colour distribution, colour saturation, faceting quality and transparency. Simply be guided by your preferences and pocket, bearing in mind that top quality Sapphires can be some of the world's most pricey gems.

While both Ruby and Sapphires are classed as Type II gemstones, meaning they typically grow with some minor inclusions in nature that may be eye-visible, Sapphires are usually cleaner (and larger) than Ruby, with an eye-clean clarity (no visible inclusions when the gem is examined six inches from the naked eye) being the typical standard. Once you've settled

Pink Sapphire

Ranging in colour from pink to purplish-pink, Pink Sapphires are differentiated from Rubies by tone (lightness or darkness of a colour) and saturation (strength of a colour). Ranging from the pastel to intense hues approaching Ruby, Pink Sapphire's more intense colours are often identified by prefixes such as 'fuchsia', 'hot' or 'magenta'. While Pink Corundum is historically considered to be 'Ruby' in Asia, due to the immense popularity Pink Sapphire has garnered over the last decade this name is now recognised globally. As red and pink are technically the same colour, and because Rubies are worth more than Pink Sapphires,

arguments over where pink stops and red begins were once common. To resolve these disputes, in 1989 the ICA (International Coloured Gemstone Association) sensibly stated: "Pink is really just light red. The ICA has passed a resolution that the light shades of the red hue should be included in the Ruby category since it was too difficult to legislate where red ended and pink began. In practice, pink shades are now known either as Pink Ruby or Pink Sapphire".

on a colour you like, look for a good shape and overall appearance. While ovals are the most common, Fancy Sapphires are available in a huge array of shapes and cuts, almost as diverse as its colours. Just note that because the alluvial nature of Sapphire rough is well suited to oval and pears, rounds are sometimes a little more expensive. Typical Fancy Sapphires origins include Australia, Madagascar, Sri Lanka, Tanzania and Thailand.

Purple Sapphire

In all honesty, this gemstone's historic name, 'Oriental Amethyst', doesn't do it justice. The brilliance and 'look' of Purple Sapphires are markedly different to Amethyst and like all tentative comparisons, no gem wins. Purple Sapphires come in various shades of bluish-purple, purple, purple-red and reddish-purple.

Sunset Sapphire

Too orange to be Ruby and lacking the pinks to make it Padparadscha, Sunset Sapphire is a relatively new Sapphire in a class of its own. Also known as Songea Sapphire, these gems hail exclusively from a deposit just outside the town of Songea in Tanzania that was only discovered in 1992. Sunset Sapphire was named in tribute to the unique beauty of the African sunset, and looking at the picture here, I'm sure you'll agree its name says it all.

White Sapphire

Reportedly finding White Sapphires on the island of Naxos in the Aegean Sea, the ancient Greeks associated them with Apollo, the god of light and the sun; truth and prophecy; archery; medicine and healing; and music, poetry and the arts. As the god of prophecy, Apollo was also the patron deity of the Delphic Oracle (Oracle of Apollo). This is why White Sapphires are rumoured to have been used as an offering to the 'pythia', the priestess who touted prophecies allegedly inspired by Apollo (although hallucinogenic ethylene gas found in the temple's local geology was probably the real source of her inspiration). Once valued in

their own right, White Sapphires are sometimes only viewed as Diamond alternatives. This is a shame given their classical history. The best White Sapphires are colourless, with gems with discernable tints of blue or yellow priced accordingly.

Yellow Sapphire

Arguably the most prized of all yellow gemstones, Yellow Sapphires colour ranges from pleasing lemon pastels through to intense yellowish-oranges. Madagascar and Sri Lanka are Yellow Sapphire's main sources.

JADE

"It is said that the Dowager Empress had trained herself to distinguish by touch Jade from any other gemstone, and further, that she had developed a faculty for discriminating, again by touch only, between one grade of Jade and another".

Louis Kornitzer, Gem Trader (1939)

If this story is true, the Dowager Empress definitely deserved her birth name, 'yu lan' (Jade Orchid). More than any other gemstone, Jade is implanted in the heart of Chinese culture and, by its influence, Southeast Asia. Treasured as the royal gemstone, Jade may have been mined in China as early as 6000 BC. Jade was called the 'stone of heaven' by the ancient Chinese, who associated it with immortality and the ability to bridge heaven and earth. The character for its name in Chinese, 'yu' (玉) embodies this belief, with the top representing 'heaven', the bottom 'earth', and the middle line 'humanity.

As illustrated by the photographs at the bottom of this page, China also has a long tradition of using Jade in carvings, sculpture, ornaments and other decorative arts. Continuing this tradition, the reverse of the 2008 Beijing Olympic Medals were made in Jade. While China, along with Burma, remains an important source for this gemstone, other Jade sources include Guatemala, Russia, Kazakhstan, Japan, Taiwan, Australia, New Zealand and the U.S.A.

Jade actually has two different varieties, but prior to 1863 it was a blanket term covering Jadeite (pyroxene group), Nephrite (amphibole group) and other similar minerals. The name

An intricate Jade carving at Wat Kow Su Kim in Chanthaburi, Thailand. This priceless creation was carved from just one piece of Jade

In ancient China, there was once a poor, but talented Jade artisan. His artworks were held in great esteem throughout the land and his style was so beautiful and unique that any respectable Jade connoisseur would immediately recognise his hand. As is always the way in these stories, he goes and falls in love with a rich man's daughter. Despite being an avid collector of all things Jade, the girl's father cites the timeless 'no money, no honey' clause, forbidding any further contact. Young and in love, they ignore her old man and elope. The young man loved the girl so much that he gave up his Jade artistry so as to keep their location secret from her enraged father. Time went by and the girl fell ill. Penniless and without healthcare, his artistic skill was the only answer. Carving a green Jade goddess of unimaginable beauty, he sold it to a merchant on the sole condition its source remained unknown. Fate being fate, the girl's father bought the piece and instantly recognised the style. The merchant being a merchant, he was eventually tempted by the small fortune offered by the father and revealed the artist's location. Dad wasn't happy, found the couple, killed the boy and took the girl home. The girl wasn't happy, took the Jade goddess and went to her lover's grave. Overcome with grief and sorrow, the girl wanted nothing more than to rest eternal in her lover's arms. But as the moon rose, the young man's spirit, who had taken refuge in the Jade goddess, re-entered his body giving him life. Her father, amazed at the miracle, accepted the couple and they lived happily ever after. The Jade goddess was given as an offering to a nearby temple, where it is said to still reside today…

'Jade' originates from the Spanish conquest of the Americas, being derived from 'piedra de hijada' (colic stone), which was coined around 1565. Another Spanish name for the gem is 'piedra de los rinones' (kidney stone), which when translated into Latin, *Lapis Nephriticus*, gives us the name, Nephrite. Not incredibly romantic, these names came from Spaniards, making a tenuous curative connection between the shapes of polished Jade pebbles and kidneys. The French mineralogist, Alexis Damour worked out that some Chinese Jade (Nephrite) and Burmese Jade (which he named 'Jadeite') are different minerals with a similar appearance and properties. Believe it or not, Jadeite actually has a surprisingly short history in China and wasn't especially coveted until the 18th century. Even so, the finest specimens, possessing a high clarity and rich 'emerald' green, were so coveted by Chinese Emperors they received the moniker, 'Imperial Jade'. Jadeite was also known as 'Kingfisher Jade' (fei cui 翡翠) due to greens the colour of a kingfisher's plumage. Today, Jadeite is the more valuable of the two varieties.

Unlike Asians, Westerners don't have a comparable Jade heritage, leaving many of us a bit clueless when it comes to understanding this gemstone. The first thing to get your head around is that the term 'Jade' is considerably broader in Asia than in the West. 'Yu' means 'precious' or 'ornamental' stone, and while it typically isn't used on its own to denote Jadeite or Nephrite, some ornamental non-Jade minerals also incorporate the character 'yu' in their name. I speculate that this cultural perception has resulted in misnomers such as 'Australian Jade' for Chrysoprase (see page 111 for more).

Jadeite comes in shades of blue, brown, cream, green, grey, lavender, orange, red, violet, white, yellow, and combinations thereof, including mottling. Jadeite's reddish coloration is caused by iron trace elements, while its greens are due to the presence of chromium. Nephrite comes in fewer colours than Jadeite, including browns, greens, greys, yellows, and whites. Mottling occurs, as do red, yellow and brown streaks, through oxidation. This is particularly evident in Nephrite found along streams and rivers. Along with yellows, the most coveted Nephrite is a pure translucent white called, 'yangzhi yu', which means 'Mutton Fat Jade' (this doesn't sound attractive, but it is actually very apt). Nephrite's colour is determined by the amount of iron present, with a higher iron content producing the darker colours. Jadeite is called 'ying yu' (硬玉), meaning hard jade, and is harder than Nephrite but not as tough. While Nephrite is called 'ruan yu' (軟), meaning soft Jade, this has nothing to do with its hardness. Instead, it comes from this Jade's characteristic silky, soft feel and appearance, as well as its softer, more subtle colours. Nephrite is actually neither very hard nor soft, but along with Jadeite, is tougher than Diamonds. Jade are some of the toughest gemstones on the planet, making it ideal for intricately detailed carvings that have become so synonymous with this gemstone.

Jade is semi-transparent to opaque, with a high degree of transparency, along with deep colours and a good overall appearance (finish) being the key factors in judging its quality. While colour preferences are subjective, a bright, even 'emerald' green with no mottling commands the highest prices. Despite this, mottled patterns, spotting and veins that contrast with the body colour are also considered attractive, especially when incorporated into the

Jade 925 Silver Ring

The Colours of Jade

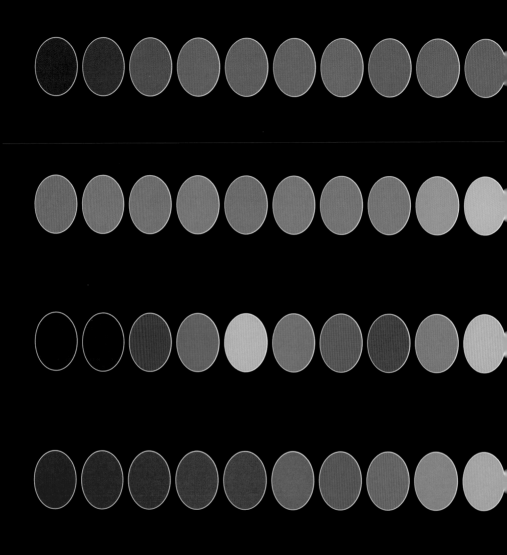

features of beautiful carvings. Jade's transparency depends on grain size and texture, with a finer texture resulting in a higher transparency. While Jade that has light colours but good transparency can still command a high price, black, dark green or brown mineral inclusions that distract the eye and prevent the smooth transmission of light will affect quality, just as in other gemstones. One question I have been asked is that, *"If Jade can come in huge pieces weighing several tonnes, how come it's rare and still called a gem?"* We must remember that the finest 'gem quality' Jade is very rare, representing far less than one percent of all Jade mined. So much so, that 'Imperial Jade' can command some of the highest prices of any gemstone, even greater than Diamond, Ruby and Sapphire. Nevertheless, Jade that has a grainier, less translucent appearance can still be attractive because of its colour, often finding its way into beautiful, yet affordable ornaments that bridge the gap between jewellery and art. While there are exceptions, Jade used in carvings is generally of a lower quality than those used in cabochons. Assessing cabochons is straightforward. Just look at their finish, shape and proportion. While carvings are probably best left to personal preferences, as a general rule, look for the intricacy of detail and the position of colour within the context of the design.

The true emperor of Chinese jewellery, Jade might inexorably be a 'Chinese' gemstone, but it has also played an important role in Mayan, Olmec, Toltec, Aztec, Native American and Maori cultures. Much like we have taken to chopsticks, fireworks and feng shui, Jade is also increasingly becoming a gemstone appreciated by the Western palate.

KUNZITE

"The very pink of perfection".
Oliver Goldsmith (1730-1774)

Oliver Goldsmith, an Irish writer, poet and physician, never saw Kunzite, but he aptly described it! While gemmologists describe Kunzite's colours as coming in pink, bluish-purple, purple, reddish-purple, purple red or purplish-red, these 'precise' descriptions are perhaps a little clinical for the layperson. Instead, try picturing the delightful range of colours that lay between pastel pinks and rich orchids.

Kunzite was discovered in California around 1902 and was named in honour of George Frederick Kunz, the gemmologist credited with its identification. Mr. Kunz is a legendary figure in the world of gems and the 'gem bug' certainly got him young. Self taught from books and practical research, he collected 4,000 mineral specimens while still in his teens! Ultimately, his knowledge saw him employed as the resident 'gem expert' at that iconic jeweller, Tiffany & Co., becoming their vice president by the age of 23. Also a wonderful author, Kunz's gemstone books are still readily available today. Interestingly, 'Kunzite' wasn't the only name for this gemstone; it was also initially traded as 'California Iris'. But like all gemstone variety names, it's all about usage. Today, Kunz's namesake remains, while 'California Iris' has fallen by the wayside.

A 20th-century gemstone, Kunzite has no real 'mythology' per se, other than its colour. Kunzite is a quintessentially feminine gemstone; after all, pink has long been regarded as

George Frederick Kunz (1856-1932)
Image courtesy of the Mineralogical Record Library

When most of us think of Afghanistan, images of conflict are probably the first thing that come to mind. What many people are unaware of is that Afghanistan has a gemstone history that may date back to as early as 6000 BC. Exported along ancient trade routes to Mesopotamia (modern-day Iraq), Egypt and India, Lapis Lazuli was mined in the Hindu Kush during antiquity (a mountain range located between Afghanistan and Pakistan). Long regarded as an excellent source of spectacular mineral specimens, Afghanistan is a country rich in gemstone deposits. Gemstones occurring in Afghanistan include Aquamarine, Emerald, Garnet, Kunzite, Lapis Lazuli, Ruby, Sapphire, Topaz and Tourmaline. Today, Afghanistan is a major supplier of Kunzite, with many excellent examples being sourced from the Kunar Valley, which is located in the north-eastern part of the country, extending from Afghanistan into Pakistan. Maintaining a very strong tribal identity, Pashtuns make up the vast majority of the Kunar Valley's population. I know rough buyers who routinely make the journey to this province, suitably garbed of course, so as not to attract unwanted attention. Unfortunately, I've been threatened with divorce should the idea ever cross my mind! Typically extracted by people living in villages surrounding the deposits, gemstone mining in Afghanistan faces many challenges, such as remoteness, primitive mining techniques and political instability. Thankfully, the Afghani government is addressing these issues so that gemstones play a key role in this country's revival. Let's hope Afghanistan's future is as bright and colourful as its gemstones.

the most romantic of colours and is typically associated with love and romance. According to colour psychologists, pink also has calming qualities. Metaphysically, Kunzite is sometimes connected to the heart chakra, the body's fourth energy point, linked with the emotions of love and compassion.

Kunzite is a colour variety of Spodumene, from the Greek 'spodumenos', which means 'burnt to ashes', in reference to Spodumene's light grey colour. This mineral's colour variants are due to trace elements of iron (yellow to green), chromium (medium to deep green) and manganese (pink to purplish-red). When coloured by chromium, Spodumene is called Hiddenite. An extreme rarity, and scarcely seen, Hiddenite was discovered in 1800 by mineralogist and mining director William Earl Hidden. While Spodumene's other colour variants are technically called '[Colour Prefix] Spodumene', the commercial names 'Green Kunzite', 'White Kunzite' and 'Yellow Kunzite' are also sometimes used. Kunzite is predominately mined in Afghanistan, Brazil, Madagascar and Pakistan, although its original deposits in California occasionally still yield the odd gem quality specimen.

Kunzite's most important consideration is its colourful brilliance, with the deeper shades commanding higher prices. Kunzite's crystals occur with reasonably few inclusions, so the standard is eye-clean (no visible inclusions when the gem is examined six inches from the naked eye), with some inclusions under magnification. While various shapes are seen, the most common are oval, emerald and cushion. Regardless of the cut, look for an even colour and good brilliance. An interesting characteristic of Kunzite is its 'phosphorescence', which is its ability to glow in low light conditions after exposure to the sun's ultraviolet rays. This, coupled with Kunzite's love of incandescent lighting (candlelight), gave rise to its common name, 'the evening gemstone'. Kunzite is also strongly pleochroic, which means that its colours and their intensity change when it is viewed from different angles (see page 33 for more). As the top and bottom of

Kunzite crystals have the deepest colours, the lapidary must take care to orientate the crystal to accentuate its most desirable colour. If you follow my 'even colour' caveat, the negative aspects of pleochrism should be a non-issue when purchasing Kunzite from reputable sellers.

You can be 'pretty in pink', 'tickled pink', 'in the pink' and apparently, being 'dressed in pink makes the boys wink', but I can't say I've ever felt that effect. For me, Kunzite is simply a beautiful gemstone, whose colours, whether pastel or intense, combine with its breathtaking clarity to create a truly splendid gemstone. And, as an added bonus, it was named in honour of a legendary gem expert I greatly admire.

Kunzite & Diamond 9K White Gold Ring

LAPIS LAZULI

"I will have harnessed for you a chariot of Lapis Lazuli and gold, with wheels of gold and 'horns' of Amber".
Epic of Gilgamesh (2650 BC)

Dating back to 2650 BC, the 'Epic of Gilgamesh' is a celebrated poem from Ancient Mesopotamia (modern-day Iraq) and is one of the earliest works of literary fiction. It is the story of the adventures of the king who 'surpasses all other kings', Gilgamesh and his 'wild man' sidekick, Enkidu. Apart from being a cracking yarn, Lapis Lazuli scores a mention in the poem, illustrating its importance and value to the people of the time.

More than any gemstone, one deposit has defined Lapis Lazuli. In the rugged Kokcha Valley of northern Afghanistan's remote Badakhshan district lays the famous Sar-e-Sang deposit. Producing continuously for over 7,000 years, this deposit is home to some of the world's oldest gemstone mines. Sure, there are other Lapis Lazuli deposits, but Afghanistan by reputation and experience remains the finest. During antiquity, Afghani Lapis Lazuli was exported along ancient trade routes to Mesopotamia, Egypt, Greece, Rome, India, China and even Japan. The medieval Persian geographer Estakhri visited the Afghani Lapis Lazuli mines in the 10th century and when Marco Polo visited them in the 13th century, he wrote: *"There is a mountain in that region where the finest Lapis Lazuli in the world is found".*

Not used until the middle ages, the name 'Lapis Lazuli' is from the Latin 'lapis' (stone) and 'lazulum' (blue or heaven, which was probably derived from the Persian 'lazhuward', their name for the Afghani deposit and also the origin of the word 'azure'). While in ancient

Lapis Lazuli was mentioned in the 2650 BC Sumerian 'Epic of Gilgamesh' (pictured)

Greece and Rome Lapis Lazuli was called 'sapphirus' (blue), today this name refers to the blue variety of Corundum, Sapphire.

Given its long history, Lapis Lazuli is a gem with a diverse and colourful mythology that alludes to why it was once as valuable as gold. Attributed with mystical purifying and curative properties, this ancient blue gem captivated Pagans, Jews, Christians, Buddhists and Muslims. Apart from Persian texts, it was also mentioned in the bible (Exodus 28:15-30) and in the Egyptian 'Book of the Dead'. The ancient Sumerian city of Ur had a thriving trade in Lapis Lazuli and its royal tombs, excavated in the late nineteen twenties, contained more than 6,000 exquisite Lapis Lazuli statuettes, dishes, beads and seals. From around 3000 BC, it was the darling of Egypt and used in religious ceremonies, for personal adornment (inlaid jewellery as well as amulets and talismans), and even as an eye shadow cosmetic. The Greeks and Romans weren't far behind and in the 1st century the Roman historian Pliny the Elder described Lapis Lazuli as, *"a fragment of the starry vault of heaven"*. A big hit with ancient alchemists, Lapis Lazuli was even used in medicine and as a pigment (the colour 'ultramarine' was once produced from crushed Lapis Lazuli, but has been made synthetically since 1828).

An opaque gemstone, Lapis Lazuli is actually a rock comprised primarily of Lazurite and several other materials, including Calcite and golden sparkling flecks of Pyrite ('fool's gold' know as Marcasite when used in jewellery). When judging Lapis Lazuli, the finest colours are

Pyrite (Marcasite)

Apart from being an attractive inclusion in Lapis Lazuli, Pyrite is also a regular feature in jewellery, albeit under a different name. Incorrectly called Marcasite, this nomenclature overlap dates back several hundreds of years due to the visual similarities between Pyrite and Marcasite. True, Marcasite is too unstable to be used in jewellery. Pyrite appears in golden metallic colours, which has led to its historic confusion with gold. In truth, experts should easily be able to tell the two apart, hence the common name, 'fool's gold'. Pyrite (Marcasite) jewellery gained popularity in Victorian England, where they were cut and 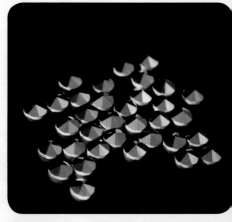 *polished in circular or square outlines and pave set so they sparkled like little Diamonds. Pyrite (Marcasite) sterling silver jewellery is still hugely popular today, often appearing in designs inspired by Queen Victoria's renowned passion for fine jewellery.*

regarded as an even royal blue (rich purplish blue). Uneven colour or hints of green will generally negatively affect the gem's beauty and value. According to Persian treatises on the gem, Lapis Lazuli's colours can be broken down into three classifications: *nili* (dark blue), *assemani* (light blue) and *sabz* (green). While some prefer Lapis Lazuli that is a solid pure azure, the presence of flicks of Pyrite is coveted by many and will not adversely affect this gem's beauty if relatively small in size and well balanced in distribution. For me, the presence of Pyrite adds a certain mystical quality I find both alluring and attractive. In general, Lapis Lazuli that contains too many eye-visible Calcite or Pyrite inclusions is regarded as not as beautiful and is valued accordingly. But as with all gems, how you define 'too many' is best left to the individual. As with all gems, cut quality is also a consideration. For Lapis Lazuli the only limits are the lapidary's imagination, so whether selecting cabochons, tablets, beads, carvings or figurines, simply look for shapes and proportions pleasing to the eye. It can be difficult to find solid blues, and pieces between 10 to 20 carats in size are considered exceptionally rare.

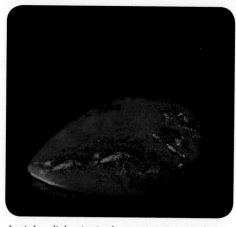

Lapis Lazuli showing its characteristic Pyrite inclusions

The best thing about Lapis Lazuli is that while it remains one of the world's most enduring and beautiful opaque gemstones, it is not expensive. It's not often that a gem with such intense colours, unique inclusions, and a rich history and mythology, is still incredibly affordable. This, along with the fact that its finest deposit has remained unchanged for thousands of years, is why I regard Lapis Lazuli as one of the world's most beautiful blue gemstones.

MOONSTONE

"I loved to think that Moonstones were made by the breaking-off of minute portions from the moon itself, which after travelling about a while in space finally reached earth".

Louis Kornitzer, Gem Trader (1939)

'Gem Trader' is one of the coolest books ever written on gemstones. I especially like Louis' imaginary lunar origin for Moonstone. Interestingly, 31 years later, Moonstone was made Florida's official state gem to commemorate the 1969 moon landing. Also known as Selenite and Adularia, Moonstone is aptly named for its likeness to the moon. Selenite is from the Greek 'selene', meaning moon and also the name of the moon goddess in Greek mythology (selenology being the study of the geology of the moon). Adularia is named for a variety of Moonstone found in the European Alps and also lends its name to the optical phenomena unique to Moonstone, called adularescence (read on for more).

There is something magical about Moonstone. With some gems you struggle to understand their lore (who would think to string a Perdiot on a donkey's hair as protection from evil spirits?), but Moonstone's mythology is immediately understandable. Given the importance of the moon to the ancients and Moonstone's lunar association, the reverence afforded this gem is no surprise. In both ancient India and Rome, Moonstone was believed to be mystically created by rays of moonlight, probably due to the silver to bluish-white light that magically dances across the gem. Considered a sacred gem in India, the Hindi name for Moonstone is 'chandrakant', meaning 'beloved of the moon'. Based on Moonstone's mythical moonlight

To commemorate the 1969 moon landing launched from the J. F. Kennedy Space Centre, Moonstone was made Florida's official state gem in 1970

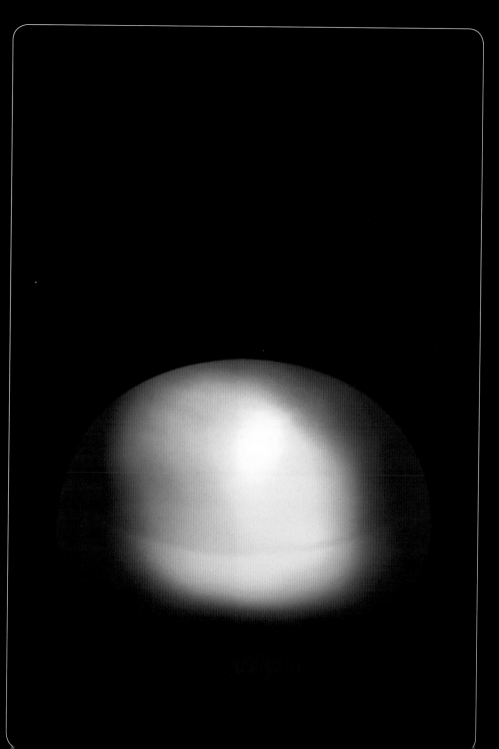

origin, the name is derived from the Sanskrit 'chandra' (moon) and 'kanta' (beloved). The Romans thought Moonstone's appearance changed with the waxing and waning of the moon, going as far to think their moon goddess (Diana) was pictured in every Moonstone. A recurring theme in Moonstone's mythology is divination, which is not surprising considering it is regarded as a feminine or 'goddess' gemstone. In mythology, divination was usually a feminine trait, so much so that during antiquity, men used to cross dress with a Moonstone in their mouths to see the future. The gem of 'tender passion', Moonstone's mythology also makes numerous references to its ability to influence that most powerful and positive of all emotions, love.

On a visit to Sri Lanka, an important source for Moonstone, a local gem dealer told me Moonstone means 'no tears' because when there is a moon in the sky, there is no rain. But

Labradorite

Named after the Labrador Peninsula in Canada where it was first discovered, Labradorite is a plagioclase Feldspar that is mined in China, India and Madagascar. Labradorite is available in transparent specimens (usually red, orange, yellow or colourless) as well as smoke grey varieties that show a striking metallic coloured iridescence, aptly called 'labradorescence' (see page 32 for more). This phenomena displays rainbow coloured reflections as light strikes the gem from different angles, and it is judged by observing the strength, intensity and range of colours. Colloquial names include 'black rainbow' and 'firestone' (the name used by the Native Americans of Labrador who believed the gem possessed mystical qualities).

one thing to cry about is the declining availability of gem quality Moonstone. Always scarce, Moonstone is one of the most coveted varieties of Feldspar.

Feldspar (derived from the German 'feldt spat', meaning 'field stone' because of its ability to enrich the soil with plant nutrients) is a mineral family especially known for gems with beautiful optical phenomenon, such as adularescence, aventurescence and iridescence (see page 32 for more). Its two subgroups are the plagioclase group and the potassium group. Distinguished by their calcium and sodium content and ratio, the plagioclase group includes most gem varieties. Gems in the potassium group share the same chemical composition, but are distinguished by their crystal structure. One important thing to remember is that many Feldspar gems look similar. Often confused due to their similar compositions and trade names, some gemmologists love to debate the differences. My advice is not to worry

Sunstone

Named for its resemblance to the sun, Sunstone is a plagioclase Feldspar that is typically yellow, pink, orange, red or colourless. Sunstone's most important attribute is its aventurescence, the beautiful glittering sunlight effect caused by tiny metallic inclusions (see page 30 for more). Predominately mined in India, Madagascar and the U.S.A. (Oregon Sunstone has been the State of Oregon's official gemstone since 1987), Sunstone was once coveted for its purported ability to guide its wearer through the journey of life. Considering its name, it's not surprising that legend also connects Sunstone to the sun. According to one story, Pope Clement VII (1478-1534) possessed a Sunstone with a golden spot which moved across the gem in motion with the sun.

The chorus in Cat Steven's classic song 'Moon Shadow', *"Oh, I'm being followed by a moon shadow"*, is eerily appropriate for me. I grew up in an Australian suburb called Jannali, which is an Aboriginal word meaning 'place of the moon' and have ended up living in Chanthaburi, Thailand, which means 'city of the moon'. An interesting connection, lent further coincidence by Moonstone being one of my wife's favourite gems. A few years back, upon learning I was off to Sri Lanka for work, she requested a Moonstone. Only having been together a short while, I wanted to get her the very best I could find when I visited Meetiyaguda, the source of Sri Lankan Moonstones located in the island's south. Me being me, I immediately launched into a long treatise on quality in the species, recommending a specimen with the bluest sheen. I was told that she wanted a light grey body colour with a silver shimmer, just like the moon. And no, she didn't care what I thought. Remember what I said about gemstone colour subjectivity on page 16? Ultimately, it doesn't matter what the 'experts' say, with gemstones it's all about you, and for my wife it was, *"By the light, of the silvery moon..."*

Rainbow Moonstone 9K Yellow Gold Ring

about this too much; some Feldspar gems are so close in composition that even some gemstone laboratories find it difficult to tell them apart. A member of the potassium Feldspar group, Moonstone is closely related to Labradorite and Sunstone (also covered in this section).

Some books confusingly make no distinction between gemstones and minerals, leading some to question the rarity of their gems after they read statements like, *"probably the most abundant minerals on earth"*. Organic gems aside, all gems are minerals, but not all mineral specimens possess the three attributes of beauty, rarity and durability necessary to make them a gemstone.

Moonstone occurs commercially in a few isolated deposits in India, Madagascar, Sri Lanka and Tanzania, making it far rarer than many better known gemstones. It comes in a variety of colours including brown, green, grey, pink, rainbow, white, yellow and colourless. Moonstone has a silver to bluish-white sheen (adularescence, see page 28 for more), is semi-translucent to translucent and often displays a very high clarity. Having said this, 'gem quality' Moonstones are increasingly difficult to obtain, especially over 1 carat. Technically, Labradorite Feldspar in composition, Rainbow Moonstone is an optical phenomena 'double whammy'. It displays a bright blue adularescence as well as an iridescence that breaks white light into its spectral components (see page 32 for more).

For the professional, the 'best' Moonstone has a blue sheen that moves smoothly across the gem as the viewing angle changes, high clarity, and a colourless body colour. Adularescence is the real magic behind Moonstone. Once you've collectively judged a Moonstone's cut (shape, proportion and finish), colour, transparency and clarity, adularescence is this gem's key quality and value determinant. Obviously, for Rainbow Moonstone iridescence also plays a part. While Moonstones were traditionally cut as cabochons, they are also increasingly faceted.

Due to its sparkling interaction with jewellery metals, Moonstone is one of those gems that just loves being set in jewellery. As mentioned previously, gem quality Moonstone is getting scarcer by the minute, so if you are enamoured by the magic of Moonstone, there has never been a better time to add one of June's birthstones to your collection.

Rainbow Moonstones displaying bright blue adularescence

PARAÍBA TOURMALINE

"There is always something new out of Africa".
Pliny the Elder (23-79 AD), Historia Naturalis

Without a doubt, Paraíba Tourmaline is the pop sensation of the Tourmaline family and a true gemstone superstar. Unearthed just under 20 years ago, in the relatively short time since its discovery, it has not only redefined the perception and appeal of Tourmaline, but also gemmological beauty itself. The late Masashi Furuya, former director of the Japan Germany Gemmological Laboratory, described Paraíba Tourmaline as *"electric blue brilliance burnt into our minds"*, and looking at the picture opposite, you'll see exactly what he meant. But we're getting ahead of ourselves; let's take a moment to meet the Tourmaline family.

If Tourmaline was a human family they would have an ethnic diversity that would put the United Nations to shame. Even its name alludes to this multiplicity, Tourmaline is derived from the Sinhalese, 'turmali' ('mixed parcel' or 'stone with mixed colours'), which hints at some of the historic confusion its many colours have propagated with other gems. But more on this in Rubellite on page 188. Similar to Garnet, Tourmaline is a group of related minerals whose differences in composition result in a plethora of colours. While there are 13 different mineralogical varieties of Tourmaline, you only really need to worry about Elbaite. Named after the island of its discovery (Elba) in Tuscany, Italy, Elbaite is the backbone of Tourmaline gemstones. A source of minerals during antiquity, Elba is best known as the island of Napoleon's exile in 1814.

Heitor Dimas Barbosa, the discoverer of Paraíba Tourmaline

Whether you give Tourmaline the distinction of coming in more hues than any other gemstone or attribute this to Diamonds or Fluorite, one thing's for certain, Tourmaline definitely puts the 'C' back in colour. Name a hue and in all likelihood you'll find it in Tourmaline, sometimes within the same gemstone! Even pure 'amethyst' purples have appeared since the discovery of Mozambique Paraíba deposits (see one on page 49). Tourmaline's different colours are either identified by a colour prefix, such as blue-green,

Apatite

Apatite is not a Tourmaline, but since the discovery of saturated neon 'Paraíba' blues in Madagascar near Fort Dauphin in 1995, Apatite has garnered increased recognition. This is the popularity power of Paraíba Tourmaline. Not only has it secured its own superstar status in the gem world, but it has also propelled interest in other Tourmalines as well as similar vividly coloured gemstones. Apatite's name comes from the Greek 'apatao', which means 'to deceive' and looking at this example, it is certainly apt; superficially, it's a pretty convincing Paraíba Tourmaline substitute. Also available in 'emerald' greens, Apatite is rare over 1 carat.

Blue Green Tourmaline

Too green to be Indicolite and too blue to be Green Tourmaline, this spectacular gem from the Democratic Republic of the Congo clearly shows the effects of Tourmaline's signature diochrosim, a type of pleochroism showing two colours (see page 33 for more). Depending on how they are cut, lighter toned specimens like this gem sometimes display the primary and secondary dichroic blues and greens sparkling on neighbouring facets, creating an attractive mosaic effect. In this book, I have separated the bluish-green 'peacock' hues of these Tourmalines from Green Tourmaline and Indicolite for ease of comprehension.

green and pink, or a variety name or prefix. These include Bi Colour Tourmaline (two or more colours, see page 193 for more), Canary Tourmaline (intense yellow from the African nations of Malawi and Zambia), Cat's Eye Tourmaline (chatoyant Tourmaline, see page 31 for more), Colour Change Tourmaline (green to red), Cuprian Tourmaline (non-Paraíba hues, but still coloured by copper and manganese), Indicolite (blue), Paraíba Tourmaline (blue to green, coloured by copper and manganese), Rubellite (red, see page 188 for more), and Watermelon Tourmaline (pink inner green outer, just like the fruit). Another prized, but exceedingly rare variety is Chrome Tourmaline, a vivid pure green East African Dravite coloured by chromium and vanadium, the same elements that *make* Emerald and Tsavorite. Last is Schorl (Black Tourmaline), a variety that is naturally abundant and once popular in mourning jewellery, yet now commercially scarce because it is rarely faceted. Nevertheless, interest in both Black Tourmaline and Black Spinel has increased due to the popularity of Black Diamonds. Due to its double refractivity, Tourmaline is strongly pleochroic (see page 33 for more) or getting more technical, Tourmaline is the most dichroic of all gemstones.

Cuprian Tourmaline

Cuprian Tourmaline is the name for the copper-rich (Cuprian) Mozambique Tourmalines that do not fall within the acceptable colours for Paraíba Tourmaline. Extremely collectable for the true Tourmaline connoisseur, Cuprian Tourmaline is a fairly new gemstone, only appearing commercially since the discovery of Paraíba Tourmaline's Mozambique deposits. As Cuprian and Paraíba Tourmaline are the same except for their colour, apply similar evaluation criteria. The colours seen in Cuprian Tourmaline include burnt oranges, dusty roses, lavenders, purples, reddish-purples and yellows. As with all gems, especially unusual exotics, your personal preferences regarding beauty should be the deciding factor.

This means that each Tourmaline crystal has two colours (dark and light), whose intensity changes when viewed from different angles. This is covered in more detail shortly. While some gemstones look better in natural daylight and others in artificial (incandescent) light, a gemstone's colours should ideally remain beautiful in any light source. Despite this, all Tourmalines are 'day gems', meaning they typically look their very best in natural light. The yellow glare of artificial lights will *sometimes* accentuate grey and brown tones which may otherwise be invisible. As always, be guided by common sense and your preferences, paying heed to the inherent characteristics of each type.

Any historical contempt for Tourmaline's look-alike abilities evaporated overnight when Paraíba Tourmaline hit the world market. The beginning of this gem begins with one man,

Green Tourmaline

Whether vividly trying to look like Emerald or embodying lighter tones reminiscent of Paraíba Tourmaline, Green Tourmaline is a gem worthy of consideration. In fact, just like Tourmaline's blue and red varieties, Green Tourmaline often has a beautiful distinctive 'green' all of its own (see page 188 for more). The 'green' of Paraíba and Green Tourmaline are fairly discernable, particularly when they are viewed together. Green Tourmaline's colours range from pure 'emeralds' to yellowish-greens. Like most gems, we are looking for the happy medium, intensely colourful, but not too light nor too

dark. Different Tourmalines have different degrees of clarity and unlike Paraíba Tourmaline and Rubellite, Green Tourmaline is usually eye-clean. So much so, that I'd steer clear of visually included examples. Darker specimens lose brilliance and beauty, and this is why Tourmaline's darker blues, reds and greens are oriented by the lapidary to display the lighter of its two dichroic (pleochroic) colours. As Tourmaline crystals are typically elongated, especially when mined from their host pegmatite (a coarse-grained rock with exceptionally large crystals formed from magma with a high proportion of water), they are often cut into baguette or octagon-shaped gems. Too much yellow or brown can result in combat greens. The main sources for Green Tourmaline are Brazil, Namibia, Nigeria, Madagascar and Mozambique.

Heitor Dimas Barbosa, the discoverer of Paraíba Tourmaline. In the early eighties, he was a 'garimpeiro' (small-scale miner) who became infatuated by the beautiful brilliance of blue Tourmaline crystal collected by a friend. Heitor was no quitter and around 1987 he hit pay dirt in mines near the village of São José da Batalha in Paraíba, Brazil. Named for the location of its discovery, by 1989 Paraíba Tourmaline was shifting perceptions and paradigms, making any respectable gem dealer go weak at the knees. In his book, 'Gemstones: Quality and Value, Volume 1', Yasukazu Suwa nicely sums this up stating, *"The appeal of Paraíba Tourmaline far exceeds that of other gems, to the point where they are desired even by people who are accustomed to seeing a variety of gemstones"*. The main reason for this is its vivid colours, characterised by a sizzling, electric, neon or fluorescent appearance as well as a

Indicolite

Visually distinct from Paraíba Tourmaline, Indicolite (also spelt Indigolite or indigolith) is derived from the Latin 'indicum' (a blue dye obtained from various plants) and from the Greek 'lithos' (stone) for its indigo hues. Due to its geological rarity, after Paraíba Tourmaline and Chrome Tourmaline, fine pure blue Indicolite is more valuable than Rubellite, Bi Colour Tourmaline, Pink Tourmaline and Green Tourmaline. The propensity of pleochroism (dichroism) to darken Indicolite so it loses transparency, brilliance and beauty can sometimes make it a difficult gemstone for lapidaries. All Tourmaline can be challenging

to cut, but in Indicolite, the table of the gem has to be orientated to not only achieve the best possible weight and clarity, but also to minimise the impact of its darker colour. Similar to Green Tourmaline, Indicolite is usually eye-clean. In his book, 'Secrets of the Gem Trade', Richard Wise compares the search for a Sapphire Blue Tourmaline to that of the Holy Grail and in my experience, he's right on the money. In my years in the gem industry, the Indicolite pictured here comes closest to looking visually similar to a Blue Sapphire. I debated on whether to include this photograph as it's definitely the exception rather than the rule. Most fine Indicolite I have seen is much darker, but with distinct neon flashes. Whilst the historic source of Sapphire Blue Indicolite is Brazil, this gem hails from the Democratic Republic of the Congo. In my opinion, blue characterises this variety and specimens with visible greens should not be called Indicolite.

distinctive transparency that affords Paraíba Tourmaline's fine brilliance. In a way, colour in Paraíba Tourmaline is perhaps a dichotomy, in that its typically medium toned, sometimes almost pastel hues, still have intensity. This is unusual and a big reason for its appeal. Clarity and size play second fiddle in Paraíba Tourmaline; colour is the beauty gauge. Variously described as Caribbean blue, peacock, copper-green, neon-aquamarine, swimming pool blue or turquoise blue, from a gemmological perspective, the colours range from bluish-green, blue-green, greenish-blue, blue and bluish-violet. As these finite colours, along with its composition, now define this gemstone, I've included a handy colour chart to show you the accepted range. While its vivid blues are the most popular and expensive, all its colours are unique, with gems displaying a greater neon intensity increasing in value. Like Emerald, Paraíba Tourmaline often has visible inclusions, although this varies somewhat depending on origin, with Mozambique Paraíba Tourmaline typically far cleaner (and larger) than those from Brazil. While Paraíba Tourmaline is not always eye-clean, this is tolerable as long as it doesn't nullify beauty. Paraíba Tourmaline's transparency is sometimes a double-edged sword, in that its shows inclusions that wouldn't be visible in other gems. Large eye-clean

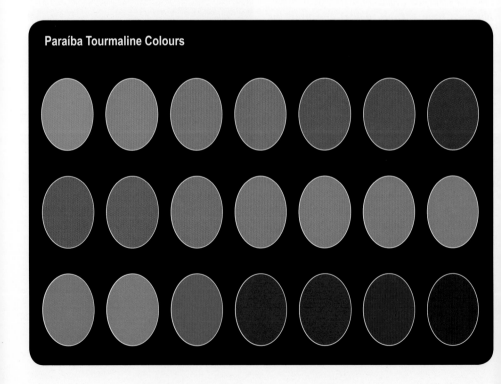

Paraíba Tourmaline Colours

Prefixes like 'Ceylon' or 'Kashmir' not only denote a Sapphire origin, but also *imply* a quality expectation. The biggest thing to remember for Paraíba Tourmaline is that it's a lot more than an origin. Tourmaline's array of colours is typically down to trace amounts of chromium, iron, manganese and vanadium, but with Paraíba Tourmaline it is copper and manganese, an uncanny combo for Tourmaline, that not only makes it beautiful, but also geologically scarce. While the original Batalha Mine in Paraíba was ostensibly exhausted several years after its discovery, new but limited Brazilian deposits were later discovered in the neighbouring state of Rio Grande do Norte in 1991 (Mulunga Mine) and 1995 (Quintos Mine), and again in Paraíba in 2006 (Glorious Mine). But just as Pliny said in the 1st century, *"there is always something new out of Africa"*. The newer African discoveries, first in Nigeria (Edoukou and Ofiki circa 2000) and then in Mozambique (Mavuco 2001, although the gems didn't appear in the marketplace until 2005) have helped fulfil the demand for this 'aristocratic' Tourmaline, not only making it more available and affordable, but also promoting it as a mainstream jewellery gemstone. The discovery of non-Brazilian Paraíba wasn't without controversy and led to marketplace terms such 'Paraíba Africana' and 'Paraíba-type'. In 2006, the LMHC (Laboratory Manual Harmonisation Committee) decided that because they are indistinguishable using standard gemmological tests, blue (electric blue, neon blue or violet blue), bluish-green to greenish-blue or green copper-rich Cuprian Elbaite Tourmaline with a medium to high saturation and tone of any origin can be called 'Paraíba'. As gemstones don't recognise borders, origin typically doesn't define a variety, yet some in the gem biz continue to disagree with the LMHC's decision. This came to a head when David Sherman (Paraíba.com) brought a lawsuit against the AGTA (American Gem Trade Association), claiming that use of the name 'Paraíba' for any copper-bearing Tourmaline regardless of origin has hurt him financially. As reported by JCK (Jewellers Circular Keystone) on 31st October, a federal court dismissed the case. The truth is 'Paraíba' was never just a place name; it is all about copper and colour. For me, I'm listening to the seven gemmological laboratories that make up the LMHC and the endorsement by CIBJO (see page 255 for more) for the use of 'Paraíba' for other origins. To use an old analogy, if it looks like a duck and quacks like a duck, it must be a duck. Nevertheless, all things being equal, Paraíba Tourmaline with a certified Brazilian origin will typically demand a premium. Just make sure you're paying for quality, not just pedigree.

(no visible inclusions when the gem is examined six inches from the naked eye) electric blue specimens, like the 8.7 carat gem pictured at the beginning of this section, are rare and priced accordingly. Once you've settled on a Paraíba Tourmaline colour and clarity that fits your taste and budget, look for a good shape and overall appearance. Available in a variety of shapes and cuts since the discovery of the Mozambique deposits, Paraíba Tourmaline are most commonly seen in ovals and pears.

While Paraíba Tourmaline is hugely popular, it's currently difficult to purchase any rough on the open market; anyone who has it appears to be sitting on it. As with anything scarce, beautiful and in demand, its prices reflect its popularity. With mechanised mining now happening in the Mozambique Paraíba Tourmaline deposit and further exploration of the surrounding area, it's likely Africa not Brazil will secure the future of this uniquely beautiful gem.

RATANAKIRI ZIRCON

"White or colourless Zircons are used in lieu of Diamonds by wealthy natives in Ceylon."
A. H. Church, Precious Stones (1905)

Before I begin my take on this gem, I've got a bit of a confession. Ratanakiri 'Blue' Zircon is one of my favourite gemstones. Apart from being December's birthstone (my birth month), Ratanakiri Zircon has a uniquely attractive blue colour that you won't find exactly in any other blue gemstone. Sure, other blue gems can come close (or perhaps Blue Zircon comes close to them), but either way, for me this gem has a certain unexplainable, *'je ne sais quoi'*. Another gemstone writer, Yasukazu Suwa agrees with this view, describing its colour as possessing *"a character that is not seen elsewhere, even in Sapphire or Aquamarine"*. He continues, adding: *"If a fancy Blue Diamond showed this colour, it might exceed $80,000 for a 1 carat stone"* (2001). For most of us, this is well outside our gemstone budget, so thankfully Blue Zircon is far more affordable.

Ratanakiri Zircon is a commercial name for Blue Zircon from Cambodia or more specifically, Blue Zircon from Ratanakiri, a Cambodian deposit noted for yielding some of the world's finest specimens. Cambodia is generally regarded as the world's premiere source for this gemstone and its other Zircon deposit is located at Preah Vihear, about 100 kilometres north of the famous Angkor Wat. But in my mind, Ratanakiri is 'the place' for Blue Zircon. Out of the way and exceptionally beautiful, 'Ratanakiri' means 'gemstone mountain' in Khmer. Ostensibly named after the element 'zirconium' present in its chemical composition, the

Famous for Angkor Wat (pictured), Cambodia is also the world's premier source for Blue 'Ratanakiri' Zircon

gem name 'Zircon' has two possible etymologies; one is the Arabic 'zarkun' (red), another is the Persian words 'zar' (gold) and 'gun' (colour). However, don't be confused by the colours indicated by its word origins. Zircon comes in an array of colours, including blue, champagne, coffee, cognac, golden, green, honey, orange, red, white (colourless) and yellow. It also has an assortment of historical and commercial names, which at times can get pretty confusing. Jargon is pale yellow; Jacinth is red; Hyacinth is yellowish-red (or perhaps even blue); Matara Diamond or Ceylon Diamond is white (more on this colour shortly); Starlite or Siam Zircon is blue; and Ligure is apparently generic.

Ratanakiri Zircon 9K White Gold Ring

A gemstone since antiquity, Zircon has been found in some of the world's oldest archaeological sites, which is no surprise given the mineral's durability. As mentioned previously in 'A Gemstone's Journey' (Chapter 1), a tiny mineral fragment of Zircon discovered in Western Australia is the earth's oldest known object.

Zircon is rich in history and legend, appearing in several ancient texts, including the bible and the Hindu poem of the mythical Kapla Tree, which was bejewelled with leaves of Zircon. Some sources mention a Jewish legend that names the angel Zircon as the guardian appointed to watch over Adam and Eve in the Garden of Eden (given how this played out, it must have been a thankless task). Called by its ancient names, Ligure and Jacinth, Zircon

White Zircon

As alluded to this section's opening quote, Zircon is the natural gemstone that possesses a sparkle and looks most similar to Diamonds. Historically, its use as a Diamond substitute probably originates in Ceylon (Sri Lanka after 1972) in the late 18th century when white (colourless) Zircon was mined at Matara, which is located on the island's southern coast. It is from this locale we get the historic commercial names 'Matara Diamond' or 'Ceylon Diamond'. Please note that marketing Zircon solely using these names today would be misleading as it is not 'Diamond' in composition. Zircon's high index

of refraction (see page 249 for more) give this gem its visual resemblance to Diamonds, resulting in a sharp brilliance, playful scintillation (sparkle), Diamond-like lustre (variously described as adamantine or sub-adamantine, see page 14 for more) and high fire (also known as dispersion, this is the splitting of light into its component colours). With the advent of manmade synthetics, such as cubic zirconia and moissanite, Zircon is no longer the pre-eminent Diamond substitute, but thankfully, this fantastic gem is today valued for what it is, rather than for just looking like something else.

One thing that gets me frustrated is when poor old Zircon gets unfairly confused with that cheap synthetic Diamond imitation, cubic zirconia. While their names sound similar and White Zircon was once regarded as an excellent Diamond alternative, this is where any similarity ends. Zirconium oxide was discovered in 1892, but it wasn't until 1937 that cubic zirconia was discovered in its natural state. In nature, cubic zirconia's crystals are way too small to be cut as gemstones, so the two German mineralogists who made the discovery didn't even think the mineral important enough to give it a formal name. In the seventies, Soviet scientists at the Lebedev Physical Institute in Moscow perfected growing cubic zirconia crystals in a laboratory. They named the jewel 'fianit', but unfortunately for our friend Zircon, the name didn't catch on outside the USSR. The institute published their results in 1973 and by 1976, cubic zirconia was being produced commercially under the trade name 'djevalite'. By the eighties, cubic zirconia was mass marketed as the Diamond substitute of choice. In my mind, gemstones are formed within the earth, not a laboratory. Remember, for a gem to be a gem it must be beautiful, durable and rare. As they can be made anytime, man-made gems are not rare, so are these 'impostors from the factory' even really gems? Zircon is a real gemstone and cubic zirconia is not, please don't confuse the two.

gets several mentions in the bible. Firstly, as one of the 'stones of fire' (Ezekiel 28:13-16) that was given to Moses and set in the breastplate of Aaron (Exodus 28:15-30) and secondly, as one of the 12 gemstones set in the foundations of the city walls of Jerusalem (Revelations 21:19). Andreas, the Bishop of Caesurae, who wrote in the late 10th century, was one of the earliest writers to link the apostles with the 12 gems of Jerusalem. He associated Jacinth (Zircon) with the Apostle Simon. According to its mythology, Zircon represents purity and innocence. Like so many other gems whose changes in their colours or lustre are said to be indicative of their wearer's mood, health or fate, Zircon's loss of lustre apparently means danger is looming.

As a jewellery gemstone, Zircon has enjoyed several peaks in popularity. In 16th-century Europe, Italian jewellers featured Zircon and later it was also used in Victorian jewellery, but it wasn't until the 'roaring twenties' that Blue Zircon got its first taste of modern popularity.

Ratanakiri Zircon comes in unique blues, often due to greenish tints, and is typically eye-clean (no visible inclusions when the gem is examined six inches from the naked eye), although you can expect some inclusions under magnification. As Ratanakiri Zircon's transparency can decrease in the darker tones, gems with medium to light colours are generally preferred. This will maintain the gem's beauty by affording visibility to its other optical attributes. Zircon is strongly doubly refractive, which means light splits into two rays as it passes through the gem. This is immediately visible, even to the untrained eye, as a doubling of the facets, although this is somewhat dependant on the angle of observation. More pronounced in thicker gemstones, double refractivity does not make the gem more brilliant per se, but often results in beautiful sparkling mosaic patterns and optical depth. Other key attributes of Zircon are its beautiful Diamond-like sparkle, brilliance, fire and lustre (more below). In order to maximise these optical properties, Ratanakiri Zircon needs to be carefully cut. Thankfully, well cut Blue Zircons are usually available. While some sources maintain that round cuts are most commonly seen, in my experience, all the classic shapes and cuts are available, including emerald, heart, marquise, oval and pear, as well as rounds. Although it is mined in Cambodia, most Ratanakiri Zircon, as well as Zircon from Nigeria and Tanzania, is cut in my adopted hometown of Chanthaburi, Thailand. At present, this town is the only primary source for finished Zircon, with gems over 1 carat increasing in rarity, availability and price. Another source for Zircon is the alluvial (sedimentary) deposits of Sri Lanka. During my years of living in Chanthaburi, I have heard the odd 'rumour' that Zircon is still mined in Thailand, but I have yet to find any hard evidence to support this.

Its Diamond-like characteristics, along with its versatile colours continues to make Zircon one of the most desirable gemstones for those wise enough to appreciate the differences between this genuine gem and a similar sounding synthetic. While its other colours are attractive, it's the exquisitely unique blues of Ratanakiri Zircon that has captured my imagination since I first saw it almost a decade ago.

Zircon & Diamond 9K Yellow Gold Ring

RHODOLITE

"By her, who in this month is born, no gems save Garnets should be worn; they will insure her constancy, true friendship, and fidelity".

Unknown Author, Pamphlet Published by Tiffany & Co. (1870)

Unknown to many, I was a gardener for three years straight out of high school. While the pay was terrible, I did attend horticultural college where I gained an appreciation for botany. One of my favourites was the purplish-red blossoms of the rhododendron, so you can imagine how chuffed I was to learn that there is a Garnet with similar colours. While I try not to play favourites, you have to agree that the delightful cocktail of cranberries, grapes and raspberries embodied by Rhodolite demands your attention.

Like many people, I initially perceived Garnets as 'little red gemstones'. While actually incorrect, this is not surprising given this gemstone's history. Used in adornment for over 5,000 years, red Garnets were a big hit in the land of the pharaohs around 3100 BC, being used as beads in necklaces as well as inlaid jewellery (gems set into a surface in a decorative pattern). Our name for this gem is derived from the Latin 'granatus' (from 'granum', which means 'grain' or 'seed') due to *some* Garnets resemblance to pomegranate seeds. Interestingly, the Romans didn't know this fruit by this name; they called it *Punicum Malum* (Carthaginian apple) because they received it from Carthage (the hometown of Hannibal, this ancient Phoenician civilisation was centred in modern-day Tunisia). For the Greeks, pomegranates were an important symbol in Hades' mythological abduction of Persephone, which explains the excavation of ancient jewellery set with red Garnets in aciniform pomegranate designs. As alluded to the opening ode to January's birthstone, Garnets are regarded as a symbol of

Reminiscent of the rhododendron (pictured), Rhodolite was first used to describe Garnets discovered in North Carolina in the late 19th century

everlasting friendship, faith, truth and protection. For more Garnet lore, visit Spessartite on page 204.

Skipping ahead to the 19th century, jewellery featuring clusters of cute little red Garnets from Bohemia (modern-day Czech Republic) were all the rage. These deep fiery red Bohemian Garnets are gemmologically known as Pyrope, from the Greek 'pyropos', which means 'fiery eyed'. Bohemian Garnets were made the 'fashion gemstone' of this era by the emerging middle-class, who purchased them in quantity while holidaying in this region's famed hot springs. In his classic work, 'Precious Stones: A Popular Account of Their Characters, Occurrence and Applications', Professor Max Bauer notes that Garnets dominated the displays of jewellery stores at the time. Max has an interesting link to a legendary gemmologist we've met once before and are about to meet again. According to Mr. John H. Buck, writing for the New York Times in 1904, Max's book was, *"prompted by the desire of the publishers to present to*

Rhodolite & Diamond 9K Yellow Gold Ring

the German public a work on precious stones similar in character to that admirably supplied in American literature in 'Gems and Precious Stones of North America' by Dr. G. F. Kunz". Regardless, of his impetus, his observation of the prodigious nature of Garnets helps explain why many Rubies of this period were later found to be fine Pyrope.

In truth, Garnets are a lot more than little red gems. Sure, there are the 'classic' reds, but Garnets also come in an array of other colours including chocolates, greens, oranges, pinks, purples and yellows. Blue had never been seen in Garnets before the discovery of certain colour change varieties from Bekily in southern Madagascar in the late nineties. According to gemstone author Antoinette Matlins, *"the Garnet family is one of the most exciting families in the gem world"* and I couldn't agree more, but boy can they get confusing. A group of minerals possessing similar crystal structures, Garnets vary in composition, giving each type different colours and properties. As 'self coloured' gemstones (see page 18 for more),

Mozambique Garnet

Mozambique Garnets are actually pure Almandine (Almandite) or an Almandine and Pyrope blend, similar to Rhodolite Garnet. A darker red colour than Rhodolite, sometimes with hints of chocolate, Mozambique Garnet is named after the east African country they come from. Mozambique Garnet is wonderfully affordable, possessing the warm 'classic' red colours typical of the Garnets of antiquity. Similar to the Bohemian Garnets of the 19th century, Mozambique Garnet often looks like dark Ruby to the untrained eye.

you'd think things would be simple, but Garnets are a friendly family that like to mix and match in nature. To put this in context, several years ago I compiled a list of 38 different current, historic and commercial Garnet names. It took me a while to get my head around the Garnets, so to make it easier for you I've included a handy chart on page 53.

If Garnets are the 'Queen of Gemstones', then in my mind, Rhodolite is the 'Queen of Garnets'. Rhodolite was discovered in 1882 in Macon County, North Carolina and was named by the acclaimed gem expert, George Frederick Kunz, after its colour resemblance to the mountain rhododendron (*Rhododendron Catawbiense*) that grows in North Carolina. Deriving its name from the Greek 'rhodo' (rose) and 'lithos' (stone), Kunz described Rhodolite as, *"pale rose-red inclining to purple like that of certain roses and rhododendrons"*. While the original American deposit was exhausted by 1901, Rhodolite had actually been mined in Sri Lanka for over 2,000 years. Today, the primary sources for Rhodolite are India, Sri Lanka and Tanzania. Secondary sources include Brazil, Kenya, Madagascar and Malawi.

Mozambique Garnet & Diamond 9K Yellow Gold Ring

Like some other Garnets, Rhodolite is a 'maverick mixture' of two different 'pure' types; in this case, a naturally occurring blend of Almandine and Pyrope (see page 53 for more). Colour wise, Rhodolite looks very different to the 'classic' Garnet reds, coming in combinations of pink, red and purple. Uniquely beautiful, the key differentiators for Rhodolite when compared to its Almandine and Pyrope cousins are its purple shades and a high level of transparency that results in good brilliance. Its purple hue should be lively, immediately noticeable and command your full attention. While colour preferences are subjective, I favour Rhodolite with a rich rhododendron purplish-red colour of a medium tone without any brownish tints. While bigger gems are usually redder with attractive violet flashes, Rhodolite can lose its transparency, brilliance and beauty if too dark. Commercial colour prefixes and names are sometimes used to describe certain Rhodolite colour varieties. Unfortunately, these 'trade names' can sometimes be confusing as they are not always consistently applied. While names like 'Raspberry Rhodolite' (a fine purplish-pink colour resembling the fruit) or 'Grape Garnet®' (named for its intense purple red colour reminiscent of fine merlot or cabernet wine) can be useful, at the end of the day, you should purchase based on what you see.

Transparency is also important for Rhodolite, and as a Type II gemstone (see page 10 for more) it typically occurs with some minor inclusions that may be eye-visible. While a few inclusions that don't overly mess with beauty are acceptable, avoid Rhodolite that is overly cloudy or silky. Once you've settled on a colour with a high level of transparency, look for a good shape and overall appearance. While you'll occasionally read that 'so and so source' has the best colours, clarity, etc., in reality, there are no significant differences between any of the major Rhodolite deposits. As with all gems, country of origin can be indicative, but never implies a quality.

RUBELLITE

"The Red Tourmaline (Rubellite) is occasionally so nearly ruby-red in colour as to necessitate care".

Augusto Castellani (1829-1914), Gems: Notes and Extracts

Tourmaline frequently garners the nickname, 'the chameleon gem', not only because of its multitude of colour varieties, but also because of its historic propensity to copycat other, often more valuable gemstones.

In the 16th century, the Portuguese thought they'd found Emerald in the Brazilian gem fields of Minas Gerais (general mines), but 300 years later science caught up with the dupe and 'Brazilian Emerald' was correctly identified as Green Tourmaline. On the other side of the planet, Dutch trading ships arrived in Sri Lankan waters around 1590 and by 1703, Tourmaline were being marketed throughout western and central Europe. This resulted in more cases of mistaken identity with both Ruby and Sapphire, leading some to stake its appeal purely on its ability to look like something else. Even its name reveals some of the historic confusion its many colours have brought.

Tourmaline is derived from the Sinhalese 'turmali', which means 'mixed parcel' or 'stone with mixed colours' and are a group of related minerals whose differences in composition result in a plethora of colours. I've reviewed all the main Tourmaline varieties in Paraíba Tourmaline (page 168), but also included a handy chart on page 56.

Peter the Great (1672-1725) reportedly commissioned many items of 'Ruby' jewellery for the Russian Imperial Court that were later discovered to be Rubellite

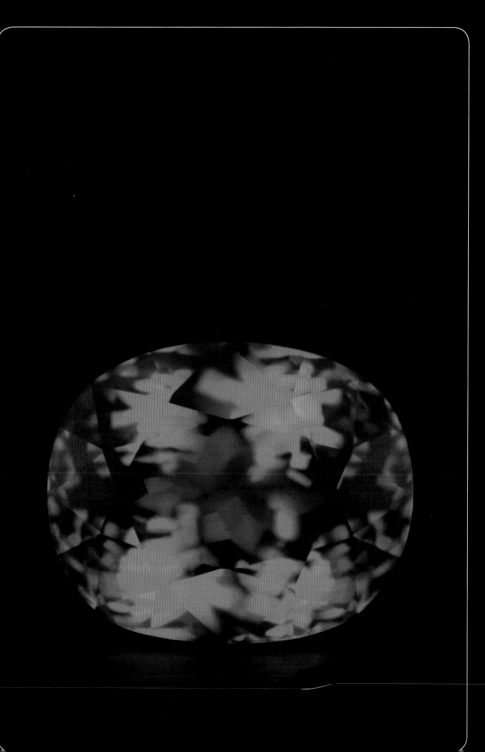

The opening quote is cautionary, alluding to the historical propensity for Rubellite to be confused with Ruby. This is echoed in Professor Max Bauer's classic 1904 work, 'Precious Stones: A Popular Account of Their Characters, Occurrence and Applications', when he warns, *"The colour may be so like that of certain Rubies that is difficult, even for an expert, to discriminate between these two stones on mere inspection"*. While this helps explain why items of 'Ruby' jewellery reportedly commissioned by Peter the Great (1672-1725) for the Russian Imperial Court were later discovered to be Rubellite, it also begs the questions: is the comparison really fair? Does Rubellite really look like Ruby? The last thing I want to do is offend the ghosts of Augusto or Max, and while the layperson might initially see some similarities, Rubellite for me has always looked like, um, Rubellite. Why? Rubellite is a commercial name derived from the Latin 'rubellus' (reddish) and the Greek 'lithos'

Rubellite & Diamond 9K Yellow Gold Ring

(stone). While Rubellite, like Ruby, is doubly refractive, making Ruby slightly pleochroic (see page 33 for more), Tourmaline is strongly pleochroic or getting more technical, it is the most dichroic (two-coloured) of all gemstones. This means each Tourmaline crystal has two colours (primary and secondary), whose intensity changes when viewed from different angles. Finished Rubellite will typically have the primary pure reds visible in combination with the secondary purples or pinks. Although the more pure the red the higher the value, Rubellite's purplish-reds constitute the vast majority. In my opinion, they are distinctive and define this beautiful gemstone.

While the 20th century has seen Tourmaline come into its own, it was also known in classical times. In the 3rd century, Theophrastus (the successor of Aristotle's school of philosophy) called it 'lyngourion', and a Green Tourmaline seal stone sporting the likeness of Alexander

Pink Tourmaline

One common question is what is the difference between Pink Tourmaline and Rubellite? After recognising that red and pink are technically the same colour, Rubellite is distinguished from Pink Tourmaline by its deeper tone (lightness or darkness of a colour) and greater saturation (strength of a colour). Confused? To help, I've included a nifty colour chart to show you where Pink Tourmaline ends and Rubellite begins. One thing to remember with Pink Tourmaline is that is usually less included than Rubellite. Classed as a Type II gemstone, Pink Tourmaline typically grows with some minor inclusions in nature which may be eye-  *visible. Despite this, most Pink Tourmaline is eye-clean and I favour intense medium-toned examples with this clarity. Historically, carved pink and red Tourmalines were a big hit in China. The Dowager Empress was not only enamoured with Jade, she also loved Tourmaline so much that she reportedly purchased almost a tonne of Californian Tourmaline, an important deposit in the late nineteenth and early twentieth centuries.*

the Great dating to the same period is believed to be the oldest known example. Believing it to possess arcane influence, the Romans apparently used Tourmaline in animal-themed carved brooches. Coming into the business while Tourmaline was still riding the wave of popularity following Paraíba's 1989 debut and the discovery of one of the world's most significant Tourmaline deposits in Nigeria (circa 1998), I never really understood why some authors would describe Tourmaline as *"confused"*, *"misunderstood"* or *"historically maligned"*. For me, it was always an important gem, both aesthetically and commercially, and the first three gems I ever purchased were Tourmalines (a pink and green for friends and a lovely bicolour for my mother).

Today Rubellite, along with Paraíba Tourmaline, Chrome Tourmaline and Indicolite, are the rarest and most valuable Tourmalines. Rubellite is a lustrous transparent gemstone that comes in red, strong purplish-red and slight purplish-red. As stated previously, pure reds with virtually no secondary purples are exceptionally scarce and demand a premium. While sometimes attractive, Rubellite with visible brownish mahogany tints will be priced

Pink Tourmaline & Diamond 9K Yellow Gold Ring

cheaper. As usual, colour preferences in gems are subjective, but you should be aware of the marketplace dynamics. For Rubellite, heed the old Goldilocks' maxim (see page 16 for more); look for a happy medium that is as intense as possible, but not too dark or too light.

In Rubellite, the trace element that lends its delightful purplish-reds is manganese, but this is a double-edged sword. More manganese gives Rubellite a deeper tone and saturation, but also increases the prevalence of inclusions. This is why a clean intensely coloured Rubellite, especially over 4 carats, is a veritable scarcity. Taking this into account, Rubellite, like Emerald, is classed as a Type III gemstone (see page 10 for more), meaning they typically grow with many inclusions in nature. Most Rubellite is going to have eye-visible inclusions, although this can vary a little from locale to locale. Like all Tourmaline, Rubellite can be a challenging gem for the lapidary due to areas of internal tension inside Tourmaline crystals and its inherent pleochroism (dichroism). On the other hand, the two-colours of Rubellite's crystals are less of a concern for the lapidary than with Green Tourmaline and Indicolite because the secondary colour isn't as dark. Expect a variety of shapes and cuts for this gem,

Bi Colour Tourmaline

Mentioned as a gemmological curiosity in early 20th century texts, by the seventies Bi Colour Tourmaline was coveted as one of the rarest of all bicolour gems. Typically showing either a green and pink split or a brown and green split, combinations of apricot, blue, bluish-green, colourless, green and pink are also possible, sometimes with more than two colours in a single gem. Bi Colour Tourmaline's unique colours are down to environmental changes during formation due to the depletion of the trace elements that lend Tourmaline its plethora of colours. The problem with these disturbances during the gem's formation is 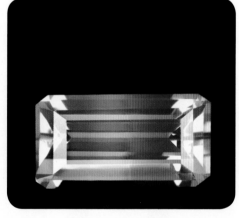 *that it results in inclusions that are usually eye visible. Eye-clean Bi Colour Tourmalines with the signature pink/green split are rarer than rare, and are priced accordingly. Deliberately cut to accentuate its split personality, any bicolour gem should ideally show a fairly even split of colour. Don't confuse Bi Colour Tourmaline with Watermelon Tourmaline; this gem has a pink inner and green outer, just like the fruit.*

Rubellite & Pink Tourmaline Colours

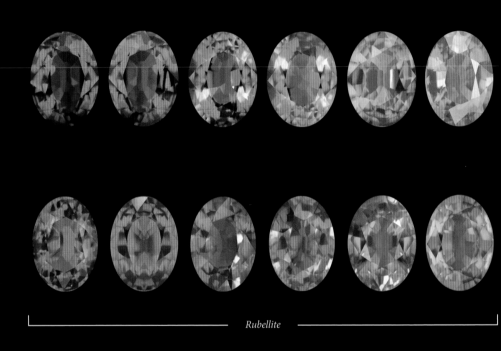

Rubellite

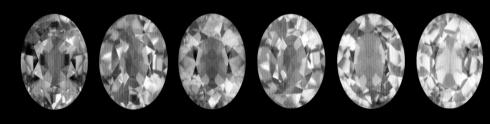

Pink Tourmaline

such as ovals, pears and rounds, often with extra pavilion facets to scintillate its colourful brilliance. As usual, look for a good shape and overall appearance.

Origin is important for Rubellite and with only four modern commercially significant deposits, it's an easy thing to get a handle on. Brazil's Cruzeiro Mine, located in São José da Safira in Minas Gerais, was an important deposit in the late seventies and eighties, but it was the Tourmaline deposit's unearthed near the city of Ibadan in Nigeria, West Africa from 1998 onwards that really turned heads. Nigeria is noted for yielding extremely fine Rubellite (as well as other Tourmalines), sometimes in larger sizes than usual. The next were the deposits near the town of Betafo, located in Madagascar's central highlands, which were discovered around 2005. This deposit divides opinion, with some viewing its output as globally insignificant and tainted by too many brownish chocolates, and others praising its more ruby-like specimens. The most recent, albeit short-lived discovery, is from Shimoyo (also spelt Chimoio) in Mozambqiue's Manica Province. Only in operation from around January to April 2008, this deposit's Rubellite is characterised by an unusually high 'eye-clean' clarity and a 'classic' colour, with very little secondary brownish tints. It is no surprise that its reported output of only 10 kilogrammes was quickly snapped up by big rough buyers.

Incredibly scarce, particularly when eye-clean, Rubellite is one of those rare gemstones whose opulent purplish-reds demand a place in your gemstone entourage. But don't just take my word for it. Friend, gem dealer, lapidary and colourful raconteur, Brazilian Tony Diniz, sums Rubellite up as follows: *"There is Ruby red and then there's Rubellite red. Almost every jewellery lover has a Ruby, but with only a handful of deposits, owning Rubellite is the hallmark of a true gemstone romantic".*

RUBY

"The Ruby not only stands in the very foremost class of coloured gems, but it occupies among precious stones in general a position which is unquestionably supreme".

Edwin Streeter, Precious Stones and Gems (1898)

The mighty 'rubinus lapis', the red stone, Ruby is without a doubt the pin-up girl of the gem world. She's the fiery scarlet starlet everyone wants to love. The oriental 'gem of the sun', Ruby was once known to the Indians as 'ratnaraj', the king of gems, but for me, Ruby will always be a queen. The colour of passion, love and romance, Ruby's intense crimson colours have mystified, entranced and romanced since she burst on to the scene over 2,500 years ago. Like many a schoolboy, I read Sir Henry Rider Haggard's classic adventure, 'King Solomon's Mines', filled with captivating fables, exotic locales and colourful 'stiff upper lip' characters, but little did I know that one of them was real. Edwin Streeter, the legendary Victorian gemstone connoisseur, actually existed and having made (and lost) his fortune trading gemstones, he's an intriguing personality. But my passion for Ruby was born in Thailand, the middle point for 90 percent of the world's Rubies, as they journey to waiting admirers around the globe.

Ruby is the 'big red' in the 'big four' quartet, along with Diamond, Emerald and Sapphire. Ruby and Sapphire are colour varieties of the mineral Corundum (crystalline aluminium oxide), which derives its name from the Sanskrit word for Rubies and Sapphires, 'kuruvinda'. Corundum produces 'other coloured' gemstones (see page 18 for more), meaning that trace amounts of elements such as chromium, iron and titanium are responsible for producing

Edwin Streeter, author and renowned Victorian gemstone merchant and jeweller, was so famous he received a cameo in Sir Haggard's 'King Solomon's Mines'

its rainbow of colours. Corundum's reds are called 'Ruby' and its other colours are called 'Sapphire'. You can learn about Blue Sapphires on page 96, its other colours on page 140, and the differences between Ruby and Pink Sapphire on page 145. Ruby gets its name from the Latin 'ruber', which means red. While many red gems were called 'Ruby' until the development of scientific gemmology in the 18th century, during antiquity, Ruby, Garnet, Spinel and other red gemstones were collectively called 'carbunculus' ('little coal' in Latin). Known as 'anthrax' (live coal) to the ancient Greeks, these gemstones were beautiful deep red gems that became the colour of glowing coal embers of a fire when held up to the sun. Believe it or not, they were apparently sourced from the East Indies! Before you discredit the likelihood of our European ancestors having access to Asian gemstones, note that Sri Lankan Rubies may have been available to the Greeks and Romans as early as 480 BC. Carbunculus is 'carbuncle' in English and this word was also once used to describe red gemstones. For example, in the King James Bible, Ruby and its namesake 'carbuncle' score several mentions.

Not surprisingly, the myths and historical allure associated with Rubies is as colourful as its red hues. Ancient Indians believed Ruby to possess an internal fire that would not only

Ruby & Diamond 18K Yellow Gold Ring

endow a long life, but could even help you bring the kettle to the boil! In the middle ages, Rubies, like so many other gems, were believed to possess prophetic powers, deepening in colour if bad moons were rising. Worn by the Burmese as a talisman to protect against illness, misfortune or injury (not surprising, considering their 'blood-like' colour), Rubies were once known as 'blood drops from the heart of the mother earth'. In the 19th century, Ralph Waldo Emerson penned one of my favourite poems, describing Ruby as *"drops of frozen wine from Eden's vats that run"* and *"hearts of friends, to friends unknown"*. Today, Ruby is the official birthstone for July.

Tanzanian Ruby, also know as Songea Ruby, is from a deposit just outside the town of Songea in Tanzania that was only discovered in 1992. The 'AAA' prefix is occasionally used to denote top qualities (colour and clarity)

Ruby is one of the rarest of the better-known gemstones. Far rarer than Diamonds, and excluding Imperial Jade and some uncanny natural Diamond colours, Ruby is also the world's most expensive gemstone. To put this into context, in 2006 a London jeweller, Laurence Graff, parted with a record-setting $3.6 million for an 8.62 carat Ruby ring, which works out to an amazing $425,000 per carat! Just remember, even though they are one of the world's most expensive gems, as with everything, quality determines price. When it comes to Ruby, the intensity and purity of its signature reds are where the value lies. While Ruby's 'pure' reds are the Holy Grail, they seldom exist. As a diochroic (two-coloured: purplish red and orangey

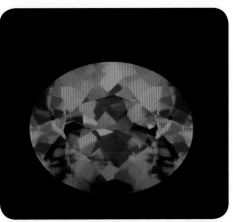

Until the beginning of the 20th century, there was a historical propensity for Rubellite to be confused with Ruby. You can read more about this on page 188

red) pleochroic gemstone (see page 33 for more), even the 'finest' Ruby is still going to be only around 80 percent pure red, with secondary splashes of orange, pink, purple and violet. With Ruby, colour preferences are extremely subjective and even experts disagree on what's best. The reliable Goldilocks maxim, not too dark or too light, just right, is good advice, certainly with respect to getting your head around paradigms and prices. While intense bright colours are the happy medium and the marketplace ideal, you should always listen to your heart. Ruby that is too dark (garnet-esque), too light, too orange or too purple will be priced accordingly. The problem is how dark, light or secondary-coloured a Ruby is subjective.

Some favour a splash of violet or purple that gives heart-warming burgundies, while others prefer a bit of orange. In Ruby, a touch of orange is the steroid that gives it Ferrari racing car reds. Lastly, other people are seduced by the oft unattainable perfection of the classic fire engine reds. To further confuse the situation, the less intense shades often look better in low lighting conditions, such as candlelit dinners, where jewellery is frequently warn. I actually favour a richer crimson than most, the historic 'beef blood', as long as its faceting affords brilliant flashes of red. The aesthetic impact of colour unevenness due to zoning (location of colour in the crystal versus how the gem is faceted) or excessive windowing (areas of washed out colour in a table-up gem, often due to a shallow pavilion) is also an important value consideration for Ruby. Finally, pay attention to how transparency and inclusions affect Ruby's colour, beauty, and subsequently value. While a gemstone's colours should ideally remain beautiful in any light source, Rubies usually look their best when viewed outdoors in natural light or under incandescent lights. This is the exact opposite to their Corundum cousin, Blue Sapphire, who loathes incandescent light. Most Rubies display a strong glowing

Star Ruby

Due to an optical special effect called 'asterism' or the 'star effect', parallel needle-like inclusions create a reflected luminous star of light that moves across the gemstone. For Corundum, reflections from a whole host of tiny rutile needle inclusions, also known as silk, cause their stars. A unique and rare gemmological phenomenon, Star Rubies were sometimes known as 'the three swords' in Europe, due to their alleged ability to banish evil, bring good luck and help find a good spouse. All star gems are dependent on a gem being cut 'en cabochon' (cut in convex form and highly polished, but not faceted). Assessing cabochons 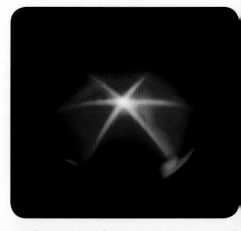 *is straightforward - just look at their finish, shape and proportion, favouring attractive smooth domes with a desirable symmetry. While asterism is most visible in a direct, single beam of light, a well-cut star gemstone has a distinct star whose rays are straight and equidistant. The norm is a six-rayed star, but 12-rayed stars also occasionally occur. In Star Ruby, the distinctiveness, intensity and transparency of the red body colour are also important value considerations. Star Rubies that are too dark, too grey or too violet will be priced accordingly. While the gem gravels of Sri Lanka are the world's 'classic' source, having supplied this gemstone for over 2,000 years, other modern sources include Burma, India, Madagascar and Mozambique.*

electric red fluorescence in natural light and, along with silk (see below), this softens the impact of areas of darkness in a table-up gem (extinction). While Thai, Cambodian and Tanzanian (Songea) Rubies lack strong fluorescence due to their high iron content, its absence isn't the 'kiss of death' and doesn't necessarily denigrate. At the end of day, beauty might be in the eye of the beholder, but it will always be tempered by what you can afford. A couple of antique terms used to describe colour in Ruby, which are actually a little yucky, are 'pigeon's blood' (a rare and valuable Burmese Ruby colour) and 'beef blood' (richer reds, perhaps somewhat reminiscent of red Garnets). Not resonating with modern times, these have pretty much fallen by the wayside.

Chromium is the trace element that gives some Rubies their characteristic reds, but as far as clarity is concerned, it's a double-edged sword. Just like it does with the clarity of Alexandrite and Emerald, chromium throws an inclusion fiesta in Ruby. While both Ruby and Sapphires are classed as Type II gemstones (gems that typically grow with some minor inclusions in nature that may be eye-visible), Rubies are usually more included and smaller. While an

Star Ruby & Diamond 9K Yellow Gold Ring

eye-clean clarity (no visible inclusions when the gem is examined six inches from the naked eye) is desirable, ultimately your tolerance for inclusions is best left to your own judgement. Just consider how clarity impacts a Ruby's colour and beauty. My wife is a July baby and the Ruby I selected for her has a few eye-visible inclusions. For me, these are totally acceptable, lending the gem character. The confusing thing is that fine microscopic rutile inclusions (called 'silk') in some Rubies can actually softly distribute light, boosting both beauty and

Noble Red Spinel

Spinel derives it name from either the Latin 'spina' (thorn), for its characteristic octahedral crystals or the Greek 'spintharis' (spark), in reference to its bright red hues. This is despite the fact that Spinel actually occurs in a plethora of colours, including blue, orange, pink, purple and red. While Noble Red Spinel was recognised as a separate gem species in 1587 and scientifically distinguishable from Ruby since 1783, it continued to be confused with Ruby until the 19th century. Both the legendary 352 carat 'Timur Ruby' and the 170 carat 'Black Prince's Ruby' in the British Imperial state crown jewels in the Tower of

London are… you guessed it, Spinel! Because it is the 'master of disguise', Spinel has scant historical references, but they were reportedly used by practitioners of the 'dark arts' to summon demons. Confused due to the proximity of their deposits and trace amounts of chromium, Noble Red Spinel and Ruby are actually fairly easy to tell apart. Spinel is singly refractive, while Ruby is doubly refractive. While highly saturated pure reds with good transparency are the benchmark, simply select a colour you find beautiful, with a good shape and overall appearance. Spinel that is too brown or too pale is priced accordingly. A colour variety related to Noble Red Spinel is the aptly named, Flame Spinel (orange-red), while 'Balas Ruby' is a historical name for Noble Red Spinel originating from either Badakshan in Tajikistan or the Balaksh region of Sri Lanka. Good cutting that accentuates its inherent brilliance is also an important value consideration. While Spinels are Type II gemstones, meaning they typically occur with some minor inclusions that may be eye-visible, the standard is eye-clean (no visible inclusions when the gem is examined six inches from the naked eye), except in lighter colours or in larger gems. Usually cleaner than Ruby, Spinel is also rarer and more affordable; all things being equal, a Noble Red Spinel will cost much less than a similar quality Ruby. One of the gem industry's best kept secrets, this beautiful gemstone's public recognition and marketing impact is limited by its low production. Sources include Burma (Mogok), Madagascar, Sri Lanka, Tajikistan, Tanzania and Vietnam.

value. Just remember that perfection in nature is a rare commodity indeed; an eye-clean Ruby is extremely rare.

Once you've settled on a colour you like, look for a good shape and overall appearance. Any fine quality Ruby above 3 carats is difficult to source, but when a fine quality Ruby clears 5 carats you've got a trophy gem on your hands. While ovals are the most common, Rubies are available in a huge array of shapes and cuts. Ruby is also cut 'en cabochon' (see page 34 for more), not only for its star varieties, but also for examples whose clarity makes them unsuitable for faceting.

While Sri Lanka might be the oldest source, the 'classic' origin for Ruby is the Mogok

In July 2008, President Bush enacted the Tom Lantos Block Burmese JADE Act. Designed to punish Burma's brutal ruling military regime, this act closes previous loopholes, totally banning the importation of Burmese Rubies and Jade into the United States. One can only guess how this will work in practice as Burmese Rubies share mineralogical similarities with Rubies from some other locales. The ICA (International Coloured Gemstone Association), of which I am a member, criticised the legislation's effectiveness out of a concern as to how it impacts independent and poor populations engaged in mining, processing, and trading activities in Burma and other countries, with ICA President Andrew Cody stating, *"Those who will suffer are the very people that the legislation was intended to protect".*

Valley in north-central Burma. Today, Ruby is also mined at Möng Hsu (pronounced 'Mong-Shoe') in Burma's northeast. Burma is still regarded as the world's finest source because of its Ruby's classic colours (body colour plus fluorescence) and transparency. Burma was so synonymous with Ruby that 'Lord of the Rubies' was one of the titles of the ancient kings of Burma. Other sources for Ruby include Afghanistan, Cambodia, China, India, Kenya, Mozambique, Pakistan, Sri Lanka, Tanzania, Thailand and Vietnam.

In 'The Book of Marvels', published in the 13th century, famed traveller Marco Polo says, *"You must know that Rubies are found in this Island (Sri Lanka)… and the King of this Island possesses a Ruby which is the finest and the biggest in the world… It is about a palm in length, and as thick as a man's arm; to look at, it is the most resplendent object upon earth; it is quite free from flaw and as red as fire".* Now you're clever to the intricacies of judging quality in Ruby, you can only imagine the ticket price of this gemstone if it still existed today. But whether you're a billionaire or a bargain shopper, there is still a Ruby for you. One of the most seductive gemstones, Ruby has been the gemstone beauty queen since antiquity; I just hope she remembers to call!

SPESSARTITE

"According to the Talmud, the only light which Noah had in the Ark was afforded by a carbuncle (Garnet)".

Marcell Nelson Smith, Diamonds, Pearls and Precious Stones (1913)

One of the rarest members of the Garnet family, Spessartite has only been around for less than 200 years. Despite this, when I think of the radiant Garnet that could have illuminated Noah's ark to salvation, the fiery oranges of Spessartite immediately come to mind.

Named after its original source in Spessart in the German state of Bavaria, Spessartite was discovered in the mid 19th century. Also known as Spessartine, it was subsequently also found in Virginia's Rutherford Mines. While Spessartite has been mined in Australia, Brazil, Kenya, Madagascar, Mozambique, Pakistan, Sri Lanka, Tanzania and Zambia, it is Namibia and Nigeria that really define this gemstone. If you've read my take on Rhodolite on page 182, you will already be familiar with the Garnet family's diversity. Coming in a range of colours, including blues, chocolates, greens, oranges, pinks, purples, reds and yellows, Garnets are a group of minerals possessing similar crystal structures, varying in composition. As each type has different colours and properties, Garnets can be potentially confusing for the beginner. To help, I've included a handy chart on page 53.

Garnet's many myths frequently portray it as a symbol of light, faith, truth, chivalry, loyalty and honesty. For example, Garnet (carbuncle) was one of the gems in the 'breastplate of judgement' (Exodus 28:15-30), the impetus for birthstones in Western culture (see page 250 for more), and Crusaders considered Garnet so symbolic of Christ's sacrifice that they set

A mosaic of Noah in the Basilica di San Marco, Venice. In Judaism, a Garnet is said to have illuminated Noah's Ark

them into their armour for protection. In Islam, Garnets illuminate the fourth heaven, while for Norsemen they guide the way to Valhalla. One of my favourite Garnet stories is the Grimm's fairytale that tells of an old lady, who upon rescuing an injured bird was rewarded for her kindness with a Garnet that glowed, illuminating the night.

As 'self coloured' gemstones (see page 18 for more), the manganese *always* present in Spessartite's crystal structure means that it is *always* going to be a shade of orange. But remember what I said on page 186 about Garnets being a friendly family that like to mix and match in nature? When the iron of Almandine Garnet lends some of its flavour, deeper reds and reddish-browns also come into play. As a result, the colours typically seen in Spessartite are orange, deep reddish-orange, rich golden orange with red flashes, yellowish-orange

Spessartite & Diamond 9K Yellow Gold Ring

and deep red. Sometimes, brownish 'dark chocolate' tints are also present, which causes Spessartite's burnt orange colours. As with all coloured gemstones, beauty is in the eye of the beholder. While the more intense, vibrant reddish-oranges and 'classic' rich oranges typically command the highest prices, your preference should dictate your choice. Just always look for good brilliance, a characteristic of Spessartite due to its high refraction (see page 249 for more). This is important as Spessartite has the fifth highest refractive index, after Diamond, Sphene, Zircon and Demantoid (a variety of Andradite Garnet). Mandarin Garnet is a variety of Spessartite with a pure, almost neon, vivid mandarin colour, just like the fruit. The most valuable of all Spessartite, Mandarin Garnet was discovered in Kunene in northwest Namibia. Also known as 'Kunene Spessartine', Namibian Mandarin Garnet was first mined

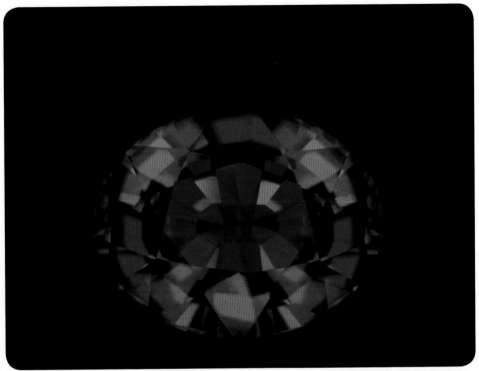

While still brilliant, this Nigerian Spessartite is almost pure red with a dark tone and strong saturation due to its higher iron content

in 1991 and is typically differentiated from Spessartite from other origins by its inclusions and graining, giving it a 'sleepy' appearance. While some in the gem biz view Mandarin Garnet as exclusively Namibian, Marlene A. Prost, in her 'Life in Orange' article published in 'Coloured Stone' (March-April, 2002), said it is: *"a term that today is often applied to all Spessartite, regardless of origin"*. In my experience, this is true. I'm not too puritanical about this, as long as the gem's colour matches its name, but fine Mandarin Spessartite with an authenticated Namibian origin will command a premium. Since 1994, Nigeria has become one of Spessartite's most important sources.

Although Spessartite is regarded as a Type II gemstone (occurring with some minor inclusions that may be eye-visible, see page 10 for more), favour eye-clean gems (no visible

Hessonite Garnet

A big hit with ancient Indians, Greeks and Romans, Hessonite is the orange version of Grossular Garnet (see page 53 for more), Tsavorite being its green variety (see page 135 for more). Hessonite comes in shades of orange, sometimes with hints of red and brown, resulting in this colour being aptly called the 'cinnamon stone'. Hessonite's entomology can confuse because the Greek 'esson' actually means 'inferior'. While softer than other Garnets, Hessonite is still a durable jewellery gemstone. In Vedic astrology, Hessonite is known by its Sanskrit name 'Gomedha' (cow urine), with Hessonite of this shade considered

the most desirable for this purpose. As my experience with bovines doesn't go much further than a barbeque grill, we're going to have to take their word for it. But before you cringe at the comparison, remember cows are sacred animals for Hindus. According to Vedic tradition, setting Hessonite in gold is believed to result in a powerful double whammy, increasing both your happiness and lifespan. For me, the best Hessonite is an intense golden honey orange with good brilliance. A clean Hessonite is the exception rather than the rule, due to the prevalence of inclusions giving it a streaky, toffee-like look. Most Hessonite continues to be obtained from its classic source, Sri Lanka.

inclusions when the gem is examined six inches from the naked eye), remembering that lighter coloured and larger examples, as well as Namibian Mandarin Garnet, may have more inclusions. During the middle ages, if your Garnet became less sparkly, trouble was on its way and in Spessartite this rings true; good cutting accentuates its innate brilliance. Once you've settled on a colour with good brilliance, look for a good shape and overall appearance. As production of fine examples from any locale is usually sporadic, the fiery oranges of Spessartite remain a rarity, whose purchase is the hallmark of a true connoisseur.

When I first came to Chanthaburi, Thailand, I was surprised at some of the colloquial terms some African rough dealers used to describe the different colours of Spessartite. Totally enchanted by the magic of gemstones, I was horrified (as you can imagine) to hear the terms Coke, Fanta and Red Soda (a Fanta variety marketed in Thailand) being casually used to describe raw crystals that would soon be faceted into beautiful, rare gemstones. Well they mightn't be very romantic, but years later I can see how apt these everyday terms are at communicating colour. We mightn't all think of the same thing when I say 'burnt orange', but a glass of Fanta with a splash of Coke quickly gets the message across, regardless of the language barrier.

TANZANITE

"Tanzanite is the most important gemstone discovery in over 2,000 years".
Henry B. Platt, Former President & Chairman, Tiffany & Co.

A big claim from the bloke who introduced it to the market, but with just over 40 years under its belt, Tanzanite is a gem people still rave about. The quintessential 'haute fashion' gemstone of the 20th century, Tanzanite is one of the best selling coloured gemstones of all time. In recognition of the enormous popularity it garners, Tanzanite joined Turquoise and Zircon as the official industry birthstones for December in 2002. As a December baby who has visited the world's only source of Tanzanite, this was also personally significant. Undeniably drop-dead gorgeous, glamorous, exotic and rare, the question still remains, why is Tanzanite so coveted? Colour baby, colour. Tanzanite displays some of the best 'velvety blues' in the gem kingdom and, depending on your perspective, can even give the finest Blue Sapphire a run for its money! But more on its colour complexity and comparisons in a moment, let's travel to where our story begins, beneath the shadows of Tanzania's Mount Kilimanjaro in the arid Merelani foothills that rise from the hot Sanya plains…

Five hundred and eighty-five million years ago, something so geologically unique happened beneath the earth's surface that some prophesise only a one-in-a-million chance of Tanzanite occurring elsewhere. Tanzanite's colours are down to the amount and ratio of chromium and vanadium, and it's the chance incorporation of these elements into pockets of transparent Zoisite (Tanzanite's mineralogical name) that has resulted in one of the world's most sought-after gemstones. Given that Tanzanite's sole deposit scarcely covers 20 square kilometres, it's

The Masai, a people forever linked to one of East Africa's most spectacular gems, Tanzanite

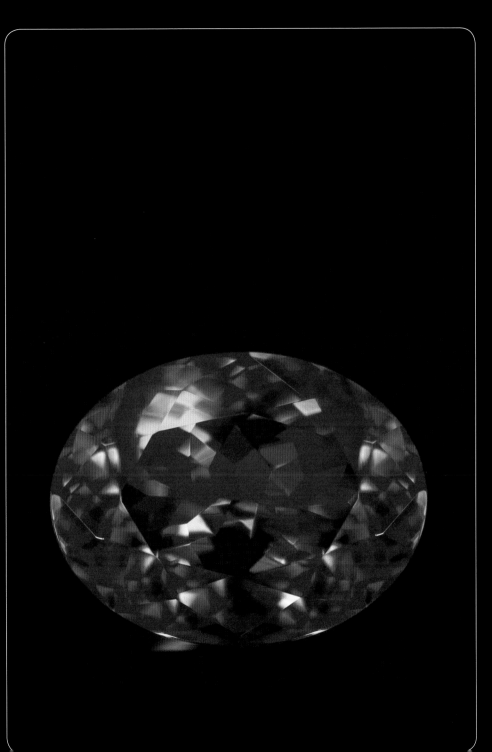

no surprise that it is routinely described as *"a thousand times rarer than Diamonds"*. Much like Zultanite, which also only comes from a sole deposit, Tanzanite is as much defined by its rarity as its beauty. Now the cynics out there will probably doubt the *"a little over a decade of mine life remaining"* claims, but do try to remember that prophesising the life of a gemstone deposit is a lot more complicated than scheduling a train timetable, and we all know how wrong they can be! Even though the odd included Blue Zoisite crystal has been found in Pakistan, Tanzania has the world's only commercial deposit. The deposit has been segmented by the Tanzanian government into four 'blocks' (A, B, C and D) and while production in at least one block has increased, overall Tanzanite production is decreasing. Unless discovered elsewhere, newly mined Tanzanite will largely disappear in years to come, probably within my lifetime.

AAA Tanzanite & Diamond 18K White Gold Ring

According, to popular myth, the first Tanzanite aficionados were nomadic Masai herdsmen. Apparently, they spotted beautiful blue Tanzanite crystals which had been transformed from their typical bronzy greyish brown by a grass fire. While this romantic story alludes to how Tanzanite's colours blossom with a little gentle heating, it seems unlikely that a grass fire could hit the temperatures needed (around 520°C). Perhaps this may have happened over time under the hot African sun, but again, this hypothesis reads more like urban legend (virtually all Tanzanite is heated to permanently enhance its colour, see page 265 for more). Whatever the truth, the Masai are a people forever linked to Tanzanite and by sheer coincidence, the Masai regard blue as a sacred spiritual colour. Once bestowing blue beads and robes to women who have born children, the Masai have now adapted this old tradition. Today, Masai chiefs give Tanzanite to wives on the birth of a baby as a blessing for a healthy, positive and successful life.

Myths aside, in 1967 a 'man' discovered some sparkling Tanzanite crystals and as they say, the rest is history. The problem is, which 'man'? Variously attributed to Ali Juuyawatu, Ndugu Jumanne Ngoma and others, visit any pub in Arusha, located 25 kilometres north of the Tanzanite deposit, and you're bound to be told one version of the story. However, three things are for certain: Manuel D'Souza staked the first claim; legendary Scottish geologist Campbell Bridges (the discoverer of Tsavorite, see page 135 for more) was the first person to bring Tanzanite to the GIA (Gemmological Institute of America) for identification; and Tiffany & Co., specifically Henry B. Platt, great grandson of Louis Comfort Tiffany, coined 'Tanzanite' and launched it to a willing world. While Czechoslovakian Baron Zois von Edelstein, for whom 'Zoisite' is named, was cheated out of better recognition, I think we all agree that 'Blue Zoisite', which for Henry echoed 'blue suicide', just doesn't fit. Christened Tanzanite in tribute to the land of its birth, it quickly became one of the world's most popular gemstones due to its dramatic beauty and pretty cool name.

But what good is a clever name if you can't back it up with beauty? As mentioned previously, Tanzanite is all about colour, so it will come as no surprise that its grading systems mostly critique colour quality. Tanzanite is pleochroic (see page 33 for more) or getting more technical, trichroic (three-coloured). This means each Tanzanite crystal has three colours, blue, purplish-red and greenish-yellow brown (bronze), whose intensity changes when it is viewed from different angles. While heating minimises Tanzanite's bronze hues, maximising the blues, violets and purples, this is dependant on the natural characteristics of each crystal and doesn't produce consistent results. While Tanzanite's rarest and most valuable colour is typically a strong daylight 'sapphire-esque' blue, most of the time, Tanzanite's final colour is a combination of its three trichroic hues, depending on the prominence of pleochrosim in each finished gem. This is because Tanzanite with more blue than purple or violet is faceted along the width, not length, of the crystal to accentuate the purity of the blue colour. This is an inherently more expensive proposition because weight and size is sacrificed for colour. While Tanzanite's colours are typically blues, bluish-purples, bluish-violets, purples, violets, violetish-blues and combinations thereof, highly collectable greens, pinks and yellows are also known to exist. Tanzanite exhibits a colour shift (a colour change where the two colours are near each other on the colour wheel) from its blues in daylight, to purples and violets in incandescent lighting (candlelight). This is a desirable trait, and as most of us live in mixed lighting environments, you can often see these colours simultaneously. While industry paradigms dictate that Tanzanite with a pure 'closest-to-sapphire' blue equals a higher value, Tanzanite should never be viewed merely as a Sapphire substitute. Even its finest pure blues will display some violets and purples in incandescent light, so while it's tempting to make comparisons, Tanzanite's uniquely beautiful colours should be appreciated for what they are rather than what some would like them to be. Once you've accepted Tanzanite is hardly ever pure blue, selecting a pastel or more intensely coloured Tanzanite is simply down to your taste and budget. Just remember that colour and size in Tanzanite are irreparably linked, so you're generally not going find its richer, more intense purple-blues in smaller sizes. While gemmological beauty is in the eye of the beholder, Tanzanite with excessive pleochroism or

AAA Tanzanite & Diamond 18K Yellow Gold Ring

a vivid purple or violet in daylight will be priced accordingly. Also, be aware that Tanzanite's deeper more expensive colours are often identified by quality prefixes such as 'AAA'.

Available in an array of shapes and sizes, Tanzanite under 20 carats is most popular and practical for jewellery. Ovals and cushions are the most common cuts, but Tanzanite is also available in rounds as well as other shapes. While you should look for a shape, overall appearance and deft finish that afford good brilliance, the quality of faceting is important for Tanzanite as the visibility of its pleochroism is largely determined by the lapidary techniques used to finish the gemstone. Also, be aware that Tanzanite which is too large or poorly cut will darken, losing brilliance. Last but certainly not least, the clarity standard for Tanzanite is usually eye-clean (no visible inclusions when the gem is examined approximately six inches from the naked eye) and it can even display a good clarity under magnification. This is important, as a high transparency and an absence of inclusions accentuates its glamorous colours, and are thus signature characteristics of Tanzanite.

Despite a fleeting resemblance between Tanzanite and fine Blue Sapphire, touting Tanzanite as *"looking like Sapphire wishes it could look"* or *"sending Sapphire into a jealous rage"* ultimately seems awkward and perhaps a little silly to me. In these competitions, no gem wins. The reality is that Tanzanite is not a Sapphire substitute. As attested by its unabated popularity and enormous public recognition, Tanzanite is definitely its own gem. Despite the intrinsic scarcity associated with a sole deposit, Tanzanite is one of the most beautiful transparent blue gemstones around. When you compare its beauty to bucks, Tanzanite remains exceptional value for money.

TURQUOISE

"If cold December gave you birth, the month of snow and ice and mirth, place on your hand a Turquoise blue; success will bless whate'er you do".
Unknown Author, Pamphlet Published by Tiffany & Co. (1870)

An ancient gemstone, blessed with a rich and colourful history, Turquoise's characteristic colour fabulously suits almost every complexion. Turquoise is a true cultural chameleon, appearing in some of the world's most significant cultures. While Egyptians, Mesopotamians (Iraq), Persians (Iran), Mongols, Tibetans, Chinese and Native Americans all greatly valued Turquoise, the two geographic areas forever linked with this gemstone is the Middle East and the Americas. Today, Turquoise is Iran's national gemstone and also strongly associated with Native American jewellery, such as Zuni bracelets and Navajo belts.

Despite its long history, Turquoise wasn't always called Turquoise. In Persian, the gem is called 'ferozah', which means 'victorious', and until the 13th century in Europe it was called 'calläis' (beautiful stone), probably from the Roman gem names 'callainos' or 'callaina'. While some mineralogists and gemstone authors think these names represented our Turquoise during antiquity, others disagree. Like so many ancient gem names, the truth is probably lost to the sands of time. Even its modern name, Turquoise, is a bit of a misnomer. When Venetian merchants brought the gem to France, it was called 'pierre turquois' (Turkish Stone), despite its Persian not Turkish origin. Today, the name 'Turquoise' is synonymous with both its unique colour and the gemstone.

Its delightful colour aside, Turquoise's rich history and mythology are probably due to it being one of the first gemstones ever mined. Mining Turquoise dates back to 6000 BC in

The Aztecs began mining Turquoise in Mexico around 900 AD and created elaborate mosaic masks like the one pictured above

Egypt and 5000 BC in Persia, which is pretty old. In fact, a Turquoise and gold bracelet excavated in 1900 from the tomb of the Egyptian Queen Zer (5500 BC) is one of the world's oldest pieces of jewellery.

In the Americas, the Aztecs, Mayans, Anasazi, Zuni, Navajo and Apache people were so taken by the beauty of Turquoise that by the 16th century ingenious cultures in the American southwest were using it as currency. Crafted by the Aztecs into elaborate masks, the treasure of Moctezuma II (1466-1520), the ninth Aztec emperor and ruler at the beginning of the Spanish conquest, includes a serpent carving covered by a mosaic of Turquoise.

A gemstone of prosperity in many cultures from the Persians to the Apache, Turquoise is purported to lighten or darken in colour based on the mood or health of its wearer. While such ability was historically attributed to many gemstones, in his book 'Gemmarum et Lapidum Historia' published in 1609, Anselmus de Boodt cranks it up a notch, claiming that Turquoise grew paler as its wearer sickened, lost its colour entirely on their death, but recovered when worn by a new, healthy owner. He also claimed if the wearer fell, the Turquoise would crack in place of their bones! *Kids, this is 'mythology', please don't try this at home.* In general, the Europeans were a little slow to jump on the Turquoise bandwagon. Despite Theophrastus (the successor of Aristotle's school of philosophy) noticing the gem in the spoils brought home from Persia by Macedonian soldiers, Turquoise did not make a big impact on European fashion until the middle ages.

Moving from history to science, Turquoise is a hydrated phosphate of copper and aluminium. Coming in various intensities of blue and greenish-blue, Turquoise's sky blue colours of a medium tone and saturation are historically considered the 'best', with greenish hues being less valued. But as always, colour preferences in gemstones remains highly subjective. If you find greenish-blue Turquoise more desirable, then this colour preference should dictate your selection. Turquoise is often mottled with veins of matrix (host rock), typically brown limonite or black manganese oxide. Whether you choose mottling (called 'spider web' due to the pattern's appearance) in Turquoise or not is largely up to individual taste. Attractive well-balanced patterns don't affect Turquoise's value. As an opaque gemstone, Turquoise is polished as cabochons, with ovals being the most common. Regardless of the shape, simply judge the overall appearance of the gem along with its colour and mottling. While Nishapar in Iran, by historical reputation and experience, is still regarded as one of Turquoise's finest sources, today Turquoise is also commercially mined in the U.S.A. (Arizona and Nevada) and China. One potentially misleading phrase to be aware of is 'Persian Turquoise', as it is sometimes incorrectly used to indicate a sky blue colour grade rather than its origin.

Turquoise is one of those gemstones that has transcended both time and culture. It is as captivatingly beautiful today as it would have been to the ancient Egyptians circa 5500 BC. To finish my take on Turquoise, I'm going to paraphrase the 17th century advice of Anselmus de Boodt: *"no gentleman thought his hands properly ornamented, or his elegance complete, without the acquisition of a fine Turquoise".*

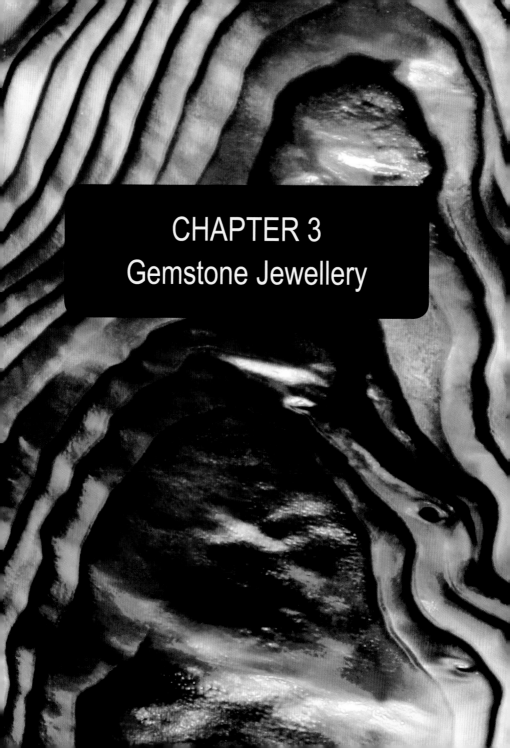

CHAPTER 3
Gemstone Jewellery

JEWELLERY SETTINGS

"For we are told by tradition, that he (Prometheus) enclosed a fragment of this stone in iron, and wore it upon his finger; such being the first ring and the first jewel known".

Pliny the Elder (23-79 AD), Historia Naturalis

If you believe Greek mythology, apart from being the guy who gave us fire, Prometheus was also responsible for getting us into jewellery. To the uninitiated, jewellery looks incredibly complex, but this couldn't be further from the truth. Gemstones aside, simply judge the balance (symmetrically or asymmetrically), proportion and finish of the metal work.

Most rings are crafted from three basic parts: the band (the ring itself also known as the 'shank'), the gallery (also know as the 'head') and the gemstone. These basic parts, along with the 'findings' (the collective name for posts, clips, chains, and hinges), are used in combination to make every piece of jewellery imaginable. The following pages introduce you to the main setting types as well as the names of jewellery components.

Bar Setting

Description: A variant of channel setting, bar setting is not the 'ambiance' at your favourite pub. In bar settings, the gemstones are individually set between short strips of precious metal, like sleepers on a railway track.

Cuts: This setting is best suited to rings featuring baguette, emerald, oval, princess, round and square-cut gems.

Jewellery: Classic yet contemporary, in bar settings the sides of the gemstones are open, optimising brilliance and scintillation (sparkle).

Opposite: Green Tourmaline & Diamond 18K Yellow Gold Pendant

Bezel Setting

Description: A bezel setting has a metal rim that precisely encircles the sides of a gemstone, extending slightly above. The rim or collar can have straight or scalloped edges that stretch around the gem's entire perimeter or only around a portion of it, as in semi-bezel or half-bezel settings. The bezel setting is an ancient technique that can appear very contoured, slightly retro yet contemporary. Bezel setting is labour intensive as it must be balanced and straight from angle to angle.

Cuts: While all cuts can be bezel set, it is easier to use this setting for ovals and rounds. Bezel setting gemstones with sides and angles are considered especially difficult.

Jewellery: Since the bezel setting securely protects the gemstone's edges, girdle and pavilion, it is great for people on the go. Good for designs with bigger shoulders or bigger gemstones, the bezel setting is used in earrings, bracelets, necklaces and rings.

Channel Setting

Description: Channel setting is where the gems sit girdle to girdle in a channel created by two long tracks of precious metal. Jewellery with a groove setting is also sometimes referred to as a channel setting. While this setting allows gems to display their maximum brilliance, its success is dependent on using gems with precisely cut pavilions.

Cuts: Although not always the case, channel setting is typically used for small gems of equivalent size. It is increasingly common in modern designs featuring round, baguette, emerald, oval, princess, round, and square cut gems. Channel set princess, rectangular and square shapes are particularly striking as there is no metal or spaces between the gems.

Jewellery: Channel setting is widely popular in bridal jewellery, such as the ubiquitous 'white Diamond white gold' wedding band, and tennis bracelets. It is said the 'tennis bracelet' was born at the 1987 U.S. Open when the clasp of an inline Diamond bracelet, worn by former world number one Chris Evert, broke. The game was actually interrupted to allow Chris to recover her bracelet. The rest is channel setting history…

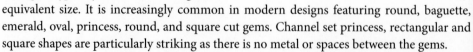

Flush Setting

Description: A variant of the bezel setting, flush setting is made by creating a tapered hole in which the gemstone sits with the surrounding metal pressed around its rim. Unlike bezels, the metal does not fold over the top of the gem.

Cuts: This setting provides good protection for all gemstone cuts. As the crown rises from the setting, flush set gemstones still catch the light.

Jewellery: Flush settings provide a smooth, sleek, elegantly tailored, contemporary appearance.

Pave Setting

Description: Pave is pronounced 'pa-vay' and is the French word for 'paved'. Using multiple gemstones to display an illusionary bigger look, pave settings look like little gemstone cobblestones laid close together with only a small amount of precious metal visible. The gems are separated and secured by little beads of the setting metal, resulting in a sparkling field of gemstones.

Cuts: This setting is most suitable for baguette, emerald, oval, princess, round, and square cut gemstones.

Jewellery: This setting is often combined with other settings.

Prong Setting

Description: Prong setting, sometimes known as claw setting, is the most commonly used technique to set gemstones. To create a prong setting, a gem is inserted into three to six equidistant prongs that form a basket-like base. The ends of the prongs are bent over and shaped so that they rest against the gem, holding it snugly in place. While standard prong settings use four prongs, the more prongs used the more secure the gemstone. A prong's visible ends can be rounded, oval, pointed, chevron, flat or formed into ornamental shapes called 'enhanced prongs'.

Cuts: Because it is relatively easy to adjust for individual cuts, most gemstones can be prong set. Its high position also freely allows the movement of light, allowing your 'rock' to sparkle!

Jewellery: All jewellery types can be prong set, but specifically solitaire rings, engagements rings and bridal jewellery. For example, the ultimate engagement ring, the celebrated six prong 'Tiffany' style setting, has become the 'the ring of rings' since it was developed by the founder of the iconic New York jeweller Tiffany & Co. in 1886. Combined prong and pave settings are suited to designs with smaller shoulders or smaller gems.

Parts of Rings

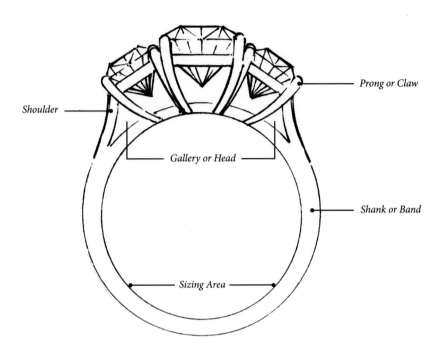

Prong or Claw

Shoulder

Gallery or Head

Shank or Band

Sizing Area

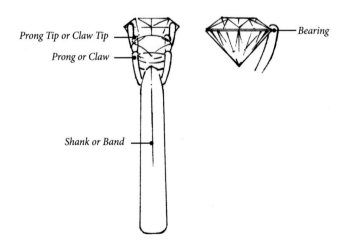

Prong Tip or Claw Tip

Prong or Claw

Bearing

Shank or Band

Parts of Pendants & Necklaces

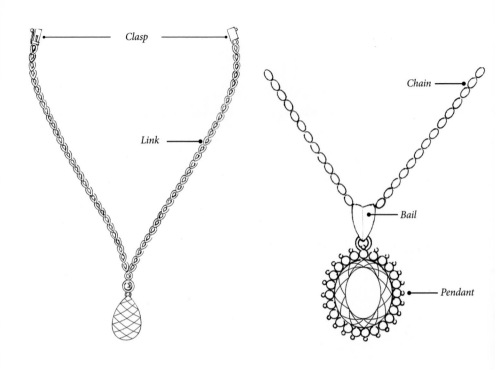

Clasp

Link

Chain

Bail

Pendant

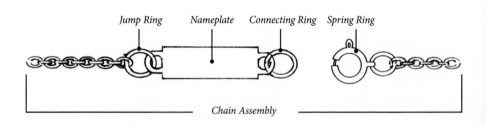

Jump Ring   Nameplate   Connecting Ring   Spring Ring

Chain Assembly

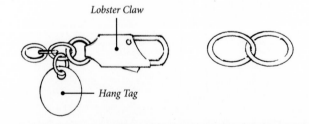

Lobster Claw

Hang Tag

Earring Types

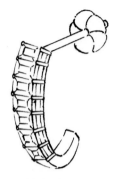

Friction Post

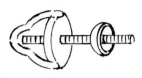

Screw Post

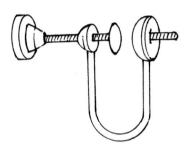

French Back

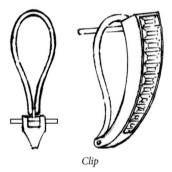

Clip

Hook

Lever Back

Parts of Bracelets

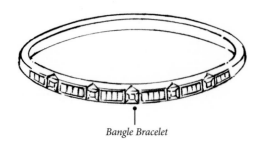

Bangle Bracelet

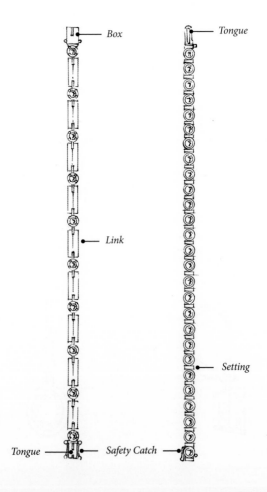

Box

Tongue

Link

Setting

Tongue   *Safety Catch*

Parts of Watches

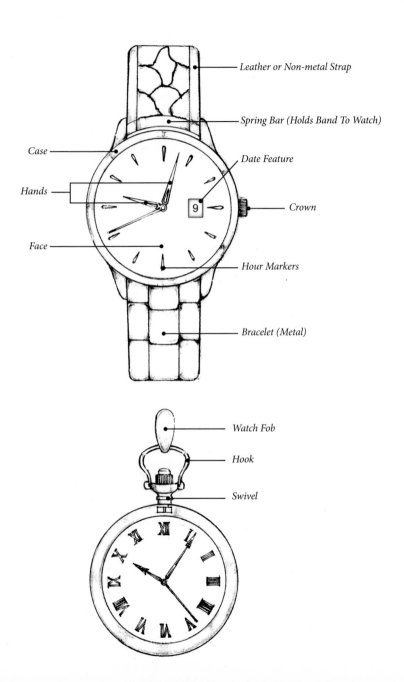

Leather or Non-metal Strap

Spring Bar (Holds Band To Watch)

Case

Date Feature

Hands

Crown

Face

Hour Markers

Bracelet (Metal)

Watch Fob

Hook

Swivel

JEWELLERY WEARING TIPS

"A strong piece of jewellery can make a simple outfit look elegant".

Giorgio Armani

Not known for my fashion sense, I am certainly no Giorgio Armani. With this in mind, I was a little apprehensive about including tips for wearing jewellery in this book. I needed some help. 'Jewellery Savvy' by Cythnia A. Sliwa and Caroline Stanley is packed full of good advice on how to wear jewellery that will look good on you. While I've included some of their tips below, I'd urge anyone who loves wearing jewellery to read their excellent book from cover to cover.

- Details on larger earrings bring out facial features and flatter larger ears.
- Because they don't detract from the shape of the ear, stud earrings look good on just about everyone. Just wear studs in proportion to the size of your earlobes.
- To distract the eye away from your nose, use earrings that aren't the same length or shape as your nose, don't cover the earlobes, don't dangle below the earlobes, or wear earrings that are similar shapes to your eyes or mouth.
- Earrings that work for most people are stud earrings, 1 inch diameter shell-shaped earrings, and 1 inch diameter round or oval hoop earrings.
- At the workplace, wear earrings no larger than approximately 1 inch in height and width.
- Your jaw line determines what necklaces and earrings are most flattering to you.
- Harmonise your necklaces with your necklines so you don't confuse the eye.
- Rings longer than they are narrow emphasise the length of long fingers.
- Wide bands or stacked rings make fingers appear shorter.
- A ring with an asymmetrical or diagonal setting can make shorter fingers appear longer.
- A ring that has a narrow strip that extends down the middle of you finger makes your hand seem wider.

Opposite: Mother of Pearl, Onyx & Marcasite 925 Silver Necklace

- Wearing rings across your hand on all your fingers also makes your hand appear wider.
- Wearing a ring on your pinky finger emphasises the outside edge of your hand, making it appear wider.
- Big rings look best with longer fingers or larger hands.
- Check to see how your jewellery looks in a full-length mirror before going out.
- The focus of any jewellery ensemble, the 'portrait area' is an oval approximately the width of your face, stretching from the top of your head to one head-length below your chin.

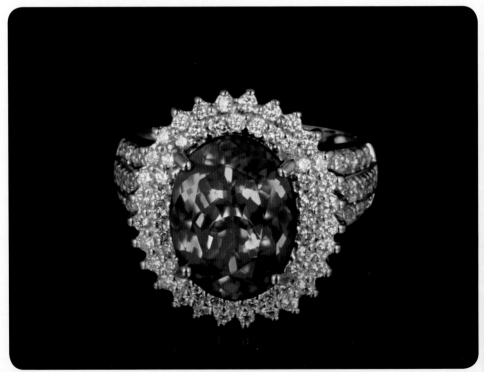

AAA Tanzanite & Diamond 18K White Gold Ring

- To get a handle on different jewellery styles, why not have a jewellery party! Get you your friends to bring all their jewellery so everyone can try it on. Make sure you take photos for later discussion.
- Jewellery is a great conversation starter in social situations, just ask my wife. As you can imagine, she has a quite a collection. I am constantly amazed how many people strike up a conversation after noticing her gemstone jewellery.

Yellow Diamond & Diamond 18K Yellow Gold Ring

ALL THAT GLITTERS

"Gold! gold! gold! gold! Bright and yellow, hard and cold".
Thomas Hood (1799-1845)

In his play, 'The Merchant of Venice', Shakespeare writes, *"All that glitters is not gold; often have you heard that told"*, and with respect to jewellery, he's right on the money. While gold remains the pre-eminent jewellery metal, there are numerous other choices available, such as brass, copper, palladium, platinum, silver, stainless steel, titanium, and tungsten. While this can make shopping for jewellery potentially confusing, the following pages guide you through the three most popular jewellery metals: gold, silver and platinum.

One common jewellery question is, *"What is a troy ounce?"* Gold, silver, platinum, and other precious metals are traditionally weighed and traded in troy ounces. Weighing 31.10 grammes, a troy ounce is about 10% heavier than the avoirdupois ounce used in cooking. Nowadays, metric units are also used to weigh precious metals, but there are no signs of the metric system replacing the troy ounce in the near future. As an Englishman once told me, *"We are going metric - inch by inch"*.

Gold

Still remembering the periodic table from my university days, gold's atomic number is 79 and its chemical symbol is 'Au', from the Latin name for gold, 'aurum'. Our modern word for this metal is derived from the Old English for yellow, 'geolo'. As a rare metallic element of high economic value, gold has long been regarded as the most precious of precious metals.

While some sources date its discovery to circa 3000 BC, it is possible that the first gold nuggets were mined in the Transylvanian Alps as early as 6000 BC! Since then, it has become a potent symbol of wealth and social status. For thousands of years, gold has been valued as a global currency, a commodity, an investment and an object of beauty. Bestowed upon people and used in worship, gold has forged civilisations and inspired legends. Gold's rich lustre and unique texture assures its place in jewellery, yet as a hard global currency, gold's economic importance is unquestioned.

Gold is a precious metal with intrinsic value. From dinky pawnshops to the venerable London Gold Exchange, enormous amounts of gold changes hands every day. Gold pricing is always based on its purity and weight. While gold reserves stopped being the basis of world monetary systems in the early nineteen-hundreds, a large proportion of the world's gold continues to be held in government reserves. Today, gold is used as an effective hedge against fluctuations in the United States Dollar (USD), the world's main trading currency.

Gold is mined from the crust of the earth and copper ores, and its leading world producer is South Africa. Since the break-up of the former Soviet Union in 1991, the U.S.A. has become

the second largest gold-producing nation, followed by Australia, Canada, China, Russia, Peru and Indonesia.

Amazingly strong, gold is also the most malleable of all precious metals. Forever glimmering and glittering, pure gold never tarnishes or corrodes. Even though about 75% of the gold produced goes into jewellery and watch production, pure gold is too soft for most ornamental applications. This objectionable inclination of pure gold has resulted in it being alloyed with other metals to improve its durability. The international measure of gold fineness or purity is 'karat', which is typically abbreviated 'K'. This should not be confused with 'carat' which is a unit of weight in gemstones (see page 10 for more). The gold content of any object is

White Gold

expressed as a ratio of 24 parts. While pure gold is 24K, the gold purities typically seen in jewellery are:

- **22K:** 91.6% pure gold (22 parts gold and 2 parts alloy)
- **18K:** 75% pure gold (18 parts gold and 6 parts alloy)
- **14K:** 58.5% pure gold (14 parts gold and 10 parts alloy)
- **10K:** 41.7% pure gold (10 parts gold and 14 parts alloy)
- **9K:** 37.5% pure gold (9 parts gold and 15 parts alloy)

Rose Gold

Gold's different colours are produced by simply varying the alloy metals. The three most popular colours are yellow, white and rose.

- **Yellow Gold:** Alloyed with silver and copper to display its timeless colour, yellow is gold's most common colour.
- **White Gold:** A popular modern alternative to yellow gold, white gold is created by bleaching pure yellow gold white. While 9K, 10K and 14K white gold is bleached white using silver, because of its higher purity (75%), 18K gold requires a stronger bleaching agent, such as palladium (Pd), a precious platinum group metal. Though nickel (Ni) can be used to alloy 18K white gold, this should be avoided as its release can cause allergic

This photograph illustrates how gold preferences vary from country to country. The Thai wedding ring on the left is 24K Yellow Gold while the Russian wedding ring on the right is 18K Rose Gold

reactions. Providing a hard, shiny, unmatched finish, rhodium (Rh) electroplating has become the international industry standard for nickel-free white gold alloys. Rhodium was discovered by William Wollaston in 1803. Approximately three times more expensive than platinum, rhodium is the most expensive platinum group precious metal.

- **Rose Gold:** Rose gold, also known as pink gold or Russian gold (this gold colour has been popular in Russia since the beginning of the 19th century), is alloyed with copper. Typically a striking pinkish rose colour, the higher the copper content, the stronger the red colouration. Interestingly, pink gold is increasingly used in men's horology (very expensive watches).

Apart from gold colours, there are other gold jewellery applications you should be aware of:

- **Gold filled**, also known as gold overlay, is a gold layer bonded to a support metal that constitutes 5-10 percent of the total weight of the item.
- **Rolled gold plate** is a variety of gold filled, where the gold layer bonded to a support metal is less than 5 percent of the total weight of the item.
- **Gold plated** is a thin plating of gold bonded to the support metal. Items that are gold plated contain less gold than those that are gold filled.
- **Electroplating**, also known as gold flashed or gold washed, is an electrical process that affixes gold, a gold alloy or another precious metal to a support metal with a minimum thickness of 0.175 microns. Heavy gold electroplating is when the minimum thickness is 2.5 microns. Items made entirely of gold can be electroplated (e.g. the rhodium electroplating of white gold).
- **Vermeil**, pronounced 'ver-may', is typically sterling silver covered with a layer of gold plate. Deriving its name from the French word for 'veneer', the original fire-guilding vermeil process developed in 18th century France has been replaced by electrolysis. Also known as onlay, double or silver gilt, in vermeil the gold must also be at least 10K and have a minimum thickness of 1.5 microns.
- **Gold leaf** is ultra thin pounded gold. Pure gold leaf has a long tradition in European cuisine, where exotic dishes are given the ultimate edible presentation.

Silver

Mined from ores such as argentite, silver's history dates back more than 5,000 years. A popular and affordable choice for jewellery, silver has been used by virtually every civilisation. Silver is also used to craft 'objets d'art', such as silverware (no surprise there) and hollowware (tableware, such as bowls, pitchers, teapots and trays that serve as containers or receptacles). The chemical symbol for silver 'Ag' is derived from the Latin word for silver, 'argentum'. Our modern name for silver comes from the Old English word 'seolfor'.

Relatively malleable, pure silver is softer than gold or platinum. As with gold, silver is typically alloyed with secondary metals such as copper for strength. Similar to platinum, silver purities are expressed as parts per thousand. 'Sterling' or '925' silver is 92.5 percent pure and the standard for high-quality silver jewellery. For every 1,000 parts in sterling silver, 75 of them (7.5 percent) is an alloy. Another commonly seen silver purity is 'Britannia' or '958' silver, which is 95.8 percent pure.

925 Sterling Silver

Platinum

Gold might be regarded as the most precious of metals, but did you know that platinum (Pt) is 60 times rarer? Platinum is also purer, stronger and denser than gold. A natural white metal, platinum's durability makes it extremely wearable. Platinum is also hypoallergenic, meaning it has a decreased tendency to provoke an allergic reaction. Discovered in 1735 by Julius Scaliger, platinum is derived from the Spanish 'platina', which means 'little silver'. While only 'officially' discovered in the 18th century, it has appeared throughout history, but not always as a unique metal. Platinum's Spanish name is likely in reference to sightings by conquistadors, who thought its small silver-coloured nuggets were undeveloped silver that had not fully matured.

While it's tempting to think of platinum as a relatively new jewellery metal, this is actually incorrect. Platinum was a big hit with the Sun King, France's Louis XIV, who declared it to be the only metal fit for kings. From the turn of the 20th century until 1940, platinum was actually the preferred precious metal for U.S. manufactured jewellery. Declared a strategic metal during WWII, platinum never regained its previous popularity.

Platinum purity is measured in parts per thousand. The most common platinum purities are 950 (95 percent pure platinum), 900 (90 percent pure platinum) and 850 (85 percent pure platinum).

JEWELLERY APPRAISALS

"Everything that can be counted does not necessarily count; everything that counts cannot necessarily be counted".

Albert Einstein (1879-1955)

I once had a simple 18K yellow gold and Diamond ring given to me as a 21st birthday gift from my parents. Unfortunately, my apartment was burgled. Ouch! Only after losing it did I recognise the real value of my ring. Jewellery is more than just a sum of its parts; more often than not, it also has an emotional or sentimental connection to the wearer. Thankfully, I had comprehensive contents insurance, but even still, its loss was heartfelt.

Emotions aside, there are occasions during your life that you may need to know the value of something you own. Having your esteemed possessions appraised will help you make decisions about how to handle and care for these belongings. While you might want an appraisal just to satisfy your own curiosity of what something is worth compared to what you paid, most people obtain appraisals to document items for insurance purposes.

There are professional appraisers who will assess everything: real estate, jewellery, antiques, small businesses, corporations, cars, trucks, corporate assets, intellectual properties and even careers. But what exactly is an appraisal? Simply put, an 'appraisal' is a statement of value and the 'appraiser' is the person who provides this statement.

A jewellery appraisal is the qualified opinion of an expert in the field of gemmology pertaining to the value of the piece described. It first requires an accurate representation of the item and its components (the gemstones and mountings), their identification, as well qualitative grading against international industry standards. A proper jewellery appraisal *should always be in writing* and reflect the average cost you would have to pay to replace the item if lost or stolen.

A jewellery appraisal will include a detailed description of each item, including gemstone measurements, metal types and weight. It should also include explanatory notes on terms and abbreviations as well as the name and professional qualifications of the appraiser, association memberships, and importantly, the tools and techniques used to perform the appraisal. For example, using relative density to calculate a carat weight estimation of the gemstones set in the jewellery (see page 246 for more). Please note that visual inspection alone is not a reliable way to identify gemstones. If a 'jeweller' just looks at your jewellery then immediately starts rattling off a 'verbal' appraisal, it's probably a good idea to make a hasty retreat. Also, how much you paid and where you purchased has no bearing on the appraisal. If the appraiser is just curious, let them know at the end of the process.

One of the most common questions I get asked is, *"who should appraise my jewellery?"* Like hiring any professional, whether it is a plumber or a lawyer, you need to get a handle on their education, credentials, reputation and experience. Basically, you need to appraise the appraiser! Start with basic questions like:

- How long have you been appraising? *As in any field, experience is of vital importance.*
- Do you have any experience appraising (insert gem here)? *Some gemstones are more marketed than others. Even if the appraiser is experienced, they might not feel comfortable appraising some of the more exotic varieties.*
- Where were you trained? What are your qualifications? What professional associations do you belong to?
- How much do you charge? *In my mind, no trustworthy appraiser charges a percentage of the item's valuation. It should always be a fixed fee based on time spent.*
- Can you give me a reference?
- How long do your keep a record of appraisals?
- When necessary, do you utilise a proper modern well-equipped gemmological laboratory?

Often, the whole process of selecting an appraiser is made simple by the fact that your insurer only accepts appraisals from selected individuals. Always check with your insurance company before getting an appraisal. One of the biggest concerns from a seller's perspective

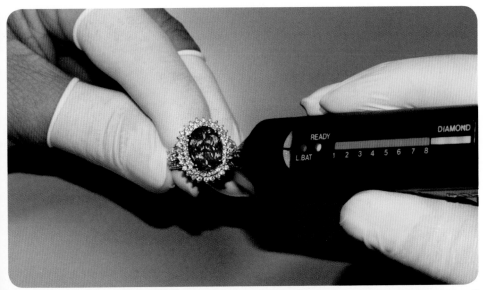

A jewellery appraiser should have access to gemmological equipment, such as an electronic Diamond tester (pictured)

is the appraiser's independence. While I prefer truly independent appraisers that do not buy or sell jewellery, finding one in your local area is not always possible. In these cases, select an appraiser that is an appraiser first, rather than a salesperson who also appraises.

After the appraisal, you'll receive a written report that is your proof of value. Appraisals sometimes also include an image of each item. Even if they don't, it's always clever to take photographs and catalogue all of your jewellery. In the day and age of digital cameras, this is a piece of cake. Keep yours in a safe place, such as with friends, relatives or your lawyer. Don't just keep a soft copy in your new notebook computer. Even portable computers disappear! This is confidential information, so secure it.

It is also a very good idea to find out from your insurance company if your jewellery collection is covered by your household policy. Insurance companies want to sell premiums and you're the buyer. Remember, it's not just about your hard earned money, it's also about protecting the 'emotional value' of what often is (or will become) a family heirloom.

Replacement value appraisals, commonly referred to as insurance appraisals, are designed to cover an individual in the event of loss of property. They are the cost to buy a new item of comparable quality in the retail market. These tend to result in higher valuations for jewellery because they are intended to provide replacement coverage in a market that has fluctuating prices. As a result, updating an appraisal every three years is a good rule-of-thumb. This will ensure you are not paying too little or too much in premiums. It is also a good idea to ask your insurance company how often they recommend you update your appraisal, and about the coverage implications of outdated appraisals.

It is the insurer's obligation to replace a lost item with one of comparable quality, but please read your policy carefully. Some insurers replace lost items with new items, while others pay cash. You need to be sure what will happen if you make a claim. We all like surprises, but getting one after the trauma of loss is no fun. Avoid disappointments by asking questions, so you're always prepared in advance.

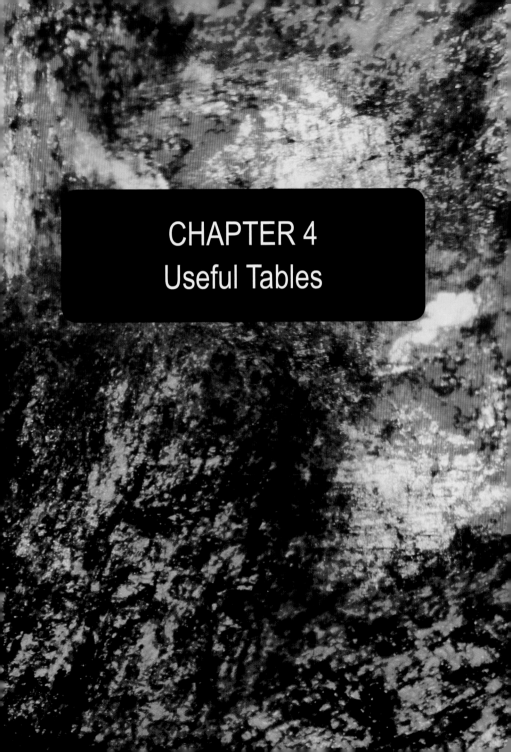

CHAPTER 4
Useful Tables

VITAL STATISTICS

There are three important measurements of a gem's physical and optical properties you should be aware of:

1. **HARDNESS:** Devised in the 18th century by Viennese mineralogist Friedrich Mohs, the Mohs' Hardness Scale measures the ability of a gem to resist surface scratching. Mohs quantified hardness on a scale of 1 to 10, with 10 being the hardest and 1 the softest. As the minerals chosen set the levels of hardness, it is a comparative not a relative scale. The hardest natural substance is Diamond, followed by Corundum (Ruby and Sapphire) then Topaz.

2. **REFRACTIVE INDEX:** Critical in gem identification, the refractive index measures a gemstone's brilliance. Developed by Dutch mathematician Willebrord Snellius (Willebrord Snel van Royen) in the 17th century, we determine a gem's refractive index by using a refractometer to measure the speed and angle of light as it enters the gem.

3. **RELATIVE DENSITY:** Due to differences in their chemical composition and crystal structure some gem types are heavier than others. Relative density (grammes per cubic centimetre on a 1 to 8 scale) has now largely replaced specific gravity (the ratio of the weight of a specific material to the weight of the same volume of water) as the index used to measure gemstone density. Relative density is what jewellery appraisers use to *estimate* the weight of gemstones without removing them from their settings. They simply measure the set gem with callipers and then extrapolate an *estimate*. While you can find a gem's exact weight by removing it from its mounting and weighing the gem on a jeweller's scale, this should generally be avoided. Doing so will expose both the gem and the mounting to increased levels of wear and tear.

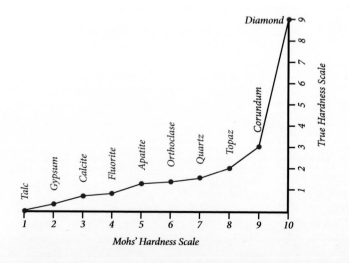

Mohs' Hardness Scale

Gemstone	Hardness	Refractive Index	Relative Density
Agate	6.5 - 7	1.530 - 1.540	2.60 - 2.64
Alexandrite	8.5	1.746 - 1.763	3.70 - 3.78
Almandine	6.5 - 7.5	1.830	4.30
Amazonite	6 - 6.5	1.522 - 1.530	2.56 - 2.58
Amber	2 - 2.5	1.539 - 1.545	1.05 - 1.09
Amblygonite	6	1.578 - 1.646	3.01 - 3.11
Amethyst	7	1.544 - 1.553	2.65
Andalusite	7.5	1.627 - 1.649	3.05- 3.20
Andradite	6.5 - 7.5	1.88 - 1.94	3.70 - 4.10
Anglesite	3 - 3.5	1.880 - 1890	6.30 - 6.39
Apatite	5	1.628 - 1.649	3.16 - 3.23
Aquamarine	7.5 - 8	1.564 - 1.596	2.68 - 2.74
Aragonite	3.5 - 4	1.670 - 1.690	2.94
Aventurine	7	1.544 - 1.553	2.64 - 2.69
Azurmalachite	3.5 - 4	1.655 - 1.909	3.25 - 4.10
Bixbite	7.5 - 8	1.562 - 1.602	2.66 - 2.87
Bloodstone	6.5 - 7	1.530 - 1.540	2.58 - 2.64
Bronzite	5.5	1.650 - 1.680	3.20 - 3.30
Calcite	3	1.480 - 1.660	2.69 - 2.71
Carnelian	6.5 - 7	1.530 - 1.540	2.58 - 2.64
Chalcedony	6.5 - 7	1.530 - 1.540	2.58 - 2.64
Chrysoberyl	8.5	1.746 - 1.763	3.70 - 3.78
Chrysocolla	2 - 4	1.460 - 1.570	2.00 - 2.40
Chrysoprase	6.5 - 7	1.530 - 1.540	2.58 - 2.64
Citrine	7	1.544 - 1.553	2.65
Clinohumite	6	1.631-1.668	3.13 - 3.75
Colour Change Garnet	7 - 7.5	1.790	3.62 - 4.18
Cuprian Tourmaline	7 - 7.5	1.614 - 1.666	2.82 - 3.32
Danburite	7 - 7.5	1.630 - 1.636	2.97 - 3.03
Demantoid	6.5 - 7	1.888	3.70 - 4.10
Diamond	10	2.417 - 2.419	3.50 - 3.53
Diopside	5 - 6	1.664 - 1.730	3.22 - 3.38
Emerald	7.5 - 8	1.565 - 1.602	2.67 - 2.78
Epidote	6 - 7	1.729 - 1.768	3.30 - 3.50
Fluorite	4	1.434	3.00 - 3.25
Gahnite	7.5 - 8	1.712 - 1.762	4.00 - 4.62
Goshenite	7.5 - 8	1.562 - 1.602	2.66 - 2.87
Heliodor	7.5 - 8	1.562 - 1.602	2.66 - 2.87
Hematite	5.5 - 6.5	2.940 - 3.220	5.12 - 5.28

Gemstone	Hardness	Refractive Index	Relative Density
Hessonite	6.5 - 7.5	1.734 - 1.759	3.57 - 3.73
Hiddenite	6.5 - 7	1.660 - 1.681	3.15 - 3.21
Howlite	3 - 3.5	1.586 - 1.609	2.45 - 2.58
Idocrase	6.5	1.700 - 1.723	3.32 - 3.47
Indicolite	7 - 7.5	1.614 - 1.666	2.82 - 3.32
Iolite	7 - 7.5	1.542 - 1.578	2.58 - 2.66
Jade	6.5 - 7	1.652 - 1.688	3.30 - 3.38
Jasper	6.5 - 7	1.540	2.58 - 2.91
Kornerupine	6.5 - 7	1.660 - 1.699	3.27 - 3.45
Kunzite	6.5 - 7	1.660 - 1.681	3.15 - 3.21
Kyanite	4 - 7	1.710 - 1.734	3.53 - 3.70
Labradorite	6 - 6.5	1.559 - 1.570	2.65 - 2.75
Lapis Lazuli	5 - 6	1.500 or 1.670	2.50 - 3.00
Malachite	3.5 - 4	1.655 - 1.909	3.25 - 4.10
Malaia Garnet	7 - 7.5	1.740	3.75 - 3.99
Mali Garnet	7 - 7.5	1.730 - 1.890	3.42 - 4.10
Mandarin Garnet	7 - 7.5	1.810	4.12 - 4.18
Marcasite	6 - 6.5	N/A	5.00 - 5.20
Merelani Mint Garnet	7 - 7.5	1.740	3.57 - 3.73
Moldavite	5.5	1.480 - 1.540	2.32 - 2.38
Mookite	6.5 - 7	1.540	2.58 - 2.91
Moonstone	6 - 6.5	1.518 - 1.526	2.56 - 2.59
Morganite	7.5 - 8	1.562 - 1.602	2.71 - 2.90
Mother of Pearl	2.5 - 4.5	1.520 - 1.660	2.60 - 2.85
Mozambique Garnet	7 - 7.5	1.790 - 1.830	3.62 - 3.87
Obsidian	5 - 5.5	1.450 - 1.550	2.35 - 2.60
Onyx	3.5 - 4	1.486 - 1.686	2.72 - 2.85
Opal	5.5 - 6.5	1.370 - 1.520	1.98 - 2.50
Orthoclase	6 - 6.5	1.518 - 1.526	2.56 - 2.59
Paraíba Tourmaline	7 - 7.5	1.618 - 1.646	2.82 - 3.32
Pearl	2.5 - 4.5	1.520 - 1.660	2.60 - 2.85
Peridot	6.5 - 7	1.650 - 1.703	3.28 - 3.48
Petalite	6 - 6.5	1.502 - 1.519	2.40
Pezzottaite	7.5 - 8	1.562 - 1.602	2.66 - 2.87
Prehnite	6 - 6.5	1.611 - 1.669	2.82 - 2.94
Pyrope	7 - 7.5	1.746	3.51 - 3.65
Quartz	7	1.544 - 1.553	2.64 - 2.69
Quartzite	7	1.544 - 1.553	2.64 - 2.69
Rhodochrosite	4	1.600 - 1.820	3.45 - 3.70

Gemstone	Hardness	Refractive Index	Relative Density
Rhodolite	7 - 7.5	1.760	3.62 - 3.87
Rhodonite	5.5 - 6.5	1.716 - 1.752	3.40 - 3.74
Rose Quartz	7	1.544 - 1.553	2.65
Rubellite	7 - 7.5	1.624 - 1.644	2.82 - 3.32
Ruby	9	1.762 - 1.778	3.97 - 4.05
Sapphire	9	1.762 - 1.788	3.95 - 4.03
Sard	6.5 - 7	1.530 - 1.540	2.58 - 2.64
Sardonyx	6.5 - 7	1.530 - 1.540	2.60 - 2.64
Scapolite	5.5 - 6	1.540 - 1.579	2.57 - 2.74
Scheelite	4.5 - 5	1.918 - 1.937	5.9 - 6.3
Sillimanite	6 - 7	1.650 - 1.680	3.24
Sodalite	5.5 - 6	1.480	2.14 - 2.40
Spectrolite	6 - 6.5	1.559 - 1.570	2.65 - 2.75
Spessartite	7 - 7.5	1.810	4.12 - 4.18
Sphene	5 - 5.5	1.843 - 2.110	3.52 - 3.54
Spinel	8	1.712 - 1.762	3.54 - 3.63
Sugilite	6 - 6.5	1.607 - 1.611	2.76 - 2.80
Sunstone	6 - 6.5	1.510 - 1.550	2.62 - 2.65
Tanzanite	6.5 - 7	1.691 - 1.700	3.35
Tiger's Eye	6.5 - 7	1.534 - 1.540	2.58 - 2.64
Topaz	8	1.609 - 1.643	3.49 - 3.57
Tourmaline	7 - 7.5	1.624 - 1.644	2.82 - 3.32
Tsavorite	7 - 7.5	1.740	3.57 - 3.73
Turquoise	5 - 6	1.610 - 1.650	2.31 - 2.84
Umbalite	7 - 7.5	1.760	3.62 - 3.87
Unakite	6 - 7	1.525 - 1.760	2.85 - 3.20
Yellow Beryl	7.5 - 8	1.562 - 1.602	2.66 - 2.87
Zircon	6.5 - 7.5	1.810 - 2.024	3.93 - 4.73
Zultanite	6.5 - 7	1.700 - 1.750	3.30 - 3.39

BIRTHSTONES

While the popular custom of wearing birthstones originated in Poland around the 15th century, birthstones first became part of Western culture through the breastplate of Aaron (Exodus 28:15-30). Also known as the 'breastplate of judgement', this was a religious garment used for ceremonial purposes by Jewish priests. It featured 12 gemstones, representing the 12 tribes of Israel, which also corresponded with the 12 signs of the zodiac and, as reported by the historian Josephus around 200 AD, also the 12 months of the year.

As it can be pretty hard to tell the difference between gems of the same colour without the benefits of scientific gemmology, gemstones were not always classified by mineral species. As many gems were once confusingly known by the same name based on their colour, there is some debate about which gemstones were actually set in the breastplate. This has seen different birthstone lists emerge, depending on where and when they were compiled.

The first 'official' birthstone list was issued in 1912 by the Jewellers of America (formerly the American National Association of Jewellers). Included below are the birthstones established in 1952 by the Jewellery Industry Council, which were revised by the AGTA (American Gem Trade Association) in 2002. While you can choose a birthstone based on a birthday, anniversary or any other significant date, did you know that birthstones were once worn each month by everyone? In the middle ages, it was believed that the powers of each gemstone were heightened during its month. This is great news for gem connoisseurs, as it gives us a good excuse to collect the full set, wearing them throughout the year!

A Jewish Priest wearing the breastplate of Aaron (Exodus 28:15-30)

January

Garnet

February

Amethyst

March

Aquamarine

April

Diamond

May

Emerald

June

Alexandrite   *Pearl*   *Moonstone*

July

Ruby

August

Peridot

September

Sapphire

October

Opal   *Tourmaline*

November

Topaz   *Citrine*

December

Tanzanite   *Zircon*   *Turquoise*

ASTROLOGICAL GEMS

Some people believe that the most accurate way to assign gemstones is according to your astrological sign, not birth month. While many lists exist, they all owe their origins to the cultures of ancient India. Included below is the most common correlation of gems with the astrological signs of the zodiac.

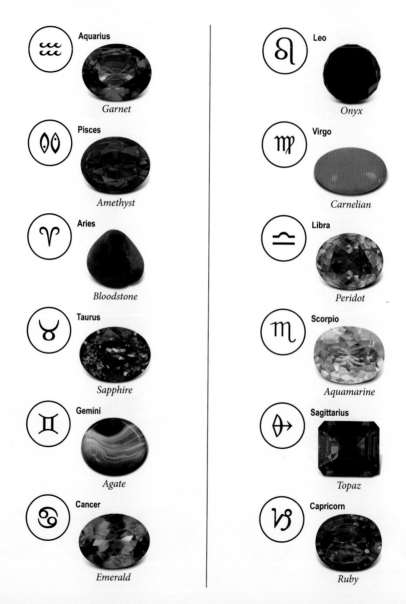

Aquarius
Garnet

Pisces
Amethyst

Aries
Bloodstone

Taurus
Sapphire

Gemini
Agate

Cancer
Emerald

Leo
Onyx

Virgo
Carnelian

Libra
Peridot

Scorpio
Aquamarine

Sagittarius
Topaz

Capricorn
Ruby

CHINESE ASTROLOGICAL GEMS

While many different lists exist, below is the most common correlation of gems with the astrological signs of the Chinese zodiac.

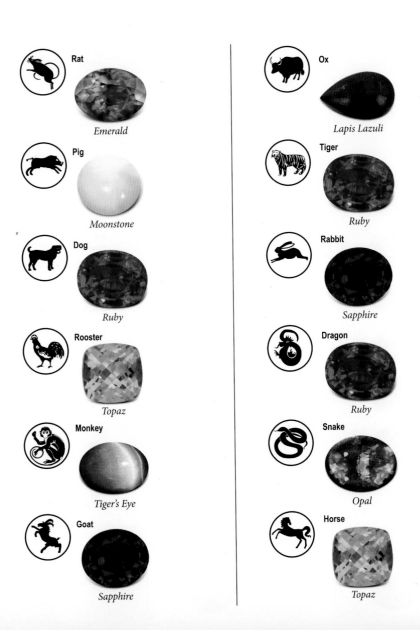

Rat

Emerald

Pig

Moonstone

Dog

Ruby

Rooster

Topaz

Monkey

Tiger's Eye

Goat

Sapphire

Ox

Lapis Lazuli

Tiger

Ruby

Rabbit

Sapphire

Dragon

Ruby

Snake

Opal

Horse

Topaz

ANNIVERSARY GEMS

Although the gift of an anniversary gemstone is traditionally reserved for wedding anniversaries, gems are the perfect way to remember any significant event. While many variations exist, the official list of the ICA (International Coloured Gemstone Association) is included below.

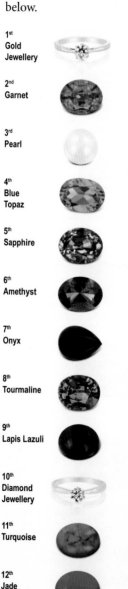
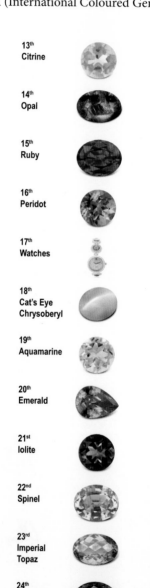

1st Gold Jewellery	13th Citrine	25th Silver Jubilee
2nd Garnet	14th Opal	30th Pearl Jubilee
3rd Pearl	15th Ruby	35th Emerald
4th Blue Topaz	16th Peridot	40th Ruby
5th Sapphire	17th Watches	45th Sapphire
6th Amethyst	18th Cat's Eye Chrysoberyl	50th Golden Jubilee
7th Onyx	19th Aquamarine	55th Alexandrite
8th Tourmaline	20th Emerald	60th Diamond Jubilee
9th Lapis Lazuli	21st Iolite	70th Sapphire Jubilee
10th Diamond Jewellery	22nd Spinel	80th Ruby Jubilee
11th Turquoise	23rd Imperial Topaz	
12th Jade	24th Tanzanite	

GEMSTONE ENHANCEMENTS & CARE

Unfortunately, gemstones don't come out of the ground ready to be set in jewellery. Raw crystals from the earth are usually called 'rough gemstones' (or just 'rough') and this is actually very apt - rough gems can look pretty rough!

To make sure each gemstone reaches its full potential, lapidaries and jewellers employ a variety of techniques. Some of these, like cutting and setting, are immediately visible, while others such as enhancements or treatments remain relatively unknown, despite being used for thousands of years. Practiced in India for over 4,000 years, the earliest known gemstone enhancement is heating a gem to improve its colour. Oiling to improve a gem's clarity is another ancient technique that has been used for over 2,000 years.

Not all gemstone enhancements can trace their origins to antiquity. Some, such as the beryllium bulk diffusion of Sapphires and the physical vapour deposition (PVD) of Mystic Topaz, are the result of more recent innovations. In the gem industry, the term 'enhancements' sometimes exclusively refers to traditional techniques that are so common they are seldom mentioned, reserving 'treatments' for more modern methods. The problem is that this is not universal - both terms are often used to refer to the same processes.

Regardless of what they are called, all gemstone enhancements simply accentuate the beautiful end results of gemstones' natural formation. Defined as any process other than cutting that improves a gem's appearance (e.g. colour, clarity, phenomena, etc.), durability, value or availability, with the vast majority of gems enhanced in some way, these processes have become an important part of the modern gemstone industry. Given the prevalence of enhancements, one term that still has a universal meaning is 'natural'. A 'natural' gemstone is one that has not been enhanced or treated in any way.

Enhancement Disclosure

In a world where many enhancements are very difficult to detect (or even undetectable) using standard gemmological equipment, enhancement disclosure can be confusing for the consumer. The World Jewellery Confederation (CIBJO or Confédération Internationale de la Bijouterie, Joaillerie, Orfèvrerie, des Diamants, Perles et Pierres) is the organisation that records accepted trade practices and nomenclature for the global gem and jewellery industry. Under their guidelines, all jewellers should be aware of how the gems they sell are enhanced, disclosing this information to their customers. Gemstone enhancements can make gemstones more beautiful, affordable and even more durable. Despite this, some gems require special care. While this section includes some simple gem grooming do's and don'ts, the big table overleaf shows acceptable enhancements applied to each gem variety, their frequency, as well as any special care instructions.

Gem Care Do's & Don'ts

While one of the defining attributes of gemstones is durability, following a few simple do's and don'ts will make sure your gemstones last for generations. Much as you wouldn't slip on Prada stilettos for a lively game of beach volleyball, gems shouldn't be worn when playing sports or doing housework. A little bit of common sense and a quick read of the following table could mean the difference between a well-maintained heirloom and a battered piece of jewellery whose shine has long since faded.

Gem Care Do's	Gem Care Don'ts
✓ Do keep your gemstone jewellery in the separate compartments of a jewellery box or in cloth pouches, always storing your gem necklaces flat. When storing chains in pouches, leaving the catch just hanging out will reduce tangles.	X Don't put on your jewellery before using cosmetics, hair spray or perfumes. Some gemstones are porous and may absorb chemicals that can discolour them.
✓ Do gently wipe your jewellery with a lint-free cloth after each wearing to remove oils and salts.	X Don't ever remove your jewellery by pulling on the gems as this can loosen their settings, resulting in them falling out!
✓ Do periodically clean your jewellery. Rings can easily collect dust, soap and grime behind the setting if you wear them regularly. While a dirty gem will lose colour and brilliance, most gemstones are easily cleaned by soaking them in water with a little gentle soap. If especially dirty, use a very soft toothbrush to gently scrub behind the gem. Organic gems like Pearls or Amber should only be wiped clean with a moist cloth.	X Don't ever store your jewellery in heaps as your gems can scratch each other. As almost every gemstone is harder than gold, silver or platinum, even the finish of your jewellery can be damaged if you throw your jewellery in a heap.
✓ Do pull out a watch's crown to the setting position when storing them to save the battery.	X Don't wear your jewellery when playing sports, doing housework or anything else that risks impact, exposure to chemicals or heat. Simply exercise common sense.
✓ Do listen to your jewellery. If you think a gem is loose in its setting, very gently tap it close to your ear. If you hear a 'rattle' the gem is definitely loose and will need to be repaired.	X Don't use a commercial cleaning solution until you have checked it is suitable for your gem.
✓ Do ask the seller about how to clean and care for the jewellery you have purchased.	X Don't use ultrasonic or steam cleaners for every gem. Check the table below to see what gems can be cleaned with mechanical cleaners, but as a general rule, when in doubt, leave it out. Ultrasonic cleaners transmit vibrating energy waves to knock dirt off the jewellery, while steam cleaners use jets of steam to blast dirt off jewellery.
✓ Do take the time to read the following table.	X Don't use silverware polish to clean sterling jewellery. Apart from getting lodged in nooks and crannies, it is not gem friendly.

Gemstone	Enhancement	Explanation & Frequency	Special Care Instructions	Steam Cleaning	Ultrasonic Cleaning
Agate (including Fire)	Natural.	N/A	None.	✓	X
Alexandrite	Natural.	N/A	None.	✓	X
Amazonite	Colourless wax or oil, paraffin or hardened resin and/or impregnated with colourless plastic or hardened resin.	Impregnation with colourless plastic or hardened resin is occasional, while colourless wax or oil, paraffin or hardened resin is usual. All improve appearance.	None.	✓	X
Amber	Heated.	Usually applied to improve appearance and/or deepen colour.	Clean by gently wiping with a moist cloth.	X	X
Amblygonite	Natural.	N/A	Can be damaged by thermal shock, do not expose to extreme temperature changes.	✓	X
Amethyst (including Rose de France and Bi Colour)	Heated.	Occasionally used to lighten colour and/or remove smokiness.	Do not wear or leave for extended periods in strong light as these gems may fade or revert to their original colour.	✓	X
Amethyst (Green)	Heated or irradiated.	Usually applied to provide/improve colour and appearance.	None.	✓	X
Ametrine	Heated.	Rarely applied to improve colour.	None.	✓	X
Andalusite	Natural.	N/A	None.	✓	X
Andesine	Heated and/or diffused.	Sometimes applied to provide/improve colour.	None.	✓	X
Anglesite	Natural.	N/A	Handle with care, very fragile.	N/A	N/A
Apatite	Heated.	Usually applied to improve appearance and/or deepen colour.	None.	X	X
Aquamarine (including AAA and Cat's Eye)	Heated.	Usually applied to remove yellow or green components to produce a purer blue colour.	None.	✓	X
Aragonite (including Capillitas)	Natural.	N/A	None.	✓	X
Aventurine	Natural.	N/A	None.	✓	X

Gemstone	Enhancement	Explanation & Frequency	Special Care Instructions	Steam Cleaning	Ultrasonic Cleaning
Aventurine (Black)	Irradiated.	Usually applied to provide colour.	None.	✓	X
Azurmalachite (also known as Azurite Malachite)	Surface waxing and/or impregnated with colourless plastic or hardened resin.	Impregnation with colourless plastic or hardened resin is rare, while surface waxing is common. All improve stability, durability, lustre and/or colour.	None.	✓	X
Beryl (Yellow)	Irradiated.	Usually applied to provide colour.	Do not wear or leave for extended periods in strong light as these gems may fade or revert to their original colour.	✓	✓
Bixbite	Colourless oil and resin.	Commonly used to improve appearance.	None.	X	X
Bloodstone	Natural.	N/A	None.	✓	X
Bronzite	Natural.	N/A	None.		X
Carnelian	Heated and/or dyed.	Dyeing is occasional, while heating is usual. All produce colour.	Do not wear or leave for extended periods in strong light as these gems may fade or revert to their original colour.	✓	X
Calcite	Natural.	N/A	Handle with care, very fragile.	✓	X
Chalcedony	Dyed.	Commonly used to improve colour.	Do not wear or leave for extended periods in strong light as these gems may fade or revert to their original colour.	✓	✓
Chrysoberyl	Natural.	N/A	None.	✓	X
Chrysoberyl (Cat's Eye)	Natural.	N/A.	None.	✓	X
Chrysocolla	Surface colourless waxing and/or impregnation with colourless plastic or hardened resin.	Occasionally used to improve appearance.	None.	✓	X
Chrysoprase	Natural.	N/A	None.	✓	✓

Gemstone	Enhancement	Explanation & Frequency	Special Care Instructions	Steam Cleaning	Ultrasonic Cleaning
Citrine (including Bi Colour and Lemon)	Heated or irradiated.	Usually applied to produce colour.	Do not wear or leave for extended periods in strong light as these gems may fade or revert to their original colour.	✓	X
Clinohumite	Natural.	N/A	N/A	N/A	N/A
Danburite (including Pink and White)	Heated.	Commonly used to improve appearance.	None.	X	X
Danburite (Brown)	Irradiated.	Commonly used to improve appearance.	None.	X	X
Diamond (all Colour Enhanced Diamonds including Black, Blue, Champagne, Green, Pink, Red and Yellow)	Irradiated and/or heated.	Always used to improve colour intensity or to produce unique colours.	None.	✓	✓
Diamond (White)	Natural.	N/A	None.	✓	✓
Diopside (including Russian and Star)	Natural.	N/A	None.	✓	X
Emerald (including AAA and Colombian)	Colourless oil, polymer, wax and/or resin in fissures, and/or open fractures or cavities filled with hardened resin.	Colourless oil, polymer, wax and/or resin in fissures are usual and open fractures or cavities filled with hardened resin is common. All improve appearance.	These enhancements can be damaged by some solvents and thermal shock. Do not expose to extreme temperature changes.	X	X
Epidote	Natural.	N/A	None.	✓	X
Fluorite (including Blue, Green, Purple, Red and Yellow)	Irradiated or heated.	Commonly used to provide colour.	None.	✓	X
Fluorite (including Bi Colour, Capillitas and White)	Natural.	N/A	None.	✓	✓
Gahnite	Natural.	N/A	None.	✓	X

Gemstone	Enhancement	Explanation & Frequency	Special Care Instructions	Steam Cleaning	Ultrasonic Cleaning
Garnet (including Andradite, Colour Change, Demantoid, Hessonite, Malaia, Mali, Mandarin, Merelani Mint, Mozambique, Pyrope, Rhodolite, Spessartite, Tsavorite and Umbalite)	Natural.	N/A	Can be damaged by thermal shock, do not expose to extreme temperature changes.	✗	✗
Goshenite	Natural.	N/A	None.	✓	✗
Heliodor	Irradiated.	Usually applied to provide colour.	Do not wear or leave for extended periods in strong light as these gems may fade or revert to their original colour.	✓	✓
Heliodor (Cat's Eye)	Natural.	N/A	Do not wear or leave for extended periods in strong light as these gems may fade or revert to their original colour.	✓	✓
Hematite	Natural.	N/A	None.	✓	✗
Hiddenite	Irradiated.	Rarely used to improve and/or provide colour and uniformity.	Do not wear or leave for extended periods in strong light as these gems may fade or revert to their original colour.	✓	✗
Howlite (Blue)	Dyed.	Commonly used to imitate Turquoise or Lapis Lazuli.	None.	✗	✗
Howlite (White)	Natural.	N/A	N/A	N/A	N/A
Idocrase	Natural.	N/A	None.	✓	✗
Iolite	Natural.	N/A	None.	✓	✓
Jade (Jadeite)	Colourless polymer impregnation and/ or polymer and colourless polymer impregnation followed by acid treatment and/or dyed.	Commonly used to improve colour and uniformity.	None.	✓	✗
Jade (Nephrite)	Dyed and/or impregnated with colourless oil, wax or resin.	Rarely used to improve colour and uniformity.	None.	✓	✗

Gemstone	Enhancement	Explanation & Frequency	Special Care Instructions	Steam Cleaning	Ultrasonic Cleaning
Jade (Cat's Eye Nephrite)	Natural.	N/A	None.	✓	X
Jasper	Dyed.	Commonly used to imitate other gemstones.	Do not wear or leave for extended periods in strong light as these gems may fade or revert to their original colour.	✓	X
Kornerupine	Natural.	N/A	None.	✓	X
Kunzite (including Green, Patroke, White and Yellow)	Heated or irradiated.	Commonly used to improve and/or darken colour.	Do not wear or leave for extended periods in strong light as these gems may fade or revert to their original colour.	✓	X
Kyanite	Natural.	N/A	None.	✓	X
Labradorite	Surface colourless waxing.	Occasionally used to improve appearance.	None.	✓	X
Lapis Lazuli	Surface colourless waxing and/or dyed.	Commonly used to provide colour and/or colour uniformity.	None.	✓	X
Malachite	Surface colourless waxing and/or impregnated with colourless plastic or hardened resin.	Impregnation with colourless plastic or hardened resin is rare, while surface colourless waxing and/or coating with colourless wax is occasional. All improve colour.	None.	✓	X
Marcasite	Natural.	N/A	None.	✓	✓
Moldavite	Natural.	N/A	None.	✓	✓
Mookite	N/A	N/A	N/A	N/A	N/A
Moonstone (including Rainbow)	Natural.	N/A	None.	✓	X
Morganite (including Bi Colour)	Heated or irradiated.	Commonly used to eliminate yellow overtones.	None.	✓	X
Mother of Pearl	Coated, dyed or bleached.	Occasionally used to improve and/or change colour and/or colour uniformity.	Clean by gently wiping with a moist cloth.	X	X
Obsidian (including Snowflake)	Natural.	N/A	None.	✓	X
Onyx	Dyed.	Always used to achieve colour uniformity.	None.	✓	✓

Gemstone	Enhancement	Explanation & Frequency	Special Care Instructions	Steam Cleaning	Ultrasonic Cleaning
Opal (including Blue, Blue Fire, Fire, Green, Jelly, Mexican Fire, Pink, Semi Black, Yellow and White)	Natural.	N/A	Keep away from heat and drying environments, these gems can crack if they lose structural water. Can be damaged by thermal shock, do not expose to extreme temperature changes.	X	X
Opal (Boulder)	Infusion of unhardened colourless substances into voids.	Occasionally used to improve appearance.	Keep away from heat and drying environments, these gems can crack if they lose structural water. Can be damaged by thermal shock, do not expose to extreme temperature changes.	X	X
Opal (Matrix)	Heated with organic substances.	Always used to improve appearance.	Keep away from heat and drying environments, these gems can crack if they lose structural water. Can be damaged by thermal shock, do not expose to extreme temperature changes.	X	X
Orthoclase	Natural.	N/A	None.	✓	X
Pearl (including Freshwater, Tahitian and South Sea)	Bleached, dyed, chemically enhanced or irradiated. Most Pearls are cultured (see page 114 for more).	Occasionally used to improve and/or change colour and/or colour uniformity.	Clean by gently wiping with a moist cloth.	X	X

Gemstone	Enhancement	Explanation & Frequency	Special Care Instructions	Steam Cleaning	Ultrasonic Cleaning
Pearl (Mabe)	A Mabe Pearl is a hemispherical shaped Pearl that is grown against the inside of the oyster's shell and is cut out of the shell with a circle-bit drill. The nucleus is replaced with resin and the back capped with a piece of Mother of Pearl. It can also be bleached, dyed, chemically treated or irradiated. These Pearls are classified as composite gemstones.	Always used to create this gemstone.	Clean by gently wiping with a moist cloth.	X	X
Peridot	Heat, colourless oil, wax or resin in fissures and/or filled fractures with colourless hardened resin.	Rarely used to improve appearance.	Can be damaged by thermal shock, do not expose to extreme temperature changes.	X	X
Petalite	N/A	N/A	N/A	N/A	N/A
Pezzottaite	Natural.	N/A	None.	X	X
Prehnite	Natural.	N/A	None.	✓	X
Quartz (excluding Blue Moon, Medusa, Phantom Rose and Rutile)	Heated, irradiated or PVD coated.	Occasionally used to improve colour or produce unique colours. Physical Vapour Deposition (PVD) is an oxide enhancement that uses optical interference to produce a variety of colours by applying a bonded layer of fine titanium atoms to a gemstone (U.S. Patent Number 5,853,826 for Azotic Coating Technologies Inc.).	Do not re-cut or re-polish gemstones with superficial colour (or phenomena) surface layers.	✓	X
Quartz (Blue Moon)	Heated.	Usually applied to provide/improve colour and appearance.	None.	✓	X
Quartz (including Medusa, Phantom, Rose and Rutile)	Natural.	N/A	None.	✓	X
Quartzite	Dyed and/or impregnated with colourless plastic or hardened resin.	Occasionally used to improve appearance.	None.	✓	X

Gemstone	Enhancement	Explanation & Frequency	Special Care Instructions	Steam Cleaning	Ultrasonic Cleaning
Rhodochrosite	Natural.	N/A	None.	✓	X
Rhodonite	Dyed.	Occasionally used for colour uniformity.	None.	✓	X
Ruby (including Star Ruby)	Heated with a high refractive index lead-glass to fill fractures and cavities and/or bulk diffused with certain additives (beryllium).	Always applied to improve clarity and/or intensify colour and/or colour uniformity and/or appearance. The lead-glass is usually yellow to orange and artificially augments the red colour of these gems as well as potentially adding weight.	These gems have fillers in voids/ cavities, fissures and/or open fractures that can scratch more easily than the gem itself as well as being more vulnerable to damage from heat or some solvents.	X	X
Ruby (AAA Tanzanian)	Heated and/or the healing of fissures and/or glass filled open fractures and cavities and/or bulk diffusion of certain additives (beryllium or borax).	Usually applied to produce, intensify or lighten colour and/or improve colour uniformity and/or appearance.	These gems may have fillers in voids/ cavities, fissures and/or open fractures that can scratch more easily than the gem itself as well as being more vulnerable to damage from heat or some solvents.	✓	✓
Sapphire (Black Star)	Natural.	N/A	None.	✓	✓
Sapphire (including Blue, Ceylon, Colour Change, Fancy, Green, Kanchanaburi, Midnight Blue, Orange, Padparadscha Colour, Pink, Purple, Rainbow, Star, Sunset, White and Yellow)	Heated and/or the healing of fissures and/or glass filled open fractures and cavities and/or bulk diffusion of certain additives (beryllium or borax).	Usually applied to produce, intensify or lighten colour and/or improve colour uniformity and/or appearance.	These gems may have fillers in voids/ cavities, fissures and/or open fractures that can scratch more easily than the gem itself as well as being more vulnerable to damage from heat or some solvents.	✓	✓
Sapphire (Padparadscha)	Heated.	Usually applied to produce, intensify or lighten colour and/or improve colour uniformity and/or appearance.	None.	✓	✓
Sard	Dyed or heated.	Dying is occasional, while heating is usual. All provide colour.	None.	✓	X
Sardonyx	Dyed.	Usually applied to improve colour.	None.	✓	X

Gemstone	Enhancement	Explanation & Frequency	Special Care Instructions	Steam Cleaning	Ultrasonic Cleaning
Scapolite (including Cat's Eye)	Natural.	N/A	Do not wear or leave for extended periods in strong light as these gems may fade or revert to their original colour.	✓	X
Scheelite	Natural.	N/A	N/A	N/A	N/A
Shell (Pink)	Dyed.	Often used to improve colour.	Do not wear or leave for extended periods in strong light as these gems may fade or revert to their original colour.	✓	X
Sillimanite (including Cat's Eye and Star)	Natural.	N/A	None.	✓	X
Sodalite	Dyed.	Rarely used to improve colour.	Do not wear or leave for extended periods in strong light as these gems may fade or revert to their original colour.	✓	X
Spectrolite	Surface colourless waxing.	Occasionally used to improve appearance.	None.	X	X
Sphene	Natural.	N/A	None.	✓	X
Spinel (including Black, Blue, Fancy, Noble Red, Pink and Purple)	Natural.	N/A	None.	✓	X
Sugilite	Natural.	N/A	None.	✓	X
Sunstone (including Star)	Natural.	N/A	None.	✓	X
Tanzanite (including AAA)	Heated.	Usually applied to produce and/or improve colour.	Can be damaged by thermal shock, do not expose to extreme temperature changes.	X	X
Tiger's Eye	Dyed, bleached or heated.	Commonly used to improve colour.	Do not wear or leave for extended periods in strong light as these gems may fade or revert to their original colour.	✓	X
Topaz (White)	Natural.	N/A	None.	X	X

Gemstone	Enhancement	Explanation & Frequency	Special Care Instructions	Steam Cleaning	Ultrasonic Cleaning
Topaz (excluding White)	Irradiated, heated, PVD coated and/or diffused.	Usually applied to improve colour intensity or to produce unique colours. Physical Vapour Deposition (PVD) is an oxide enhancement that uses optical interference to produce a variety of colours by applying a bonded layer of fine titanium atoms to a gemstone (U.S. Patent Number 5,853,826 for Azotic Coating Technologies Inc.).	Do not wear or leave for extended periods in strong light as these gems may fade or revert to their original colour. Do not re-cut or re-polish gemstones with superficial colour (or phenomena) surface layers.	X	X
Tourmaline (including Black, Blue Green, Cuprian, Fancy, Green, Indicolite, Paraíba, Pirineu, Pink, Rubellite, Shimoyo Rubellite and Santa Rosa)	Heated and/or irradiated and/or filling of colourless oil, resin and wax in fissures and/or cavities/fractures filled with colourless hardened substances.	Commonly used to improve colour intensity and appearance.	None.	✓	X
Tourmaline (Bi Colour)	Natural.	N/A	None.	✓	X
Turquoise	Impregnated with plastic and/or surface colourless waxing and/or dyed.	Dying is rare, while impregnation with plastic and surface colourless waxing is common. All improve stability, durability, lustre and/or colour.	None.	✓	X
Unakite	Natural.	N/A	None.	✓	✓
Zircon (including Cinnamon, Ratanakiri, Red, Yellow and White)	Heated.	Always used to improve colour.	Do not wear or leave for extended periods in strong light as these gems may fade or revert to their original colour.	✓	X
Zircon (including Brown and Green)	Natural.	N/A	Do not wear or leave for extended periods in strong light as these gems may fade or revert to their original colour.	✓	X
Zultanite (including Cat's Eye)	Natural.	N/A	None.	✓	X

SELECTED BIBLIOGRAPHY

Agricola, Georgius. De Natura Fossilium, Dover Phoenix Editions (1546)

Bancroft, Peter. Gem and Crystal Treasures, Western Enterprises (1984)

Bauer, Max. Precious Stones, translated by L. J. Spenser (1904), Dover Publications (1968)

Brown, Richard S. Ancient Astrological Gemstones & Talismans, A.G.T. Co. Ltd. (1995)

Castellani, Augusto. Gems: Notes and Extracts, Bell and Daldy (1871)

Church, A. H. Precious Stones, H.M. Stationery Office (1905)

Dennis, Jr. Daniel J. Gems, Harry N Abrams, Inc. (1999)

Drucker, Richard B. Gem Market News, GemWorld International, Inc.

Drucker, Richard B. The Gem Guide Colour, GemWorld International, Inc.

Drucker, Richard B. The Gem Guide Diamonds, GemWorld International, Inc.

Farrington, Oliver Cummings. Gems and Gem Minerals, A.W. Mumford (1903)

Federman, David. Coloured Stone, Interweave

Feuchtwanger, Dr. L. A Popular Treatise on Gems, D. Appleton & Co. (1859)

Finlay, Victoria. Jewels: A Secret History, Ballantine Books (2006)

Furya, Masashi. The World of Gemstones: Paraíba Tourmaline, Japan Germany Gemmological Laboratory (2007)

Hughes, Richard W. Ruby & Sapphire (Hardcover), R W H Publishing (1997)

Keller, Alice S. Gems & Gemmology, Gemmological Institute of America

Kornitzer, Louis. Gem Trader, Sheridan House (1939)

Kunz, George Frederick. The Curious Lore of Precious Stones, Bell Publishing (1989)

Linsell, Gavin. Guide to Gems & Jewellery, GemsTV Holdings Limited (2008)

Lipatatpanlop, Barbara & Michelou, Jean Claude. The ICA 2006 World Coloured Gemstone Mining Report, International Coloured Gemstone Association (2006)

Lipatatpanlop, Barbara & Michelou, Jean Claude. The ICA World Gemmological Laboratory Directory, International Coloured Gemstone Association (2007)

Lyman, Kennie. Gems and Precious Stones, Simon & Schuster (1986)

Matlins, Antoinette P.G. Coloured Gemstones, Gemstone Press (2005)

Michelou, Jean Claude. In Colour, International Coloured Gemstone Association

Newman, Renee. Ruby, Sapphire & Emerald Buying Guide, International Jewellery Publications (2002)

Newman, Renee. Diamond Handbook, International Jewellery Publications (2008)

O'Donoghue, Michael. Gems (Sixth Edition), Butterworth-Heinemann (2006)

Oldershaw, Cally. Gems of the World, Philips (2008)

Pellant, Chris. Rocks and Minerals, Dorling Kindersley (1992)

Pliny the Elder. Natural History, translated by John Bostock and H.T. Riley. Henry G. Bohn (1855)

Schumann, Walter. Gemstones of the World, Sterling Publishing (1999)

Simmons, Robert & Ahsian, Naisha. The Book of Stones, North Atlantic Books (2007)

Sliwa, Cynthia A. & Stanley, Caroline. Jewellery Savvy, Jewels on Jewels, Inc. (2007)

Smith, Dr. Herbert G.F. Gemstones and their Distinctive Characters, Kessinger Publishing (1912)

Smith, Marcell Nelson. Diamonds, Pearls and Precious Stones, Griffith-Stillings Press (1913)

Soukup, Edward J. Facet Cutters Handbook, Gems Guide Books Co. (1986)

Streeter, Edwin. Precious Stones and Gems, George Bell & Sons (1898)

Suwa, Yasukazu. Gemstones, Quality and Value. Volumes 1-3. Sekai Bunka Inc. (2000)

Vargras, Glenn & Martha. Faceting for Amateurs, Glenn & Martha Vargras (1969)

Voloillot, Patrick. Diamonds and Precious Stones, Thames and Hudson (1997)

Wallis, Keith. Gemstones, Antique Collectors Club (2006)

Wise, Richard W. Secrets of the Gem Trade, Brunswick House Press (2006)

Zoellner, Tom. The Heartless Stone, St. Martin's Press (2006)

http://www.agta-gtc.org/index.html
http://www.aigslaboratory.com/
http://www.alexandrite.net/chapters/
http://www.colored-stone.com/
http://www.faceters.com/properties/index.shtml
http://www.fieldgemology.com/index.php
http://www.gaaj-zenhokyo.co.jp/index-e.html
http://www.ganoksin.com/index.htm
http://www.gemologyonline.com/
http://www.gemstone.org.html
http://www.gemwiseblogspotcom.blogspot.com/
http://www.gia.edu
http://www.gubelinlab.com/index.asp
http://www.jckonline.com/
http://www.lapidaryjournal.com/
http://www.mindat.org/
http://www.mineralminers.com/
http://www.multicolour.com/
http://www.palagems.com/home.htm
http://www.pearl-guide.com/
http://www.preciousgemstones.com/Forecasters.html
http://www.ruby-sapphire.com/home.htm
http://www.secretsofthegemtrade.com/index.htm
http://www.tsavorite.com/index.html
http://www.webmineral.com/
http://www.yourgemologist.com/
http://www15.plala.or.jp/gemuseum/

INDEX

ABOUT THE AUTHOR

Gavin Linsell is an Australian gemstone writer based in Chanthaburi, Thailand, an international centre for coloured gemstones. He has travelled extensively to gem markets and mining centres in Asia and Africa.

Despite popular misconception, Gavin holds a bachelor of science, but he is not a gemmologist. His experience is in the buying, selling and marketing of gemstones. Gavin is a member of the ICA (International Coloured Gemstone Association), an organisation whose members include the top gemstone miners, cutters and dealers throughout the world. *The Clever Gem Buyer* is Gavin's second book.

Gavin lives in Chanthaburi with his wife Natasha and their four dogs.

Published by Rocks Holdings Limited.
Printed in Taiwan.
ISBN: 978-0-9561330-0-7